Group Projects in Local History

GROUP PROJECTS
in
LOCAL HISTORY

Edited by

ALAN ROGERS

DAWSON

IN ASSOCIATION WITH

THE NATIONAL INSTITUTE OF ADULT EDUCATION

First published in 1977

Wm Dawson & Sons Ltd, Cannon House
Folkestone, Kent, England

British Library Cataloguing in Publication Data

Group projects in local history.
1. Great Britain—History, Local—Study and teaching—Addresses, essays, lectures
I. Rogers, Alan, b. 1933
941'.007'2 DA4
ISBN 0-7129-0765-3

Printed litho in Great Britain
by W & J Mackay Limited, Chatham

Contents

List of Illustrations . . . . *page* 6
List of Tables 9
Introduction: Groups and Local History Alan Rogers 10
1 Starting the Group Lionel Munby 18
2 Reconstituting the Medieval Landscape Barry Harrison 33
3 The Study of Traditional Buildings R. A. Machin 54
4 The Hearth Tax and other Records Roger Fieldhouse . 72
5 Historical Demography Christopher Charlton 89
6 Local Nonconformist History Denis Stuart 117
7 Parliamentary Enclosure Rex Russell 140
8 Census Analysis John Phillips 159
9 Urban Housing in the Nineteenth Century
Martin Gaskell 178
10 Industrial Archaeology Michael Lewis 202
11 Change within Living Memory Rex C. Russell 221
12 Writing and Editing Bernard Jennings 229
Bibliography 239

Illustrations

The number of the Chapter precedes that of the Illustration. Chapters 1, 11 and 12 are not illustrated.

2.1 Romanby near Northallerton 37
2.2 The East Moor at Bedale 38
2.3 Three Vale of York townships 40
2.4 Seven townships in Swaledale 42
2.5 Seven townships in Swaledale 43
2.6 Bagby, near Thirsk 46
2.7 Three Northallerton townships 47
2.8 Three Northallerton townships 48
2.9 Surviving ridge and furrow 50
2.10 Distribution of medieval waste 51

3.1 Ivy Cottage, Fordington, Dorchester 58
3.2 Ivy Cottage. Ground floor 62
3.3 Ivy Cottage. Scale outline and finished drawing 66
3.4 The Green, Tolpuddle, Dorset 68
3.5 The Green, Tolpuddle. The roof 68

4.1 Map showing sizes of village communities in Cambridgeshire 76
4.2 North West Yorkshire. Percentage population change . . 77
4.3 Standard Form for Summary of Inventory Transcription 79
4.4 Social Structures from 1673 Hearth Tax 81
4.5 Cambridgeshire Hearth Tax. One hearth homes 82
4.6 Cambridgeshire Hearth Tax. Two hearth homes 83
4.7 Nidderdale Hearth Tax 1672 84
4.8 Ripon Hearth Tax 1672 85

5.1 Family Reconstitution Form 95
5.2 Baptism Form 96
5.3 Nine Year Moving Averages, Gedling 98
5.4 Graph showing cumulative natural increase 100

5.5 Graph showing maximum and minimum population levels 102
5.6 Seasonality: Burials, Burton Joyce 106
5.7 Form to record parishes of origin of Marriage Partners . . 108
5.8 Graph showing literacy figures, five yearly averages for Matlock 110

6.1 Circuit Plan for Tunstall, Staffs. 127
6.2 Two pieces of Methodist ephemera 128
6.3 Methodist Graveyard, Stoke-on-Trent 134

7.1 Enclosure Act, a copy of the first page 141
7.2 Aerial photograph of Habrough (Lincs.) 144
7.3 Map showing a typical change of alignment of roads at a parish boundary 145
7.4 Parish Boundaries in North Lincolnshire 146
7.5 Kirmington (Lincs.) enclosure map 152
7.6 Kirmington (Lincs.) the open-field system 153

8.1 A page from the unpublished enumerator's book for the 1851 census 160
8.2 A page from the printed report on the 1851 census 162
8.3 Sample card based on the census enumerator's book for Ruddington, 1851 165
8.4 Occupation Structure—Heads of Household 166
8.5 Age-Sex structure for two contrasting communities 167
8.6 Part of Chapman's map of Nottinghamshire, 1174 169

9.1 Bolton, School Hill 180
9.2 Burngreave—a suburb of Sheffield 183
9.3 Mill houses at Hyde in Cheshire 184
9.4 Houses built in 1865 by Ripley & Sons in Bradford 188
9.5 Sheffield, comparison between 1868 and 1873 Ordnance Survey maps 190
9.6 Houses in Brightside, Sheffield 192
9.7 Nineteenth century housing, Sheffield 194
9.8 Map of Sheffield 1868 196
9.9 A specimen card for recording housing character 197

10.1 Specimen completed Proforma for recording Bridges in Lincolnshire and Yorkshire 204
10.2 Rough drawing made on site: Horkstow Bridge, Lincs. . . 212
10.3 Completed drawing; Horkstow Bridge 213
10.4 Interior of Engine house of the Appleby Ironstone Mine 214
10.5 Rhosydd Slate Quarry, North Wales; underground workings 216
10.6 Rhosydd Slate Quarry, North Wales: sketch of underground workings made on site 217
10.7 Rhosydd Slate Quarry, underground workings to scale . . 218

Tables

The tables are numbered consecutively

1 Checklist for a Preliminary Survey 59
2 The Assessment of Downholme and Walburn 74
3 Nine-Year Moving Averages—Baptisms 98
4 Cumulative Natural Increases 1640–1740 99
5 Peak Months for Burials in Decades 105

Introduction
Groups and Local History

ALAN ROGERS

This book is a handbook of local history. It is primarily intended for local history groups, both informal society groups and the more formal adult education classes; but it should also prove of value to those many individual practitioners of local history who are at work throughout the country.

Local History Projects

The growth in the number of local history groups is one of the more prominent features of the present-day scene. Over the last ten years, for instance, the number of local history societies and groups in the four East Midland counties of Derbyshire, Leicestershire, Lincolnshire and Nottinghamshire has grown from about 60 to over 120. And their variation is large—from new village societies to regional industrial archaeology associations, from 'the Friends' of particular buildings or canal restoration groups to collectors of reminiscences. At the same time the older groups are to a large extent changing in their functions. Many are becoming less satisfied with a programme of outings and lectures given by visiting speakers and more anxious to engage in local history work of their own, either through sub-groups or by a society project. For some, it is a matter of running a museum or planning an exhibition or a Victorian week or something similar; for others, the aim is to secure an eventual publication on the history of their locality.

The motivation behind these two developments is complex. There is in part the search for roots in a changing society, a desire for identification with some community; there is the sense of exploration and at the same time a concern to slow down the pace of change; there is even the chance to make a genuine contribution to scholarship, to add in some small but significant way to knowledge. In all of these, as well as in the sense of comradeship engendered by a common task, the attractions of practical local history work are enhanced. So that there can be seen a marked increase in the numbers of local history societies who are practising the skills of the local historian. And with this has come an appeal for expert guidance, for help in techniques and approaches. Some societies turn themselves into adult education groups, but the majority remain as societies, informal groups under their own elected leaders.

The world of adult education, too, is not unaffected by the growing demand for active local history. Not only has it responded to the calls from the societies and other new groups, but recent trends within the discipline of adult education have come to make local history work important. For adult education is seen to be student-centred, starting from the students' own range of interests, experiences and concerns. At the same time, adult education is active, not passive; it consists of the creation of learning situations in which the students participate. Thus history (as with all other subjects) is best learned by *doing,* not just by listening to it. The value of the lecture may indeed even have come to be under-rated at times—it has its uses in some circumstances (presenting, for instance, a critical review, or developing an argument without interruption, summarizing material dealt with, or introducing new material not easily available in other form); but nevertheless it is a truism in adult education that learning is best facilitated by student rather than tutor activity. And in order to cater for this demand, history classes have tended to move towards local history for their activities—for it is here that the sources are most easily available, and it is here that the students show themselves to be most interested. As with archaeology it can be said of local history that 'one undoubted reason for the popularity of [the subject] in the last twenty-five years has been the direct contact it gives with the raw material and methods of the subject'.[1]

In both of these areas, then, in local history societies and in adult education groups, there has been a growth of project work, of practical investigation in local history. In general these trends have come to be encouraged by academic historians, for a number of reasons. First, there has developed an awareness that some of the tasks of the historians can best be done by teams. This is particularly true of the new demographic history, sponsored by bodies like the Cambridge Group for the Study of Population (CAMPOP) which has called for local groups and individuals to help it study local population trends;

but it is also true of the industrial archaeologists and the more recent collectors of 'oral history'. Secondly, there has been a growing recognition that some of the material collected needs local skills and local knowledge for its true interpretation. Hence the encouragement of local group activity by many academics.

But at the same time, academic local history has changed over the last few years.[2] There has been an enormous explosion in the range of source materials available; printed sources like the British Parliamentary Papers and unprinted collections of records have become available in embarrassing quantities. At the same time, the techniques used to analyse these sources have grown in sophistication. A whole study of any local village or town is daily growing more unmanageable and less satisfying, even one produced by a team of local historians; it becomes a sequence of 'one damn fact after another'. It seems necessary for the local historian, whether individual or group, to select his theme, to specialize; only in this way can he add significantly to knowledge. And it is to help in this process of selection that this book has been prepared.

Local History Groups

Much of the increased local history activity is of course done on an individual basis, but over the past few years there has been considerable growth in group work. This is not simply a result of the unquestioned social advantages of people coming together to engage in a common activity, but rather it springs from a recognition of the special advantages of the group over a single scholar. The very wide range of skills now required of the local historian, such as palaeography, making graphs, mapping and sketching, for instance, can more easily be met by a team than by an individual, and any group will contain within its borders a valuable range of skills and experience on which to build. Again, the area of study covered by a group can be considerably wider and the studies therefore that much more satisfying. The varying conditions of access to different types of source material, whether documents in the Public Record Office in London, in the county and diocesan record offices, in private hands or in the possession of local firms, or whether field remains such as buildings and earthworks, all call for different amounts of time and commitment, and a group of people can best provide the range of opportunities to exploit all these sources most easily: some will travel more than others, some will be freer during the day than at weekends, some will have time at home to spare for the lengthy and painstaking analysis of the sources collected by others. Further, the group is supportive, maintaining its members in their tasks. But above all, the value of the group becomes particularly clear in problem solving. Learning is, it is true, an individual process, but the process of coming to a common mind, during which each of the participants in the group changes his or her role, sometimes several times, may well create a more effective means of learning than isolated study. For few things are more conducive to learning than the necessity to teach others; and within the 'learning commune' of the group, each member will be in turn both learner and teacher. The eventual range of insights achieved, the number of new relationships between different sorts of material created, will be greater than those achieved and created by the solitary student.

There are, however, special problems attached to such group work which need to be faced. Of these, three in particular may be instanced —the creation of roles within the group (especially the position of the leader-cum-tutor), the varied pace and quality of work done by the group, and the particular methods of working as a group.

The role expectations of any group are vital to its success. Groups soon establish their own structures, their own hierarchies, without which they cannot function; but if these become too rigid, then they can prevent both the completion of the task in hand and also any learning. If for instance some members always cast themselves in the role of learners and some always in the role of teachers, some as planners and some as routine workers, it will become difficult for changed roles to come about, and without such changing roles, changed attitudes are impossible.

This poses difficulties for the leader-cum-tutor of the group. Most of the studies presented in this book are based on a good deal of experience of the adult class-tutor relationship, but much the same holds good for the group-leader relationship. His or her role may not always be that expected by the group members, who will frequently look to the tutor or leader for an understanding of almost all the matters raised during the reasearch programme. Indeed, a common fault of many local history groups has been the tendency on the part of both the leader and the members to regard the latter as a convenient source of labour to complete tasks set by the former. An early statement of the precise role to be played by the leader is here helpful; it should be accepted and clearly understood by the group and continually reiterated, both in action and in statement, as the work progresses. There is no point in the leader stating that he or she is not always going to take the role of teacher if at all stages that is in fact the role adopted. The group should be allowed, indeed encouraged, to solve their own problems rather than have all solutions provided for them. A careful balance between 'input' (the material provided by the tutor, usually in the form of lectures and/or notes) and discovery learning is required.

The exact functions, then, of the leader-cum-tutor will vary according to circumstances—the nature of the task in hand, the nature and expectations of the group and the skills available. At times he may help to choose the questions to be answered, to set the task; he may indicate and even provide access to the source material; he may train the group members in the skills required for the analysis of the sources; he may 'administer' the programme, distributing tasks and ensuring that the goals set are achieved; he may help in the provision and maintenance of motivation; he may act as final editor of the completed study. But it cannot be stressed too strongly that all or any of these tasks *can* be done often as well and sometimes indeed better by members of the group rather than by the leader.

What then are his essential tasks? Firstly, he must always keep the overall objectives (as well as the immediate goals) before the students and members—no-one else can do this. It is here that his academic expertise as well as his administrative skills are called into play. His job is to see to it that the work is indeed done and done well. Secondly, he must carefully monitor the inter-actions between the group members, to maintain harmony more than efficiency. And thirdly, he must maintain the group coherence by seeing to it that each member achieves some measure of satisfaction from the studies being undertaken. His supervisory role, however, does not inhibit him from taking other, more active, parts in the group's work, both as teacher, researcher, interpreter and learner.

If the roles of the group members pose a range of problems not seen in individualized research projects, it must also be freely admitted that the varied nature of the group will inevitably mean a slower pace of work and less coherence in the final product. A balance needs to be kept between the demands of academic standards and the best products of the group members. Particularly is this tension apparent in the speed of work throughout the project. It is usually much quicker to do the job oneself; an infinite amount of patience is called for on the part of the tutor. Some lack of willingness to work and especially of confidence will frequently be met in any group; indeed, this is often the first task which faces any leader. Careful preparation of the ground is needed; and no-one should be asked to undertake more than the simplest of tasks without the tutor first doing a sample alongside the student before leaving him on his own. Nevertheless, in the end the educational value of allowing the group members to move at their own pace rather than at that of the tutor, and indeed of allowing them to make their own mistakes, will more than compensate for all the demands on the tutor's long-suffering patience.

Then there is the problem of working conditions. How does one get a group to work on one copy of a parish register, on a single will or on the hearth tax returns? How does one fit the tasks to the different levels of motivation, educational experience and abilities of the members of the group? How does one reconcile the divergences between the varying interests of individuals within the group on the one hand and the common task on the other? It is after all easier for the group to develop into a collection of individual projects under a common banner than to keep the whole group together on a united programme while at the same time using the individual abilities of each of the members. And further, the conduct of the group sessions themselves can pose some problems—they can (and often do) polarize between the extremes of an unending and unsatisfying perpetual discussion on the one hand and of an unbroken hard grind of form filling, counting or transcribing on the other. In this respect, as in the other two, the object of this book is to be practical and helpful; it does not aim just to direct to the sources but to show how they may be used in groups. A balance between work done by individuals, by pairs and by the group as a whole, between work done in the class session or group meetings and that done between sessions is needed, and it is the purpose of these studies which follow to provide guidance in these matters.

At the same time, the book helps to indicate the range of equipment needed for each of the projects discussed. This is always a major problem for local history research groups. Photocopying facilities, frequently in bulk, are a minimum requirement; photographic equipment similarly will often prove essential. A micro-film projector (an ordinary film-strip projector will normally serve) is often of more use than a simple micro-film reader; a tape-recorder, surveying equipment, drawing boards and tools, card-index and filing systems, a plentiful supply of maps and graph paper—all of these may well be needed for even a simple local history research project. Above all, the group will need funds—for photocopies of documents, for research travel, for photographic materials, for typing and duplication, and of course eventually for publication. It will be for the leader to assess such needs realistically, as far as he is able, at an early stage of the research work.

The Scope of the Essays

This book consists of a series of personal statements, based on work done with groups. My aim as editor has been to encourage each writer to speak for himself. There are thus certain recurrent themes—and in this lies some of the value of the studies, for they are founded on practical experience.

But while each essay may stand on its own, and groups may select any one topic for research, there is nevertheless a flow in the subject matter. Thus Lionel Munby's contribution which deals with getting the group together and persuading its members to work, with choosing the questions and dividing up the tasks, forms a necessary prelude to all the other sections. Then follows a series of studies in roughly chronological order, each of them highlighting one or more of the major sources of local history, whether documentary or physical remains. Thus analyses of the medieval landscape and of methods of surveying early 'traditional' buildings lead to a discussion of some of the more important records relating to houses (hearth tax assessments and probate inventories). Population changes as reflected in parish registers, and the growth of nonconformist communities are followed here by the parliamentary enclosure movement. Nineteenth century studies are represented by work on census analysis, industrial archaeology and working class housing; and the series is completed with a study of the more recent changes in villages, as recalled in living tradition. Finally there is a section on writing up and editing the finished product—a process applicable to each of the special projects and one which continues during the whole of the group's work.

Throughout the book a balance has been kept between medieval and modern, between town and country. Some of the problems discussed, it is true, are more applicable to some parts of England than to others; parliamentary enclosures for instance will concern more groups at work in the Midland Plain than in some other parts of the country like Devon and Cornwall, where similar work based on tithe awards might be more appropriate. Nevertheless, each topic is handled in a way which can be adapted to any setting—the questions are set, the sources are discussed in outline and the problems of group work examined. Each of the authors has solved the role problems mentioned above in his own way, and in this others will find guidance for their own studies. Bibliographies of the main published works relevant to the subject in hand (what in terms of an adult education class would be termed the basic 'book-box') have been provided for each of the specialist studies.

More could of course have been added, but these topics have been selected as being among the most practical for local history groups, with sources easily accessible, with methods of analysis relatively simple, with findings at once direct and yet significant, and with a considerable body of published comparative studies with which to assess one's own findings. It is possible to build on this framework to make such project work apply to topics and sources other than those mentioned here. The aim throughout is to be practical, to provide detailed guidance for local historians. It is our common hope that individual students, local history societies and adult education groups will all benefit by being allowed to share these experiences, to see groups engaged in work within the new tradition of local history.

Notes and References

1 *See* D. Dymond, *Archaeology and History* (1974) p. 4.
2 *See* Alan Rogers, 'New Horizons in Local History' in *Local Historian* 12, no. 2 (June 1976) pp. 67–73.

1

Starting the Group

LIONEL MUNBY

Setting the Goals

There are many different reasons why groups of people come together to study local history and an analysis of these reasons is important, for to a large extent the aim which the group has in mind will determine the way it works. Throughout this chapter, it has been assumed that the common purpose which unites the group is learning about the history of their own town, or village. But there are some groups which have a more specific purpose. Thus a number of people may gather together, on a more specialized basis, to pursue the study of a particular theme in several neighbourhoods. Such a group may take as its theme some aspect of the local history of education or of religion; or it may make a study of local domestic buildings, of changes in farming or local population trends. Other groups may begin with a particular range of documents, such as wills and probate inventories, analysing them to establish variations in the social structure or economic activity of the locality. But whatever the type of group, it is hoped that all of them will find the ideas in this chapter to have some general relevance for their work. Later chapters will deal with a number of more specialized topics and how their study may be undertaken; this chapter will try to concentrate on the common problems which will be met by all such groups, the common experience acquired in their activities.

There is one important factor which should be clearly appreciated at the beginning. The motives of different individuals in the group will not always be the same; educational experience suggests that they may not even be what the individual genuinely believes them to be. But the purpose of the group can be clearly expressed. Normally it will consist of one of two possible alternatives. It may be undertaking a specific piece of research, for the satisfaction and glory of the members of the group or of their mentor, research which is believed to have some academic value in its own right; that the research project really does have this significance should be certain before a group gets too far into it. Quite different is the more general aim of getting to know one's own place, whether one is a native or an immigrant. These two objectives can be combined into one aim, but with difficulty. The former, when pursued sensitively and with a feel for the locality, can bring some of the benefits of the more general approach; while the latter, when undertaken seriously, can sometimes produce results of value to scholarship. But the two aims are different, and although they may be combined, they should not be confused. It is the second aim which I have in mind in what follows, because I believe that this is the more important socially and it is with groups with this general purpose that I have experience.

The desire to join a local history group is both deep and widespread, and the social and educational rewards are very great. In a restless and changing world, learning to understand the local past can help people to strike roots in a new environment or to strengthen their roots in their birthplace. There has been, in this age of more widespread education and leisure, a growth in the 'instinctive desire for increased self-knowledge. Genealogy is no longer a snobby hobby', as Mr. Terrick FitzHugh has pointed out,[1] while the kind of topography to which W. G. Hoskins and M. W. Beresford have opened our eyes has an immense appeal. A group of local people, meeting to make a serious study of their own 'place', can get much enjoyment out of the process. Serious study is the essence of the enjoyment, for the pleasure lies in learning how to discover and how to judge the truth for oneself. For many people, fantasy and myth, the 'ye olde' nonsense and the collecting of historical gossip soon palls. Joining a group of people with similar interests both increases each individual's pleasure (because discoveries and ideas are shared) and also develops the necessary critical sense because precious original thoughts are inevitably submitted to public examination and testing, either verbally or in writing.

Writing, however, is not the be-all of studying local history in a group. Indeed, the most memorable historical writing is produced by a single person, the man or woman who can draw on the work of varied specialists and on personal researches to present a unified view in language which bears the imprint of the writer's own personality. When one compares great co-operative works of scholarship like the

UNESCO *History of Mankind* or the Cambridge Histories with the work of a single author, such as Sir Stephen Runciman's *History of the Crusades* or Fernand Braudel's *The Mediterranean and the Mediterranean World in the Age of Philip II,* the difference is obvious. One reads the latter and consults the former. This is not to denigrate co-operative scholarship, as Bernard Jennings' comments in the last chapter of this book will show, but rather it is to accept honestly its limitations.

There are, however, good reasons for co-operative work in history. The research team has come into the world of academic history, from the natural sciences, to study large historical problems using a wider range of techniques than a single person can easily master. The process of discovery is a team effort, though the results may be written up in various ways. At first sight this may seem irrelevant to local history. The history of a big city might require this concentration of skills, but surely not that of a small market town or a village? Nevertheless the fact is that, while such a local history might not take so long as a major project in national or international history, it requires quite as wide a range of skills. Because the history of a single place covers all historical time and all aspects of human life, some understanding of all the available specialist skills is needed by the local historian. The local historian's knowledge ought to range from archaeology and architecture to palaeography.[2] The specialist backgrounds of tutors in demand by adult classes make it clear that no one person can provide for all the needs of local history students. A survey made in 1965 in the area for which the University of Cambridge Board of Extramural Studies was responsible revealed tutors at work who were archaeologists, architects, archivists, classical scholars, folklorists, geographers, librarians, museum curators, natural scientists, oral historians, sociologists, and free-lance writers. This kind of pattern would be found in any area where local history has flourished during the last twenty years. Indeed the specialisms have multiplied, as is witnessed by the rapid growth of specialist historical societies whose work closely concerns the local historian. Today we could add to the above list anthropologists, computer technicians, demographers, industrial archaeologists and urban historians. Even supposing that one man was able to master the range of skills needed, is it likely that very many places in Britain will find such a person? Norway is uniquely fortunate in having historians at work in some seventy-five to eighty per cent of the 450 *kommuners* into which that country is divided. But, if competent local histories are to be produced in many parts of Britain, they will have to be written by local people who are untrained, at least when they begin. It is in this situation that group work and co-operation are so important.

Setting Up the Group

There is, then, ample justification why anyone interested in local history, that is in using some of their spare time to learn about the local past, should want to know how best to work in a group. The first thing to appreciate is that it is both probable and desirable that any such group will contain people of varied circumstances, 'a fair field full of folk, thronged with all kinds of people, high and low together, moving busily about', as William Langland expressed it in *Piers Plowman*. Their common aim, urged on by Reason, was to look for 'a saint called Truth'. It was neither scholars nor theologians, but a simple ploughman, Piers, who showed them 'the way to his place' and he did this by making them work; they liked it! There can be no better text for those who want to enjoy local history.

Someone must take charge of the group and be accepted as its organizer and inspirer. If the group is meeting in an adult education context, as a class, the tutor will fulfil this function. This is probably the best way at any rate for a group to begin, because it will then have access to professional, technical assistance. But it is perfectly possible for a group to work without a professional adult tutor in charge of it, provided that the group has an organizer and respects him or her. Such a person needs to be reasonably efficient administratively, good at organizing, strong-minded and inspiring enough to keep the group moving through calms and stormy waters alike; but he must also be tolerant and understanding of human beings. It is no good expecting every member of the group to have either the same enthusiasm or the same capacity. The group leader has to be capable of considerable flexibility while never losing sight of the purpose which has brought the group together. This may in time result in the publication of a local history, but even if and when it does, the basic aim of the group must remain in sight, which is the deepening of the understanding and widening of the capacity for enjoyment of the individual member. For what was said by H.M. Inspectors about some adult education classes in local history in the Cambridge Extramural area in 1954 applies equally to any local history group: 'it is, in fact, the students for whom the class exists and it is what the individual student achieves in thinking, in reading, in written work that is important'.

We are not thinking here of team work by a group of already qualified people but of a group, whose members may between them have many skills and much experience of which use can be made, but who for the most part lack historical training. For this reason the first step in organizing the group will be to divide up the work to be done, to allot individual tasks, bearing in mind each person's situation, capacity and interests. In an ideal situation the group, or at least its organizer-tutor, would assess the total tasks to be undertaken at the beginning of the project. In practice things do not work out like that, for many reasons. The nature of research is such that one cannot foresee all the means to one's end; many are only discovered in the process of research. No one can foresee the full capacities of a group's members before they have started work. Accident can play an important part: who can foretell what a bulldozer may uncover or an attic reveal? The best practice is to begin with a general idea of where one is going and be very flexible as one goes along. To avoid losing one's way in detail it will be necessary from time to time to take stock and to be more specific about the route ahead and the tasks to be undertaken.

Collecting the Material

While a professional research team might well sub-divide itself by subjects, as the great collective histories show, an amateur group will begin best by dividing up the available sources. Material on which research can be done will be available in several different places. Many ordinary private people will have the deeds of their house, or at least their solicitor will: it is not the modern, legally valuable deeds but the old ones which the lawyer may discard that are most important for the local historian. There may be many other family records, letters, diaries, old photographs and drawings, a family Bible, and the memories of old people. Local institutions, church and chapel and local government, businesses and shops and local societies will all have records. The minute books of the British Legion or Women's Institute, the accounts of a village craftsman or shopkeeper, the school records, all have something to tell. Sources like these are discussed in later chapters and related to particular historical themes. The place where most unprinted original records will be found is in the County or Borough Record Office. In the local library there will be books and journals, as well as other original records. Secondary sources—that is, already published histories—can be consulted in the library, but the library may also contain much original printed source material, from theatre programmes to election posters. The first task then for the group is to identify the kinds of sources which they can consult and which are relevant to their theme, and to discover where and when these can be made available for study.

Only then can individual people or groups of people be allotted specific tasks. Those who cannot get away from their houses for long enough periods can borrow books and work through printed material, copying out relevant extracts and summarizing for the others. Those who can get out in the day may work in the reference room of a nearby public library on printed material which cannot be borrowed, for example the more expensive older local histories or files of newspapers. Sometimes books which are not locally available can be obtained and borrowed through the National Central Library inter-library borrowing scheme: this is available to anyone engaged in serious private study, not merely to full-time students, and local library staff will explain it. Other members of the group may work on record sources, in the local parish church or borough offices and, if they are mobile, further afield in the county record office. When working on original documents a pencil must be used for note-taking, never a pen, ball-point pen or indelible pencil because they might mark the document. Do not use the sharp end, even of a pencil, to point out something in a document or on a manuscript map; you will almost certainly touch and mark the manuscript. Before visiting a record office write or telephone to give the staff time to get out the document or documents you wish to examine. It is always wise to make a preliminary visit to study the indexes, calendars and filing system so that you learn how to find what you want and how precisely to refer to it when ordering. The full-time staff of record offices will usually be most helpful to those students who have tried to help themselves first.

The amateur is severely handicapped by the fact that record offices and even libraries and museums are increasingly open only in 'office hours'. No single change would do more to promote the serious popular study of our own past than the provision by local authorities of sufficient finance to make it possible for such places to open in the evenings and at weekends. The group has, however, the advantage over the lone local historian in that someone in it is usually able to get to the right place at the right time; in practice as enthusiasm mounts people use parts of their holidays and even their lunch hours, where relevant, to search for what they require. The development of facilities for copying documents has made things much easier, although it is true to say that the replacement of Xerox facilities with, presumably cheaper, photocopying reproduction processes like S.C.M. is to be deplored; they give grey copies, which are more difficult to read, fade, and cannot be copied as can Xerox. A working group needs a financial pool to buy Xerox copies of documents and photocopies of maps. Multiple copies may be made for the group's members from a quality first copy through the good offices of a member who has access to facilities at work. For the amateur who needs something to work on at home in leisure hours, microfilming is of little use.

There is an entirely different dimension which some people will make their own. Those who like cycling or walking can be given the responsibility for producing a thorough topographical study of the neighbourhood. This and other similar information can be put on maps by those who enjoy this kind of drawing. Amateur photographers can make a photographic record of the community as it is and of changes occurring in it. But it must be made clear that the most important aspect of a building or a landscape from an historical point of view is not always the most beautiful; what is wanted are accurate records of historically significant sites. Photographers can do something else of great importance: collect, and re-photograph to improve the contrast, old photographs as well as old drawings and pictures. From local postcards to family snaps and prints, and watercolours, there is an extraordinary wealth of visual historical material available in almost any village or town.

The popularity of tape-recorders can prove seductive in another pursuit, the recording of oral tradition, preserving the memories of old people. These can cover matters like the physical appearance of the locality in their childhood; the flavour of life at school, in the home, in 'service', and at work in the field, factory or office; social customs and entertainments; personalities and local conflicts. To record these properly, the informant must be put at ease; the use of a tape-recorder may tend to create an unnatural atmosphere. Much can be recorded by taking notes; the information on the tape has, after all, to be written or typed out later.

Analysing the material

As historical material begins to be accumulated, its interpretation becomes important. This is where the varied backgrounds of the group's members will prove most valuable. Those who work on farms can explain many things which may puzzle the academic or even escape his notice. What is true of agriculture is true of mill and mine and factory. The member of a chapel or a church has surely something special to give to the interpretation of its history, as has the local councillor or council official to the history of local government, the doctor or nurse to that of local epidemics, the architect or builder to the history of local buildings. History is one of the few remaining academic fields in which the amateur, the man or woman with a hobby, can make a real contribution, because they can draw on their own experience of life.

Bernard Jennings' experience in the production of two important Yorkshire histories supports this view: 'Teamwork in local history has considerable advantages.' 'The range of interests of the class has made possible a reasonably comprehensive approach. . . . Their general knowledge of the dale and its people has been of great value. This variety of experience and interests, which has enriched our discussions and writing, proved to be only one of the advantages of working as a team. We have been able to deal with voluminous records. . . . Members of the class have tracked down records in private hands, and in unlikely places, to an extent which would have been impossible for a professional historian working on his own'.[3]

What makes the historian is his judgement, his critical sense, the appreciation of what evidence to believe and what not to believe, and the instinct for when to risk a guess. It is not necessary to go to a university to acquire these skills. Many people learn them in the process of living. The advantage of working in a group is that its members foster the development of each other's judgement. Indeed it is not uncommon for a group of amateur local historians to become more critical than a trained historian working with them.

But before the historian can exercise his judgement he must have used his technical skill to find out and analyse his evidence. The local historian must be able to read old handwriting, understand the formulae of different types of documents, read a map, interpret an air photograph and know something about the history of buildings beyond the traditional 'styles' of English architecture. This is where the amateur group needs professional help and where the adult education agencies, the Workers Education Association, the Local Education Authorities and university adult education or extramural departments, should be asked to help. Asking for a course of lectures on the 'History of Little . . . ham' is much less sensible than asking for a tutor or tutors who can teach the local group how to read Secretary Hand, the writing used in ordinary documents in the sixteenth and seventeenth centuries, or how to interpret the local landscape, or how to survey and interpret local buildings—ordinary houses, not only big ones. An adult course which introduces its members to the kinds of historical evidence available to them and shows them how to make use of it will stimulate continuing work and interest, while a course of lectures on the 'History of X' may have only a passive reception.

But not only will the group members need to acquire the range of skills to analyse their sources; they will need to learn some general history, perhaps ideally focused on the county or the region, as a background against which to set their own findings. The wider context of the local study, the general history of the period or the history of the region, is an essential back-cloth for the village or town study. Without some such background, the members of the group will not be capable of judging the significance and importance of their own local history. Again, this background may be acquired by an adult class or by a series of readings in the more general histories, either a single volume history—there are many—or the volumes in the Pelican *History of England* series. It does not really matter which history is read because the purpose of this reading is merely to acquire a general impression of what follows what, or to refresh one's school knowledge. Any serious work in local history will soon lead to the recognition that statements in general histories bear only an approximate relationship to the truth whatever the point of view of their author. It is just as important to read one or two examples of really good local histories, ideally from one's own locality.

Perhaps the most important piece of self-training necessary is in achieving accuracy and system. This is fundamental to all research, but particularly important to group research, in which someone else may be interpreting the material which you have collected or you may be interpreting someone else's material. A good training in achieving accuracy can be obtained by working as a group to analyse the data from the census enumerators' books of 1841–71. If two different people, or two pairs, are set to count each item, for example the numbers of boys and girls described as 'scholars' and their ages, they will rarely achieve the same result at the first attempt. The lesson is salutary. W. G. Hoskins has pointed out, with wisdom, that 'inaccurate information is not only false: it is boring and fundamentally unsatisfying'.[4] Never rely on your memory. Make quite sure that your notes, in whatever form you take them, will provide all the information which you want to record accurately. For instance, always indicate clearly, by the use of quotation marks, whether you are exactly transcribing the original or summarizing: it is disturbing when writing up the results of a group's research to find that one has quoted what seemed to be a phrase from an original source and then to find that its originality was in the mind of the transcriber. Remember that every note must show quite clearly the source on which it is based, either by a description or by a record office reference number; and if you develop your own abbreviations, leave a clear explanation of them with the notes. Whether you transcribe the whole extract from a particular document onto a piece or pieces of paper, or put each piece of information onto a separate card, is much less important than that what you have done should be quite clear to others. There are all kinds of ways of note-taking and of analysing information and it is best to use the one which suits your own temperament.

So that the best use can be made of all the information which accumulates it is desirable to develop a system of common folders in which notes can be kept and which can be available for everyone to consult. Again and again X discovers a piece of information which only makes sense to Y. A group working effectively will accumulate an astonishing amount of paper in a remarkably short space of time. This needs proper sorting, listing and storing, and a careful record of who has borrowed what. I have suffered from perpetual frustration in failing to find a piece of information which I know has been obtained, or in not knowing who has borrowed a particular document or transcript. Ideally a group 'librarian' or 'archivist' should be in charge. The group may contain someone who has experience of, and takes pleasure in, the mechanism of analysing information. Such a person might best contribute by card indexing information collected by others. A simple card index of persons and places can be elaborate enough and sometimes too large for most groups. Punch card and computer analysis have been used successfully by several local history groups, but before embarking on such projects someone in the group must know exactly what they are about or frustration at so much wasted effort will be the only result.

Interpreting the Sources

From what has been said so far it will be apparent that the group will start its work quite diffusely, sending out probing antennae in as many directions as the group contains members and the members have interests and experience. There will be a considerable accumulation of information which can rapidly get out of hand in more ways than one. A Gloucestershire doctor once confided to me that he had been working for many years on his parish history and had a huge collection of information. All he was interested in were the many sources of information which he had not yet tackled. I pointed out to him that if he continued in that way, he would never leave anything to remind people of his labour of love except for boxes full of notes. He must stop collecting facts and begin sifting them so that he could start interpreting them. Sir Matthew Nathan's volume, *The Annals of West Coker,* 594 royal octavo pages, which opens with the words 'Nothing much ever happened at West Coker', shows the sheer size of the historical information which it is possible to collect for one not very important Somerset village. When a group has reached the stage in accumulating evidence, 'facts', which we have assumed, it might be revealing to try arranging the facts in the form of a Chronicle or Annals, at least for a few of the better researched years. It will soon be obvious that selection is essential; everything cannot be included.

Quite early in the work of a group it is, therefore, important to acquire a sense of direction, to decide the scope of its researches in time and place and to divide the whole up into relevant and coherent units for study. This is the stage at which the historian parts company with the antiquarian. In defending the antiquarian, David Cox claimed that 'there is an urge within local communities to find out detail and fact about the past life of a village' and argued that 'the study of events *per se* has always been a satisfying art. The study of trends and movements is also a satisfying art. Why need the two be combined?' Marc Bloch gave one answer when he argued that 'the nature of our intelligence is such that it is stimulated far less by the will to know than by the will to understand.' Collecting 'facts' may be satisfying, a sufficient aim for some and particularly for the 'local antiquarian . . . wedded to his material by bonds of residence, and often descent', as Cox puts it, but once the facts are to be explained to others, or indeed really understood, interpretation begins. W. G. Hoskins has criticised the failure of the local historian to go on to the next stage, kindly but firmly: 'Many local historians go on writing in this tradition, without perceiving the fundamental questions which they should be engaged in answering'; they are 'preoccupied with facts and correspondingly unaware of problems'; their works 'remain enormous collections of facts, the raw materials for history and not history itself.'[5]

Interpretation of one's material is as necessary for the amateur as for the professional, and this is one important reason for turning to writing. It helps the group to select and make sense of their material. No one wants to have their local history reviewed in terms like the following, which many local histories unfortunately deserve: 'The material collected is undigested, badly arranged and carelessly annotated. . . . It is a pity that the information collected by the authors was not properly edited for there are items of interest here which are worth the permanence of print'; or 'it is not sufficient simply to write down everything which can be found out about a parish, without pointing implications or drawing conclusions. The amateur, as much as the professional historian, must be prepared to learn the historian's craft. A craft which uses fact and anecdote not as ends in themselves, but as means to an end. This booklet, though it contains fascinating material, is not sufficiently selective.'[6]

Sooner or later more coherence, a more precise plan of campaign, has to be introduced into the group's work. This second phase of development is fundamental and it should not be delayed too long. With an experienced group it may be undertaken at the very beginning. Victor Skipp organized a series of adult classes in north Warwickshire, studying a compact block of five adjacent parishes, on these lines; it must have required remarkable organization:

> 'Classes are broken down into a number of small research teams, each engaged in a particular aspect of the overall study: for example, the topography of the parish; place- and field-names; population; the care of the poor, etc., etc. At the end of each year's work reports of the various investigations are put into duplicated form for distribution to all members. . . . Students specialize therefore, and make their own particular contribution in a narrow field, yet they are always being stimulated to take a wider interest in the full range of studies; while ultimately they have the satisfaction of seeing their own work integrated into a larger and more meaningful whole, the published history of the parish . . . the aim throughout is to train students, not only in transcription, the selection of facts and analysis, but also to confront them as far as possible with the problems of synthesis and interpretation.'[7]

Before this kind of breakdown into subject fields can be done properly the group must make an appreciation, in the military sense, of what already exists in print, and so of where they will need particularly to fill the gaps with new research rather than supplement what has been done already. In particular, as Rex Russell shows in chapter 11 below, the history of the most modern period will certainly need writing. As the Oxfordshire Rural Community Council's Handbook (1973) puts it (page 22): 'There is much work that can be done in recreating the communities of towns and villages in 19th- and early 20th-century Oxfordshire from records which are often more easily handled by the amateur than those of earlier centuries.' While the records may be easier to handle, the emphasis put on 'recreating the communities' is most important, for it is precisely in the modern period that a local history is most likely to descend into a mere chronicle, into annals. The prehistoric and early historic period may need equal emphasis because so much reinterpretation of earlier archaeological findings has been made necessary by new techniques and fresh views. In every period there will be a need to interpret or reinterpret the documentary evidence in the light of the study of material remains which has been advanced by the techniques of medieval and industrial archaeology, landscape history and the study of vernacular architecture.

Because every place is unique, its history is different from that of anywhere else, but it may help the group to develop their own local plan of campaign if they can think of their local history along broad lines, in a pattern which can provide a frame around which to arrange their multiplicity of facts. But if they do this, the frame must not become a Procrustean bed into which facts are fitted for the sake of the pattern. The frame of a village history might consist of four elements: the topography, the local population—its economic life and social structure, the government of the area, and the cultural and spiritual life of the community.[8] At any given moment in time the interrelationship of these four levels of local life can be studied. Yet each of them changes, and the changes in any one level affect all the others. The study of this complex process is what history is about. While the process of enclosure can be looked at purely as a topographical phenomenon, it cannot be understood unless it is related to economic and social changes. The full significance of these is only clear when their effect, not only on the quality of local farming but also on the quality of local life, is understood. In nineteenth century Cambridgeshire, dissent, and with dissent popular participation in local government, flourished in those villages in which enclosure was not accompanied by a concentration of landholding and tenancies into compact estates and large farms.

Writing it Up

As the group's work develops around themes and their interpretation, 'work reports' or drafts should be circulated, either by duplicating copies or by passing around a few typed texts. Bernard Jennings explains that this is what was done in preparing his two Yorkshire histories: 'All of the main themes have been discussed at length in class, and drafts circulated to the whole group for comment.'[9] Detailed critical comments, preferably in writing, should be obtained from as many members of the group as possible. The draft will be enormously improved in accuracy and lucidity and the critical sense of its author and its readers be enlarged. Working in a group will teach everyone humility and patience. The 'author' being criticised must not be too sensitive; many criticisms cancel one another out, and vigorous criticism by other members of the group can be the best aid in developing one's own capacity for self-criticism.

There is no reason why the form of these first drafts, texts written about themes, should be followed in the final 'chapters' of a published work. They may or may not prove suitable.

At this stage in their work, while drafts are being discussed, additional information may be gathered, and the market prepared for a future publication, by the production of a duplicated news-sheet in which titbits from these preliminary drafts are interspersed with requests for information. These can be sold for a few pence in a local shop or shops and will be extraordinarily popular.

Preparing drafts implies discarding fuller notes and transcripts. These should not be thrown away but filed and deposited, when finished with, in a local branch library or similar public place where they are accessible to others. This makes it possible for anyone who wishes to do so to check the sources used. Whether the final publication contains the full academic apparatus of footnote references or merely mentions the main sources used, it is important that later local historians should be able to follow in one's footsteps. The elegant and fascinating *History of Hitchin* by the late R. L. Hine is seriously marred for the scholar by the fact that some of his apparently full references are untraceable and others when traced do not completely justify his assertions. One serious critic was driven to the conclusion that some parts of the book were simply invented on the basis of parallels from elsewhere.

Of one thing there can be no doubt: whether a group publishes or not, its members will be the richer for their activity. The shallow romanticism about the past which enables so many readers of bad historical novels and viewers of bad historical films or television programmes to believe that life in the past was superior to that in the present because it was more exciting, more vivid, will vanish. As J. H. Plumb put it: 'No one in his senses would choose to have been born in a previous age unless he could be certain that he would have been born into a prosperous family, that he would have enjoyed extremely good health, and that he could have accepted stoically the death of the majority of his children'. Learning history from the original sources, learning how to write history, trains the mind. While learning to understand how society has changed in the past may not provide rules to guide us in the present, at least we will appreciate that living is change.

Notes and References

1 *The Local Historian* vol. 10 no. 8 (1973) p. 383.
2 *See* C. Taylor, 'Total Archaeology' in *Landscape and Documents* ed A. Rogers and T. Rowley (1974) pp. 15–26.
3 Bernard Jennings (ed) *A History of Harrogate and Knaresborough* (1970) pp. 13–14 and *A History of Nidderdale* (1967) pp. 13–14.
4 W. G. *Hoskins, Local History in England* (1972, 2nd edn.) p. 4.
5 David C. Cox, 'The Use of Local History: the Position of the Antiquarian', *Amateur Historian* vol. 6 no. 8 (1965) pp. 260–1; Marc Bloch, *The Historian's Craft* (1954) p. 10; Hoskins (1972) p. 23.
6 *Amateur Historian* vol. 6 no. 1 (1963) p. 30: I quote this without compunction since the second comment was made about a booklet I edited myself.
7 Victor Skipp, 'Amateur Study of Local History', *Amateur Historian* vol. 6 no. 6 (1965) pp. 184–5.
8 Alan Rogers, *This Was Their World* (1972) new edition under the title *Approaches to Local History* (1977) elaborates these four themes.
9 Jennings op. cit. 1967 p. 14.

2

Reconstituting the Medieval Landscape

BARRY HARRISON

The Theme

The rural landscape has been a favourite subject for local history projects since the mid-1950s, when Hoskins, Finberg and Beresford first demonstrated the importance of the physical 'palimpsest' to an understanding of economic history.[1] In many projects the aim has been to reconstitute the immediate pre-enclosure landscape and to assess the impact of enclosure on the village community.[2] This is a worthy enough object in itself, but such work has often left an impression that the pre-enclosure landscape was static and in some sense primaeval. While it has long been recognized that the classical two- or three-field system never existed over most of England, it has been strongly argued in recent years that even in those areas where such arrangements were found in the eighteenth and nineteenth centuries, they may be of no great antiquity.[3] Furthermore, recent studies have emphasized the flexibility of the open-field system itself and its ability to accommodate many of the improvements formerly associated with enclosure. The emphasis in landscape studies has thus shifted from the static to the dynamic, and a picture of landscape evolution is emerging in which enclosure is seen as just one important event among many.[4]

It is by no means certain that groups working on local history projects have yet caught up with these new developments. Yet it is most important that they do, for there is a real danger of the subject becoming divorced from reality. We have already had a number of studies which seem to be creating models of landscape evolution rather than landscapes themselves, a tendency which local historians, with their traditional respect for documentary evidence and the 'total' study of individual communities, could do much to correct.

There is a temptation to suppose that, in the absence of an enclosure award and map, little can be done to reconstitute the landscape. If this were so, it would be very hard on most of us who live and work in areas where parliamentary enclosure of anything beyond upland commons and a few open-field fragments was the exception rather than the rule. In some districts enclosure took place in the sixteenth and seventeenth centuries or even earlier, and enclosure awards are difficult and often impossible to find. In some places enclosure was a piecemeal process carried out over a long period of time and no enclosure award can be expected. In others, particularly in the highland zone, the whole or most of the cultivated land had always been enclosed, although small areas of open-field and of course extensive common pasture were found almost everywhere. Nevertheless, in my experience, local history students are so dominated by the idea of enclosure, the one great event which is supposed to have changed everything, that even in considering areas of known early or piecemeal enclosure, they find it difficult to resist the temptation to look for traces of two or three arable fields with simple names such as 'East Field' and 'Mill Field'. The trouble is they will probably find a few small fields with names of this kind, and it will be difficult to persuade them that they are probably of no significance whatsoever. But the greater danger in this sort of 'field-hunting' is that a mass of valuable evidence contained in seemingly inexplicable field-names, in field-shapes and in the pattern of ownership and occupation, will be overlooked. It is precisely such evidence which can throw a great deal of light on the evolution of the landscape for many centuries before enclosure and sometimes point to the origins of the open-fields themselves. T. A. M. Bishop pointed the way forty years ago in a famous article dealing with the evolution of open-fields in Yorkshire, but with a much wider relevance, yet surprisingly few scholars and even fewer local historians have followed his lead.[5] The aim of this chapter is to demonstrate, using concrete examples, how a team working on a landscape project can achieve at least a partial understanding of the origins and phases of development of their local landscape before final enclosure, whenever that might have taken place.

To begin with, it cannot be stressed too strongly that a single township is not an ideal unit of study. For one thing, the arrangement of arable fields, permanent meadow and common pasture were rarely peculiar to one township, but tended to run in broad tracts over a considerable expanse of countryside, and the pattern in one village must be examined in the context of the district as a whole. A multi-township parish may be a satisfactory unit, but more consideration should be given to geographical unity than to administrative boundaries, important though these are. At the very least it is essential to examine all the townships bordering on the one in which the group is particularly interested. Further, the interpretation of landscape development must depend very largely on field-names, and the significance of many of these will only become clear when they are plotted over an extensive area.

The Basic Sources

The starting point of the enquiry should be the tithe award and map drawn up between 1836 and about 1850. There are some parishes without awards and others in which the award contains little or no field-name detail, but for most places this is likely to be the best and sometimes the only detailed source available.[6] Fortunately, the tithe awards are of greatest value for townships which have undergone early or piecemeal enclosure, and which therefore lack a parliamentary enclosure award. When parliamentary enclosure took place, the tithes were usually commuted at the same time, and the area affected by the enclosure will be shown as a blank on the tithe map. However, areas of older enclosure will be detailed, and information about the rest can be gleaned from the enclosure award and map, where these exist. Of course, enclosure maps usually show the allotments after enclosure—'strip-maps' of the previous open-fields are very rare—but the schedule will usually relate the new allotments to the old fields and, even more importantly, to the furlongs within them, and this will allow a reasonably accurate delineation of both. One way or another, the group will be singularly unfortunate if it is unable to construct a reasonably accurate picture of the landscape of most of the townships within its area in the late eighteenth or early nineteenth century. Of course, if there are earlier detailed maps in estate archives, they may be used as a basis for the work, but it is important to be sure that no areas are missing.

There should not be much difficulty in tracking down the tithe awards and maps required. Three copies were made, one of which was to be kept in the parish, another in the diocesan registry and a third at the offices of the Tithe Redemption Commission in London. Many of the parish copies have now been deposited in county record offices, as have the diocesan copies in some areas, while the third copy will now be found in the Public Record Office from whom electrostatic prints can be obtained fairly cheaply.

Several copies of the tithe map should be made, on which to plot such things as the pattern of ownership, the pattern of occupation and field-names from the tithe schedule. If, as recommended, the group is dealing with a number of townships, each of which may have its own map, often on a different scale, it will be useful to plot the field-names on to one map covering the whole area. For this purpose my groups generally use the first edition six-inch Ordnance Survey maps, many of which were published near to the date of the tithe awards and thus show a more or less unaltered field-pattern.[7] Photocopies of these maps can be obtained from the British Library and from many county record offices. It is not advisable to plot information directly on to photocopies of tithe awards and Ordnance Survey maps since these will contain a good deal of superfluous detail and may not be very sharp. A copy of each map should be traced and drawn, preferably by a member of the group experienced in such work (for example a draughtsman, an architect or a geography teacher) and photocopies can then be made of the drawings. In most large towns there are firms specializing in the production of 'instant' photocopies, and of course many offices have their own machines for this purpose.

Interpreting the Results

The pattern of ownership may appear to be of little significance in the evolution of the landscape, but in fact it can provide a good deal of useful information. Although units of ownership may have changed hands many times and may have been sub-divided and amalgamated, there was a strong tendency for the units of the original enclosure to be perpetuated, particularly in villages where there were many small or middle-sized owners. Figure 2.1 shows the pattern of ownership in one such village. This village was enclosed in 1596, yet half a dozen of the original allotments still survived intact at the time of the tithe award, and a good deal of information about these holdings has been obtained from deeds and manor court books. Apart from individual properties, the overall pattern is also significant; the concentration of small properties to the west and south of the village represents the division of the original common (West Moor) and meadows (West Ings) respectively. Even when a full enclosure took place, such important pasture resources were often shared out in small units among smallholders with common rights and others whose main allotment was situated elsewhere. Finally, the pattern of ownership provides useful clues as to the whereabouts of documentary material, because where large landowners owned a portion of the land, even a

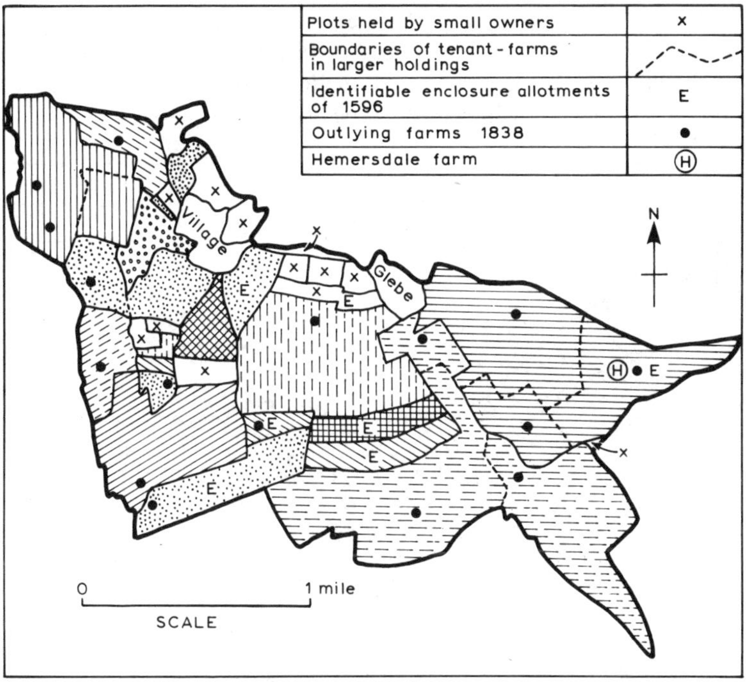

2.1 Romanby near Northallerton, North Yorkshire. Landownership in 1838

very small portion, there is likely to be information about it in their estate papers. In this particular village, we found four landowners who owned only modest plots here but substantial estates elsewhere, and this led us on to a profitable examination of archive collections we would otherwise never have considered.

The pattern of occupation is of less significance than the pattern of ownership, because larger owners could divide and re-divide their property at will; but it is still worth plotting on the map (2.2), particularly where most of the land was owned by only one or two people. Tenants with little or no land but enjoying rights of common pasture before enclosure were often granted small allotments on the former common, often as close to the village centre as possible (2.2). Farm boundaries might be altered at will, but since the framework of ridge-and-furrow, balks, field-ways, boundary banks and ditches inherited from pre-enclosure times could not easily be altered, some tenant-farms tended to remain intact from the time of enclosure onwards. Thus at Romanby (2.1) the farm of Hemersdale, once a common pasture, remained within the same boundaries from enclosure in 1596 until after 1840. Similarly, old ring-fence farms on the periphery of the open-fields and divided from them by a substantial bank or ditch, often remained unaltered through many centuries and their boundaries can still be traced on the tithe map.

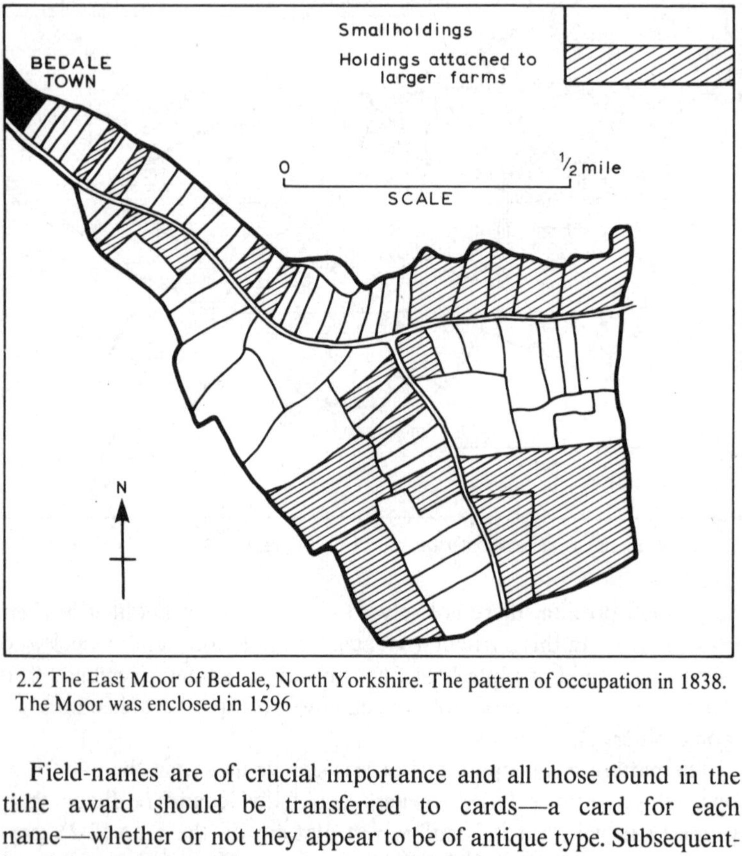

2.2 The East Moor of Bedale, North Yorkshire. The pattern of occupation in 1838. The Moor was enclosed in 1596

Field-names are of crucial importance and all those found in the tithe award should be transferred to cards—a card for each name—whether or not they appear to be of antique type. Subsequently all documentary references to each field-name should be transferred to the appropriate card. The task of plotting various categories of information on to maps and of transferring field-names to a card-index can be undertaken simultaneously by individuals or small sub-groups, but since everybody is working from the same source materials at this stage it is advisable to do this work during meetings of the whole group. Otherwise there is a danger of variable reading and interpretation of the documents. Further, field-names can be very misleading, and it is most important to take down all forms of each name if it is to be correctly interpreted.[8] The next thing is to block together all fields which carry the same name and enter these, together with any other names of an undoubtedly ancient type, on a copy of the map.

Figure 2.3 shows the results of this exercise for three townships in the Vale of York, near Thirsk. In itself this map can tell us a great deal about the medieval landscape and suggests many possible lines of enquiry when we come to consider the documentary evidence. The two large areas of moor (the usual name for all common pasture in Yorkshire) stand out very clearly as do some quite large areas of carrs (marshes) on the edge of the moor. The three villages are surrounded by fields or blocks of fields with names strongly suggestive of former open-field arable containing elements such as 'lands', 'flatts', 'dales', 'butts' and 'hills'. In non-Scandinavian parts of England many of the elements in field-names will be different, but reference to the relevant Place Name Society volume and to Field's Dictionary will usually make it clear which elements are most common in any one area.[9] To the west of our three townships, along the banks of the River Swale, lay extensive 'Ings' or permanent meadows. Thus the basic layout of the pre-enclosure landscape is already becoming clear, but we can go several steps further. To the north-west are a group of fields with names suggesting former woodland, although none was left by the early nineteenth century. On the south are large areas of 'Leas' or 'Leys' on the edge of the moor. In North Yorkshire this name usually relates to an extensive area, often on the edge of a former waste, and there is reason to believe that it was applied to former arable land carved out of the waste at the height of the medieval boom and subsequently allowed to revert to grass. Large areas associated with a particular kind of livestock, such as 'Ox Close' or 'Cow Close', are also often found near to the edge of the waste and appear to represent stinted pastures reclaimed either from the moor or from decayed arable on the moor-edge and reserved for particular animals. They represent a phase of enclosure which is often overlooked—the enclosure of blocks of better-quality pasture or old arable for the purpose of creating commons in which different kinds of stock were segregated and their numbers more closely regulated than was possible on the old wastes.

Field-names also reveal something of the process of reclamation from the waste and the creation of the fields themselves. The name 'riddings' (clearances from woodland) occurs in close proximity to other names of a woodland character to the north-west of our villages, suggesting an extensive wooded tract for which, as it turned out, there was thirteenth century documentary evidence. Other evidence of reclamation is found in the 'Out Crofts' of Carlton, an island of arable

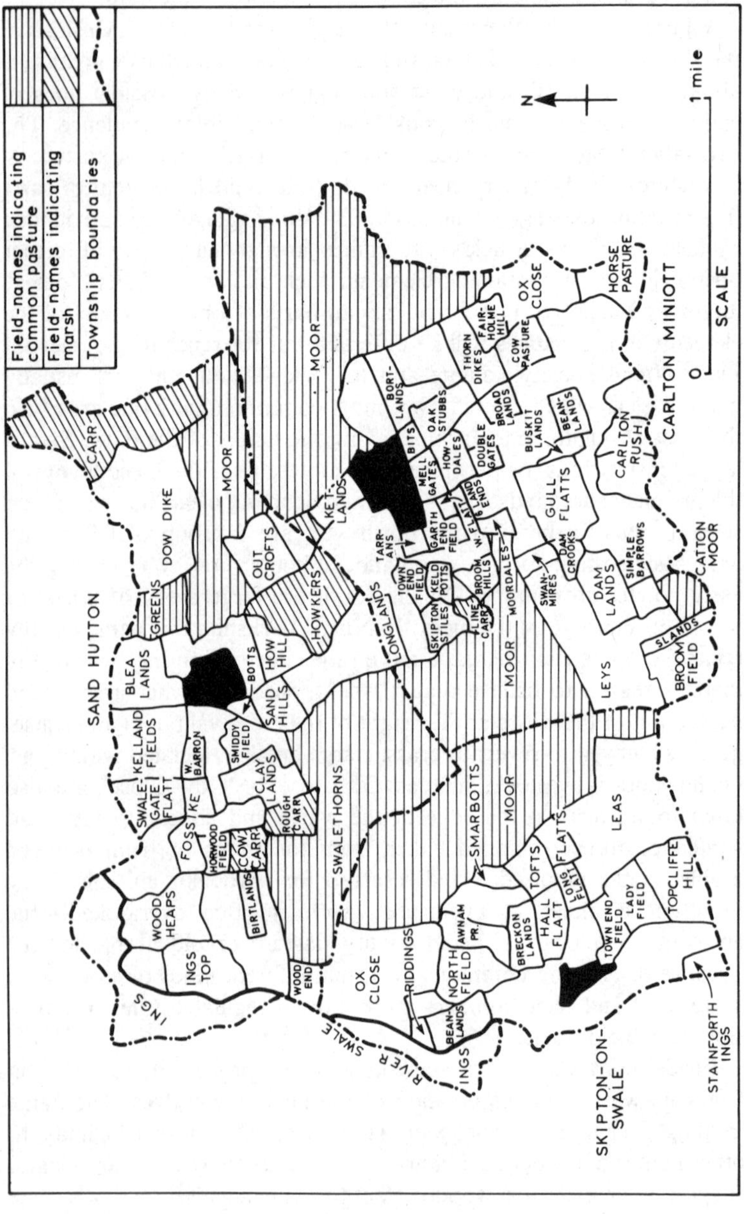

2.3 Three Vale of York townships. Field names from Tithe Awards

carved out of the moor, and in names like 'Oak Stubbs' and 'Breckon Lands'. Former boundaries of the arable, before it reached its maximum extent, may be indicated by names like 'Thorn Dikes', 'Dow Dyke' and Fossike'.

These townships have been examined at some length simply to show how much can be gleaned from the field-names in the tithe award alone, and how much a comparative study of field-names in several adjacent townships can add to our understanding of them. It will of course be necessary to test out these hypotheses against the documentary evidence, but it is not a bad idea to formulate hypotheses at this stage provided that one does not become a slave to them.

So far we have considered villages in a lowland situation in which most of the cultivated land would have been open field arable, but over large upland and woodland tracts of England small open-fields were mixed in with ancient enclosures in varying proportions. Figures 2.4 and 2.5 illustrate what the tithe awards can tell us about such an area, in this case a group of townships in Swaledale, North Yorkshire. Figure 2.4 is based on an analysis of the pattern of ownership, but for the sake of simplicity distinguishes only between areas of multiple and areas of individual ownership within sizeable blocks of land carrying the same field-name. It will be seen that the areas around the larger nucleated settlements were mostly in multiple ownership, while around the smaller villages and hamlets the balance is more even. In townships with no nucleations, however, there is little or no intermixture of holdings, and most of the isolated farms are found here, although there are also a number of small farms cultivating intakes on the edge of the moor. The ownership pattern thus suggests a correlation between the degree of nucleation of settlements and the extent of their open-fields, and this hypothesis finds considerable support in the type and distribution of field-names. Figure 2.5 shows a large concentration of open-field names around the larger villages of Healaugh and Reeth, a few around the smaller nucleations, and none in the non-nucleated townships. The existence of a 'Town Field' at both Grinton and Harkerside is interesting in that it suggests the concentration of all open-field arable into one large field, a feature which has been remarked on in some other areas with extensive wastes.[10] It is remarkable that open-fields should have existed at all in such a tiny hamlet as Harkerside, and their presence serves as a useful reminder that, wherever arable farming is found, even on a very small scale, it was usually organized on some kind of open-field basis, although the open-fields might be mere islands in a sea of enclosed pasture. As one

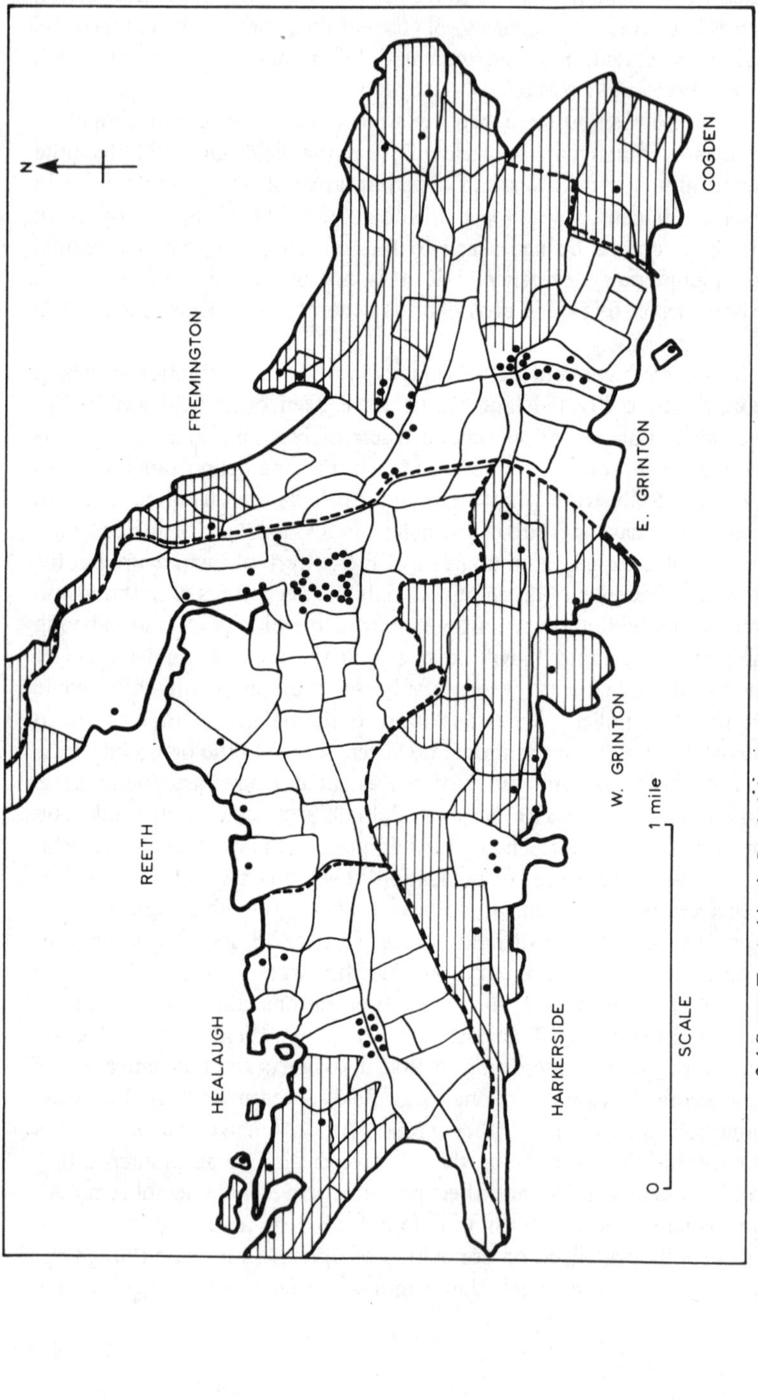

2.4 Seven Townships in Swaledale, North Yorkshire. Blocks of land in multiple ownership unshaded

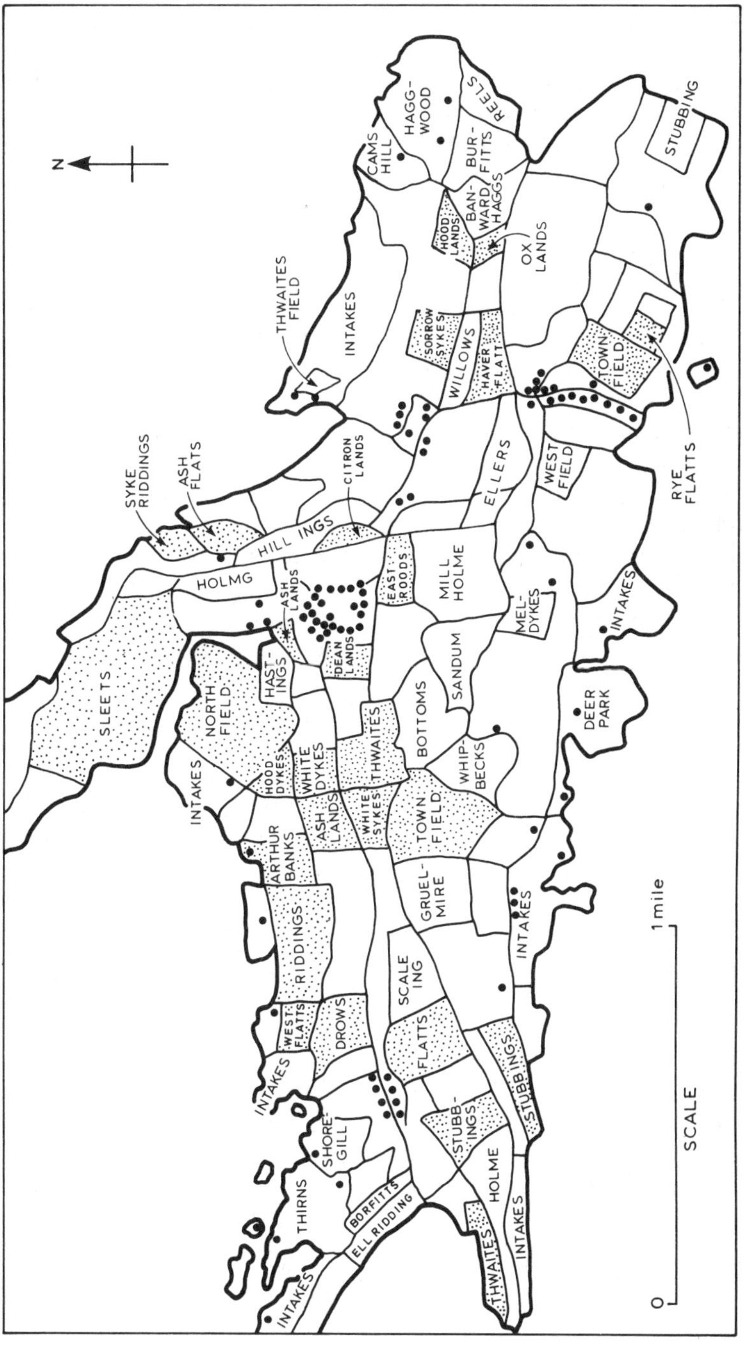

2.5 Seven Townships in Swaledale, North Yorkshire. Field Names, open-field types unshaded

might expect, the field-names in this area differ quite markedly from those in the Vale of York; very large areas known as 'riddings', 'thwaites', 'stubbings' and 'sleets', all indicating original reclamation from woodland, are found in close proximity to open-field names and often mixed in with them. There can be little doubt that the open-fields in this area were themselves reclaimed largely from virgin forest.

Other Documents

The next step in the project is to gather as much documentary material relating directly to the landscape as possible for all periods prior to the early nineteenth century. Most of the sources are well known, and it would be tedious to describe them all in detail. The main records must of course lie in estate collections, for it was the owners of property and holders of rights who were most concerned to describe their holdings at various times. Thus deeds, lease books, manorial court records, rentals and surveys may all survive in private possession or be deposited in some record office, often at a distance from the landscape under study. Other sources will prove of great value, especially glebe (or ecclesiastical) terriers, those descriptions of the property of parish churches drawn up in the seventeenth and eighteenth centuries in each parish at the request of the bishop and often preserved among parish or diocesan records; sometimes uninformative, they may nevertheless on occasion list in some detail the fields of the township in which the parish church had lands. But numerous as the documentary sources are, coverage of the study-district is bound to be uneven, since many of the most useful records, such as field-books, estate surveys and court rolls, are only likely to be found if there is a good estate archive.

The collections of information from deeds, estate records and other sources normally housed in county record offices, estate and solicitors' offices, and not therefore available at group meetings, will usually have to be undertaken by a few members of the group (although it is worth asking your local archivist if he would be prepared to open up his record office to your whole group for the occasional weekend or evening meeting). It is most important that the information collected is not transferred to cards on the spot but that a summary of the contents of each deed etc. be made for examination during group meetings. Without frequent reference to the other source materials there is real danger that field-names, many of which will closely resemble one another, will be entered on the wrong cards.

Of all these sources, deeds are perhaps the most significant. They have been consistently underrated by historians except for the medieval charters which many local record societies once devoted much of their resources to publishing. For many places it may not be possible to find more than a handful of deeds, but where they exist the information they provide is invaluable. Even eighteenth century deeds often reveal a large number of field-names which had disappeared less than a century later. Moreover, the deeds for a particular property may cover a long period since they tended to be handed down from owner to owner. In those parts of the country which experienced early enclosure, information about the enclosure is much more likely to come from deeds than from any other source. A separate card-index of deeds should be built up, containing for each deed the date, names of the parties, details of the property and any other topographical information. Field-names in the deeds should of course also be transferred to the field-name cards. Quite apart from the property which is the subject of the deed, reference will often be made to other land and landscape features which bordered it and this information can assist in placing hitherto unlocated field-names on the map.

Figure 2.6 will convey some idea of the possibilities of this approach. The tithe award for the township of Bagby was only moderately informative, but the deeds cast a good deal of light both on the meaning of some of the obscurer field-names and on the location of others. The following references to the large areas known in the tithe award as 'loscars' were assembled:

LOSCARS	1838 Tithe Award.
LOSKEWE	1583 (deed): bounded by Cockrigg Close on S. and adjoining Spital Garth.
LOSCOGH	*c.* 1170–1185 (charter): bounded by Baunelandesic, Hospital Ditch and Baggesnape Syke.
LOFTSCOGH	Late 12th century (charter): 'lucrative' land in.

The derivation of the name was now quite clear—from Scandinavian *loft* (loft) and *scogr* (wood). It was evident that this stretch of land had once been wood and that it had only recently been brought under cultivation at the end of the twelfth century—'lucrative' land has this significance in Yorkshire. There was practically no wood in Bagby in 1838 and apart from 'Loscars' no field-name suggestive of it. However, using deeds of the sixteenth to eighteenth centuries it was possible roughly to locate other areas of former woodland, to judge by the field-name elements *snape* (woodland pasture), *scoh* or *skewghe* (wood) and *with* (wood). Several of these names were found in late twelfth century charters as well, in a context that suggests rapid reclamation at that period. The original woodland character of this township goes far towards explaining the scattered character of open-field names and the fact that our only glimpse of the open fields in operation (in the late sixteenth century) shows widely separated units. By the same means it also proved possible to locate the lost medieval hamlet of Newbiggin and a small grange (Bagby Cote) belonging to Byland Abbey. The area of the grange was, incidentally, found to be tithe-free in the tithe award, a feature which might help to locate many such properties.[11]

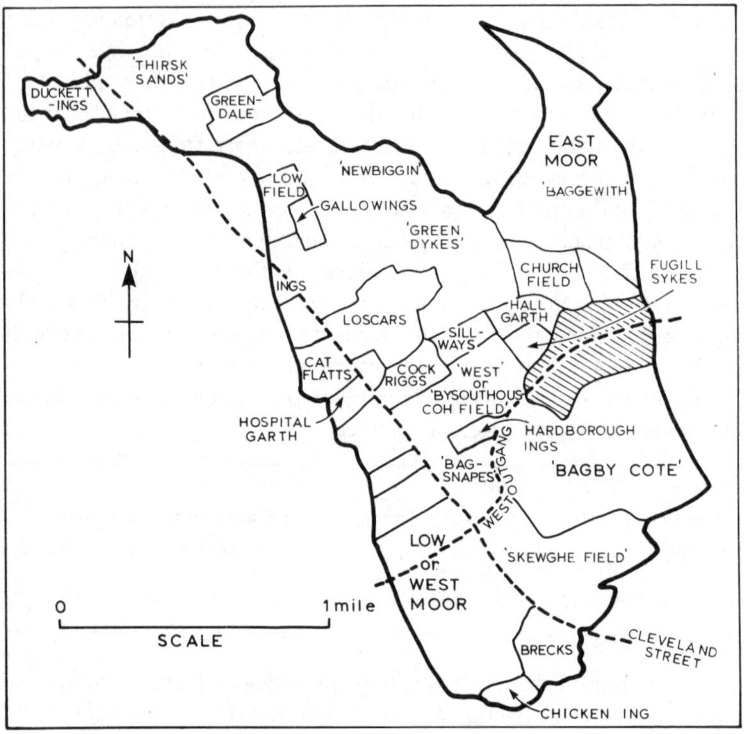

2.6 Bagby, near Thirsk, North Yorkshire. Field Names from Tithe Award and Deeds

Where there is a fairly good collection of deeds and other records, they might be used not only to help reconstitute the pre-enclosure landscape, but also to illustrate the chronology of enclosure itself, particularly where it occurred piecemeal over a long period of time. Figures 2.7 and 2.8 show the sixteenth century landscape of three townships in the northern Vale of York, and the approximate dates of enclosure, based on the evidence of tithe awards, deeds and manor

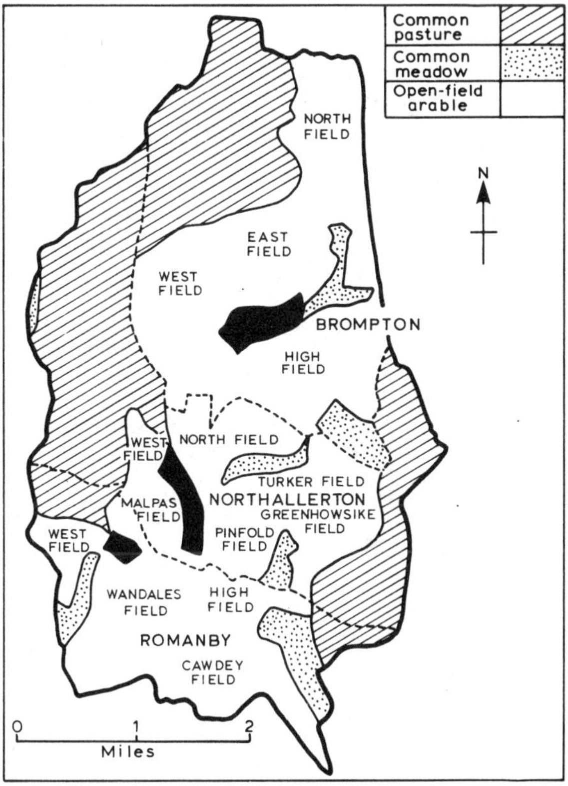

2.7 Three Northallerton townships. The Pre-Enclosure Landscape

court admittance books. The earliest enclosed land lay to the west of Northallerton near to the Bishop of Durham's castle and including a substantial part of his demesnes. This may well explain why enclosure took place so early in this area. At the end of the sixteenth century the whole of Romanby was enclosed, and so a little later was a large slice of Brompton including all the moors. It is perhaps significant that all these lands were held by copy-hold tenure. Later in the seventeenth century the rest of Brompton and most of the Northallerton commons were enclosed, leaving a block of land on the east side of Northallerton under open-fields and meadows for a further century or more. The preservation of open-fields at Northallerton alone would seem to be accounted for by the commoning rights enjoyed and jealously guarded by the burgesses of the town. The field-system in Northallerton was in a state of constant flux, as new areas were enclosed, and is scarcely identifiable from one century to another.

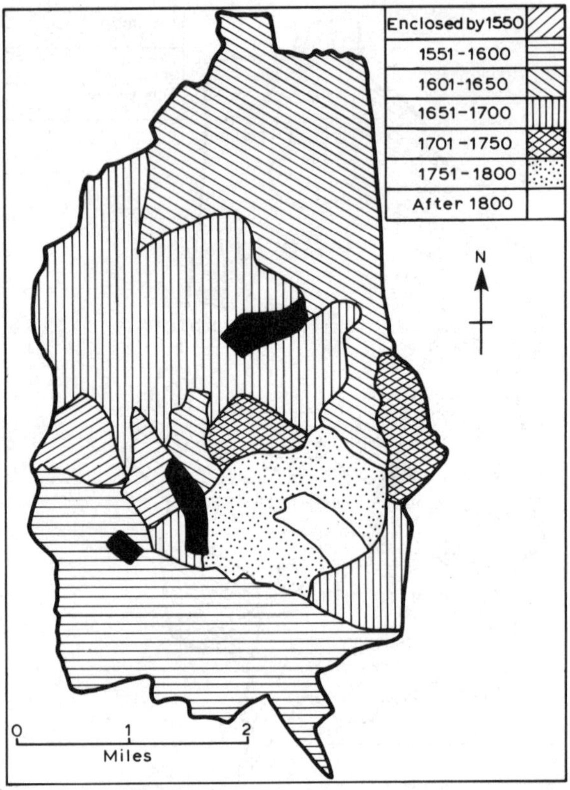

2.8 Three Northallerton townships. Chronology of Enclosure

Although it is not intended to detail all possible sources for landscape-study, it is worth mentioning one particularly valuable source—the Exchequer Inquisitions and Depositions in the Public Record Office (class E134 & E178). There are many thousands of these for the late sixteenth and seventeenth centuries and, unlike some other potentially valuable sources, they are indexed by county (although not in alphabetical order of township). They contain many cases relating to the early enclosure of lands which had at some time or other been in the hands of the Crown, usually when an enclosure was challenged by an aggrieved party, and they are full of information about the pre-enclosure landscape. As a means of tracking down early enclosures, they are second only to good deed collections. To examine this material, there is no alternative to a personal visit to the Public Record Office in London, since it is not listed in such a way as to make it possible to photocopy the indexes for any area smaller than an entire county.

The Landscape Itself

So far very little has been said about the medieval landscape as such. One might well ask precisely what, if the landscape was constantly changing, are we trying to reconstitute? It is obviously desirable to have some fixed point to work towards, whether backwards or forwards in time, and in most areas the late thirteenth and early fourteenth centuries will be most satisfactory. There is a general agreement that the peak of medieval settlement and colonisation of the land was reached round about 1300 or perhaps a little later in areas of extensive wastes, by which time arable cultivation had reached an extent which it was never to attain again.[12] It is worthwhile aiming our enquiry at this period since the topographical framework of the village lands was determined for centuries afterwards by the high medieval arable expansion. Although cropping units might change, the physical earthworks—ridge and furrow, balks, fieldways, ditches and banks—remained a permanent fact until quite recent times. Pasture farming and mixed agriculture took place within this framework and the shapes of enclosures were determined largely by the strips and furlongs of former arable fields. Thus it is only by recreating the medieval fields that we can fully understand the later development of the landscape. An appreciation of the arable bias of high medieval agriculture is also important for an understanding of the way in which the open-fields were built up; we have to appreciate that any land which could support cereals, however temporary and however poor the crop, was likely to have been put under the plough in the thirteenth century.

We cannot proceed very far with a study of the development of the open fields without documentary support, but medieval deeds and other documents are far more numerous than many people suppose. In practice, I have found very few townships with nothing at all from this period, and even a handful of charters can often supply a large number of field-names, some of which can be linked with information from the tithe award and later deeds. In many areas much material from both national and local archives has been published by record societies although not always translated from the Latin. However, it does not require much knowledge of Latin to grapple successfully with the standardized forms of medieval charters after a little experience.[13] One must not expect medieval deeds to give a very clear picture of the landscape as a whole; open fields are seldom named even where the classical system prevailed, and holdings were commonly described by reference to the various furlongs in which they lay.

The final stage in a landscape project should be a consideration of the landscape itself, not in maps and documents but in the field. Medieval farming has left many physical remains, which are being rapidly eradicated at the present time. Ridge and furrow is perhaps the most obvious, but internal boundary-banks and access roads, the large banks and ditches which once divided the common pastures and meadows from the open-fields, the abandoned sites of isolated farms and hamlets, park dykes and the township boundaries themselves, all deserve consideration and can add immensely to our understanding of the medieval landscape. Groups working in the southern and midland counties may like to try their hand at 'historical ecology', particularly the dating of hedgerows by the variety of shrubs found in them. For guidance, reference should be made to the booklet on *Hedges and*

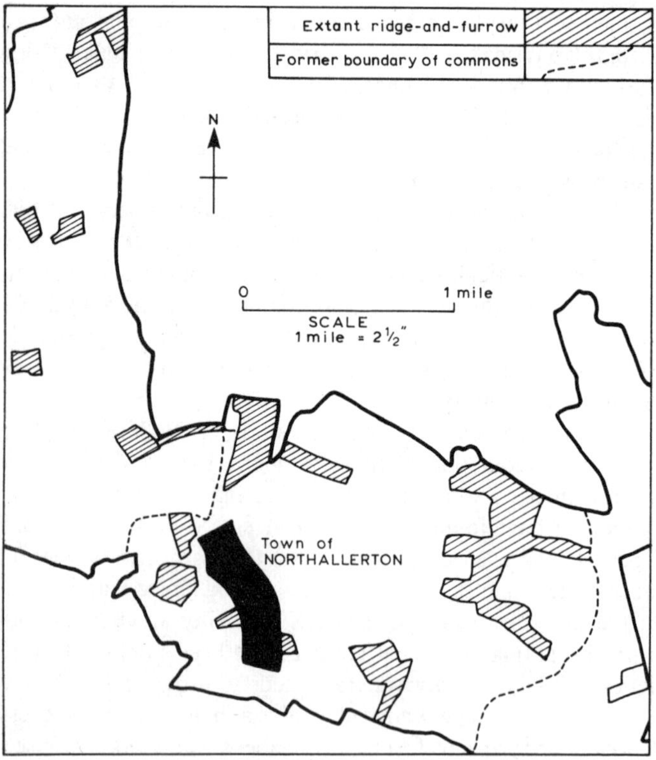

2.9 Surviving ridge-and-furrow, Northallerton, North Yorkshire

Local History and other works listed in the bibliography, although it must be noted that the techniques there described do not seem to yield such fruitful results in the northern counties.

Some of these features can be more readily identified from good air-photographs than on the ground. Most county planning offices now have full sets to which they are happy to grant access if given adequate notice. Figure 2.9 shows the distribution of ridge and furrow in the fields of Northallerton, plotted from air photographs. In general it accords well with what we have learned from the tithe award, deeds and other sources, and provides a reassuring confirmation of our conclusions. However, there are some areas of undoubted medieval ridge and furrow lying deep in the moors to the north of the town which suggest an even greater extension of arable cultivation than we had hitherto suspected.

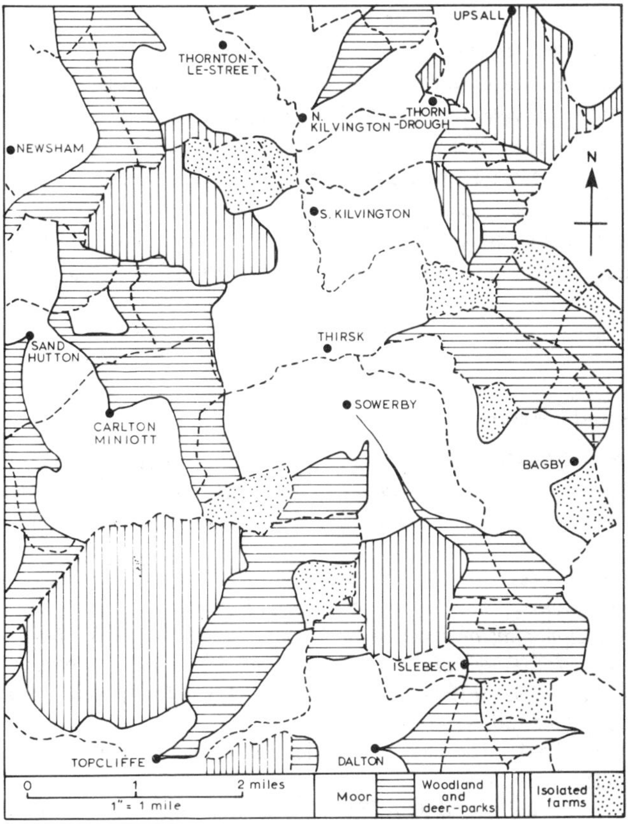

2.10 Distribution of medieval waste, Thirsk area

At the end of the project, the material collected is most unlikely to provide a uniform coverage of the whole of the area studied, but it should be possible to learn a good deal about the less well-documented townships from those which are more favoured with source-materials. Figure 2.10 shows one exercise carried out by an adult class at Thirsk, based on material collected for a study of the medieval landscape. The medieval wastes—common pastures, woods and deer-parks—for which there is clear evidence, have been plotted on the map for a large area of the Vale of York, together with any isolated farms that were to be found. The map tells a fairly dramatic story. The village fields are seen as a series of linked islands and peninsulas in a sea of waste, and this not in the remote Pennine uplands but in the middle of the fertile Vale of York. As suggested earlier, the wastes ran in great tracts separated by other tracts of field-land. Another exercise was to plot the location of field-names containing reclamation elements and these were seen to lie almost entirely on the margins of these wastes.

Once the overall pattern has been grasped, it is not too difficult to fit in those townships for which the evidence is slight. Mere guesses must be avoided of course, but the omission of a township or two is not likely to make a great difference to the overall picture. One advantage of this kind of project is that it stimulates groups in neighbouring districts to take over and extend the project area, so that gradually a broader picture emerges which might eventually form the basis for a regional study.

Notes and References

1 W. G. Hoskins, *The Making of the English Landscape* (1952); M. W. Beresford, *The Lost Villages of England* (1954); H. P. R. Finberg, *Gloucestershire: An Illustrated Essay in the History of the Landscape* (1955).

2 *See* the excellent series of studies of north Lincolnshire enclosures by Rex Russell, *E. Halton 1801–4 and N. Kelsey 1813–40* (1964); *Nettleton, Caistor and Caistor Moors 1791–1814* (1962); *Barton upon Humber 1793–6 and Hibaldstow 1796–1803* (1962); *Bottesford and Yaddlethorpe 1794–7, Messingham 1798–1804, and Ashby in Bottesford 1801–9* (1964).

3 Joan Thirsk, 'The Common Fields', *Past and Present 29* (1964) pp. 3–25.

4 A. R. H. Baker and R. A. Butlin (eds) *Studies of Field Systems in the British Isles* (1973) especially chapter 3, 'Field Systems in the British

Isles' by R. A. Butlin, chapter 6 'Field Systems of the East Midlands' by Joan Thirsk, and chapter 14, 'Conclusion: Problems and Perspectives'.

5 T. A. M. Bishop, 'Assarting and the Growth of the Open Fields', *Economic History Review VI* (1935–6) pp. 13–29.

6 H. C. Prince, 'The Tithe Surveys of the Mid-Nineteenth Century', *Agricultural History Review VII* (1959) 1 pp. 14–26.

7 For the earliest large-scale O.S. maps, *see* J. B. Harley, *The Historian's Guide to Ordnance Survey Maps* (Standing Conference for Local History, 1964).

8 For a good example of group work with tithe awards, *see* V. H. T. Skipp and P. R. Hastings, *Discovering Bickenhill* (1964).

9 J. Field, *English Field Names, A Dictionary* (1972).

10 June Sheppard, 'Field Systems of Yorkshire', in Baker and Butlin (eds) (1973) pp. 179–80.

11 For the location of former monastic granges in tithe awards, *see* C. Platt, *The Monastic Grange in Medieval England, a Reassessment* (1969).

12 J. Z. Titow, *English Rural Society 1200–1350* (1969) pp. 71–2.

13 J. L. Fisher, *Medieval Farming Glossary* (1968) National Council of Social Services; E. A. Gooder, *Latin for Local History: An Introduction* (1961).

3

The Study of Traditional Buildings

R. A. MACHIN

It is no longer necessary to argue that archaeological and documentary evidence are complementary. The local historian should be concerned primarily with the ways in which people lived and worked in the past. He ought therefore to study houses, farm buildings and workshops as carefully as any documentary source. Published work shows that this is not on the whole being done. Asked why this is the case, local historians usually reply that architectural history requires technical expertise akin to the trade mysteries of medieval guilds. This is an assumption as false as the one that it requires a degree in Latin and a certificate in palaeography to read manorial court rolls. An effort sustained by a belief that the results will be worthwhile is sufficient. This essay is intended for those local historians who want guidance on what to record, how to do it and what to do with the finished product. The advantages of group involvement in this work are clearly apparent. The study of buildings has many facets, each of which can be undertaken by one or two members of a group according to their particular interests and aptitudes. Surveying particularly may be considerably eased by team-work, and the collection and analysis of the documentary material relating to any building can form the basis of group activity.

What follows is written with minor rural houses in mind but the principles hold good for other types of buildings which have not received the attention they deserve. Despite a multitude of books we still do not fully understand the rural manor house,[1] and farm buildings remain largely unknown territory.[2] Urban houses present peculiar difficulties because of the many uses to which they are put during their life. The ground floors of town houses are remarkably uninformative and the urban architectural historian often pursues a painful course through upper floors and roofs.[3]

Before you begin

At an early stage it is essential to decide the final objective of the work, for this will determine the techniques and degree of detail of the study. Will traditional buildings be primary or secondary in the work? If they are to be the principal or indeed the sole concern, will the final product be mainly architectural—a study of building materials or stylistic features;[4] or will it concentrate on functional aspects such as the development of plan types (which is probably more relevant to the local historian)? A satisfactory result cannot be produced by working on one of these topics in isolation, but the predominant concern ought to be identified as soon as possible.

You must also decide upon the geographical range of the study. Most local historians think in terms of a parish. Few architectural studies have been published at this level, although a recent study of Stoneleigh based on work in a University Extra-Mural class shows the possibilities.[5] But usually there are not enough old buildings in one parish, and even if it is peculiarly well endowed, the significance of the buildings will not become apparent unless adjacent areas are surveyed, if only briefly, for comparisons and contrasts. A physically defined region is preferable to a parish. This again will depend upon the objectives of the work. A study of building materials requires geological boundaries, while a survey of the buildings of uniform farming practices or tenurial forms might indicate a river valley or ancient forest, an upland plateau or an aristocrat's estate. A study of plan types, on the other hand, might require a combination of these to highlight contrasts. R. B. Wood-Jones[4,5] discusses a range of criteria for defining his Banbury region: whether they are all relevant to the definition is a debatable point. P. Smith and C. E. V. Owen[6] isolated two distinctive trends in building in the upper Severn valley and related them to social development in the area. Small regional studies like these raise questions about adjacent areas. Studying plan types, S. R. Jones and J. T. Smith[7] have worked systematically across Breconshire taking a Rural District each year; using a range of regional studies, P. Smith has considered the whole of Wales.[8] The beginner will rightly feel that part of a county is more than enough; indeed, you may feel that a thorough study of two or three houses will be as much as you can manage. But traditional buildings have an insidious fascination. Sir Cyril Fox and Lord Raglan began by surveying a single threatened house; other houses were then compared to see if the first example was typical. Their weekly excursions all over the county became compulsive, and after several years the result was *Monmouthshire Houses.*[9]

Some background reading and a preliminary review of the buildings in your area are necessary to go alongside your first surveys. The books and articles that I have found most useful and stimulating are listed in the Notes and References at the end of this chapter; M. W. Barley's *English Farmhouse and Cottage* (1961) is also useful, as is Eric Mercer's volume, *English Vernacular Houses,* published by HMSO for the Royal Commission on Historical Monuments (1975). *A Bibliography on Vernacular Architecture* edited by Sir Robert de Z. Hall (1972) is exhaustive for further reading. His regional sections will show the extent of published work in your area. Further work may have been deposited at Fortress House, 23 Savile Row, London W.1, which houses the National Monuments Record (principally photographs plus some plans) and the Royal Commission on Historical Monuments (England). Even if the latter organization has not undertaken a full scale survey of your area, the 'Monuments Threatened or Destroyed' files may include details of demolished buildings. There are separate Commissions for Scotland and Wales based at Edinburgh and Aberystwyth.

However, traditional buildings may be secondary to your main historical interests. If so, the way ahead is difficult. There is an outstanding need to relate the archaeological evidence of traditional buildings to historical problems. 'Vernacular architecture' is becoming a highly technical study, and not surprisingly some of its practitioners have shown remarkable naivety in historical matters. W. G. Hoskins has made this point forcefully on several occasions, but even in his *Midland Peasant,* surely one of the best local histories ever written, the section on peasant houses and interiors forms an 'excursus' following the final chapter.[10] When a master of both documentary and field research finds difficulty integrating both aspects of traditional buildings, we might well despair of success. A pointer is supplied by Sir Robert Hall[11] who has related changes in security of tenure to new building. Despite some reservations in detail, the principle of his study is worthy of imitation. Theoretically it should be possible to relate buildings to changes in social and economic structure, population, distribution of wealth, security of tenure and other standard local history topics. This would require mastery of several technical historical disciplines which few individual workers could achieve; but a group, dividing the work and regularly pooling discoveries, might expect success.

The following is aimed at the complete beginner. I have tried to recall the difficulties I first encountered, with the addition of problems raised by my own extra-mural students asking how they might begin independent work. The section on measuring and drawing is very detailed, since this is a major psychological obstacle for the beginner. After some practice you will not find it necessary to take all the measurements I recommend; you may devise different ways of drawing or alternative methods of preliminary survey to suit your own requirements. A growing sense of dissatisfaction—perhaps hardening to disagreement—with what I have to say will be a measure of your independent ability in the basic work of studying traditional buildings.

Making a Start

There are two ways of learning a subject: reading and listening to the practitioners, or practising it yourself. In the study of traditional buildings, particularly, the two should proceed together. But all too often those who first opt for vicarious experience remain passive for ever. Go out, then, and look at the buildings around you. You say you have already done so? Then answer the following questions: what are the predominant walling materials and roof coverings? window and doorway types? external decorations? the common plan types (by relating chimneys to wall openings)? Most people fail this test because their visual sense is more inaccurate than they realize.

A simple way to sharpen one's architectural vision is to use R. W. Brunskill's *Illustrated Handbook of Vernacular Architecture* (1970) and the local statutory list of scheduled buildings produced by the Department of the Environment. Brunskill's book contains a simplified version of the so-called 'Manchester System', first published in 1966.[12] It may be that either the fuller or the shorter system will suit your needs; I find the former too complicated and the latter too simple. But whichever you choose, the *Handbook* provides an analytical framework for examining buildings. The D of E statutory list can be consulted at some libraries and museums or at the Local Authority Planning Office. It is a brief descriptive list of scheduled buildings of historic interest. The descriptions are almost exclusively external and vary greatly in detail and quality. With Brunskill's *Handbook* as an aide-memoire, the list for your area can be revised and expanded. Using a separate sheet of paper for each building, write a description following a fixed sequence, as in the table below. Much of this can be done from the roadside. It may be necessary to ask permission to make a closer inspection from the garden—unless, as often

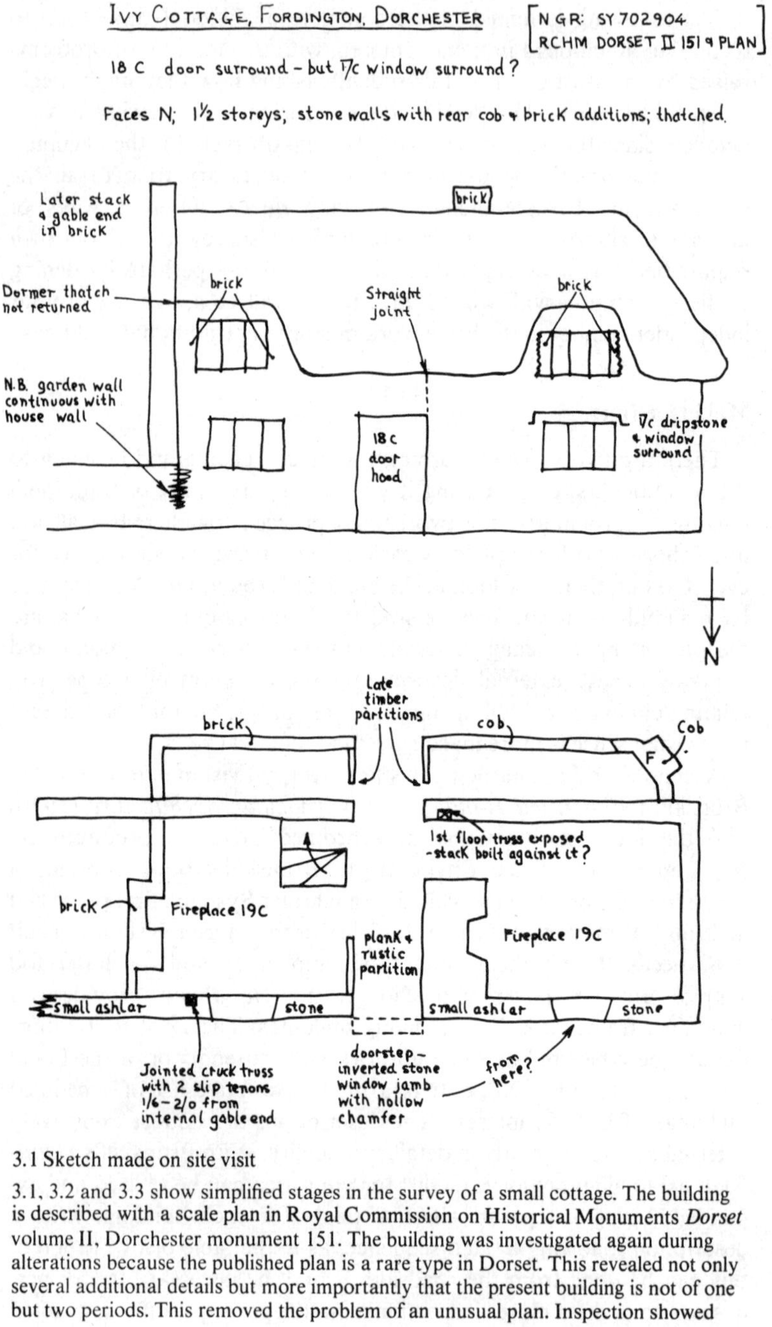

3.1 Sketch made on site visit

3.1, 3.2 and 3.3 show simplified stages in the survey of a small cottage. The building is described with a scale plan in Royal Commission on Historical Monuments *Dorset* volume II, Dorchester monument 151. The building was investigated again during alterations because the published plan is a rare type in Dorset. This revealed not only several additional details but more importantly that the present building is not of one but two periods. This removed the problem of an unusual plan. Inspection showed

happens, the occupant comes out to discover what you are doing. If so, an explanation of your serious purpose frequently leads to an invitation to look inside. If this happens, make a sketch plan with details (3.1); if not, a reasonable guess of the plan can be made by comparing the position of door, windows and chimneys. Do not force yourself upon the occupant; there will be time for a public relations exercise later, particularly when he finds that his neighbours have similarly been surveyed and burglary has not ensued!

Table 1 **CHECKLIST FOR A PRELIMINARY SURVEY**

1 LOCATION	Address and name of occupant if known plus National Grid Reference.
2 DATE	Date on datestone, fountain-head etc., or approximate date.
3 GENERAL DESCRIPTION	Aspect; height; walling materials; roofing materials.
4 EXTERNAL DESCRIPTION	Sketch front elevation and note variations in other walls. (a) Walls: materials, bonding etc., in detail; quoins. (b) Openings: doors, windows. (c) Roof: overall shape; materials; details (tabling, kneelers, dormers, etc.); chimneys.
5 INTERNAL DECRIPTION	Sketch plan: note fireplaces, beams, partitions, panelling, etc.
6 ROOF	Sketch truss stating number of trusses with sketch plan if a mixture of types. Describe general type giving details of principal rafters; apex; tie-beam, collar, collar-braces; longitudinal features (ridge-piece); purlins; wind-braces).

For definitions of these and other building terms, *see* Brunskill, *Handbook*.

A file of such sheets, with photographs if possible, is a useful record in itself—for later workers, for a Conservation Society or as a superficial account in a local history. It will certainly teach you ways of seeing a building, and add a new interest to journeys anywhere: best of all, it can be the starting point for a serious investigation. Reading these files will highlight certain houses. Dated buildings are obviously important because their stylistic features and plans provide a chronological frame of reference for other houses within the area. One or two houses may be clearly older than the others. Modernization of

that part of the rebuilt section had been demolished. The 1844 tithe map shows a much longer farmhouse; an 1864 water colour shows the building as it now stands. Presumably it was a casualty of the piecemeal enclosure of the parish. Further research is indicated in estate land tax assessments census and parish records, leading perhaps to an eighteenth century probate inventory. Rate books might indicate the precise date of the partial demolition and lead to some explanations as to why it happened

houses may reveal hitherto hidden features (3.4 and 3.5). Alteration and demolition of a listed building requires public notice, and it is thus necessary to watch the 'Public Notices' column in the local newspaper and/or to make friends with the planning official responsible. Twice in the last twelve months I have visited buildings listed as eighteenth century during alterations to find evidence of late medieval open halls. There will also be several apparently similar houses. The typical is more significant than the unique, and a detailed survey of a selection of these can be rewarding: but check for typicality, for there are several villages with distinctive house plans which are absent from the surrounding area. And this fact leads to further questions: Why are certain houses not scheduled although they look as if they ought to be on the list? On what grounds would you justify their addition to the list?

Detailed Surveys

If you have never measured a house before, it is useful to have one or two trial runs. This will inspire confidence both in yourself and in the occupants of the first houses you enter: an experienced workmanlike approach is advantageous. It is best to try surveying the houses of some of the group members, no matter if they are all modern structures. Every occupier leaves his own mark on a house, as you will discover in the older buildings. Nor is the exercise necessarily a waste of time. Most surveys of traditional buildings begin 'in the beginning' but stop somewhere in the eighteenth century. It would be interesting to see some surveys which, instead of ignoring the post-traditional buildings, illustrate the later contrasts and possible similarities. In some areas the nineteenth century labourers' cottages bear comparison with sixteenth and seventeenth century houses built for higher social groups. If local craftsmen were still working in the nineteenth century, it would not be surprising to find traces of earlier traditions.

Measuring a building is not a mystery. Our drawings will not reach A.R.I.B.A. qualifying standard but they can be adequate for our purposes. By following a few elementary precepts, *anyone* can produce a useful scale drawing of a building. The following equipment is basic:

1 a tape. Linen tapes stretch, but steel tapes break and therefore I prefer the former. 66 feet or metric equivalent is a useful length. (Whilst metric measurement is *de rigueur* for most professionals, my mind and equipment are designed for feet and inches. The metric user must make his own substitutions in what follows.)
2 a pad of graph paper.

3 a clipboard (a piece of hardboard with a bulldog paper clip will do).
4 two different coloured ball point pens.
Additional useful items are:
5 six foot spring steel tape (i.e. expanding rule).
6 a six foot rod (rigid or folding). I carry a couple of six foot laths with alternate feet painted black and marked at three inch intervals. Mine came from a Government Surplus Store but could easily be made at home.
7 a spirit level with hooks to hang on a length of string (to establish the fall of ground).
8 a plumb weight and line (to establish verticals).
9 oddments such as drawing pins, tin-tacks, plasticine, chalk, etc.

These items can all be kept permanently in a box, ensuring that nothing is left at home.

Before you begin, remember that measuring is a means to an end, which is to produce a scale drawing. Your sketches must be comprehensive, clear and simple. Study the building externally and internally and draw on graph paper the required plans, elevations and sections. The minimum requirement is a ground floor plan. Time available and the value of other features will determine whether or not you go further than this. If in doubt, work on the principle that the building may be demolished or extensively altered before you see it again.

Each drawing should be put on a separate sheet of paper, labelled with the address of the building, national grid reference and north point. Do not try to draw the first sketch to scale; aim instead at getting the proportions roughly correct. For example, if a doorway is drawn half an inch wide, the adjacent window opening can be fixed by estimating how many doorways would fit the intervening space; if four doorways, then the window reveal will be drawn two inches away (3.2). Here is one advantage of using graph paper. A decision must be taken about frames to doors and windows. Either all wall openings will be measured to the solid, ignoring the frames, or the frames will be included to provide an exact internal and external correlation of measurements at the glass.

When the sketch is completed, a different coloured pen can be used to draw in all measuring lines, around the outside of the building, around and between rooms, wall thicknesses, and diagonals of rooms which are far from square. Put a dash through these lines at every point where a measurement is required. Again graph paper makes the job easier since the graph lines match the sketch and measuring lines.

The drawing board restricts you to straight lines at right angles. Therefore irregular walls and curves must be established by off-sets at regular intervals at right angles to a datum line. I recommend that all this is done before any measurements are taken; putting in measuring lines whilst measuring leads to omissions.

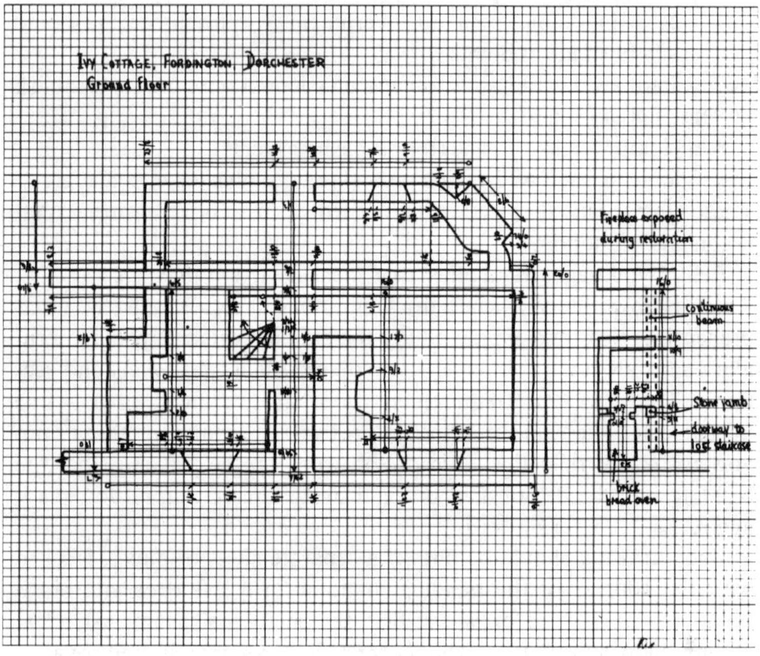

3.2 Ivy Cottage: rough measured plan

The final drawing of the sketch will be to 1/8th or 1/10th scale. It is impossible to draw anything less than an inch at these scales; therefore, except for details such as mouldings, all measurements can be taken to the nearest inch. If this appears to be inaccurate, it is worth remembering that the tape may stretch or sag, and that plastering plays havoc with real wall thicknesses. When noting measurements, turn the clipboard in the direction of travel and write measurements alongside each point. Six feet three inches should be written as 6/3: any other indication merely clutters the sketch and leads to problems at the drawing board.

The beginning of the tape has a ring; this is the first inch. There is also a moveable hook which can be attached to projections (a piece of paper or cardboard will prevent damage to door jambs etc.). The ideal measuring team is three persons, one at each end of the tape to hold it taut and horizontal along the measuring line, the third walking alongside and writing down the measurements. Here is an advantage of team work. Two teams, one working inside and the other outside, might finish a house in an hour; one team will take twice as long. Two people only will take longer still. Solo work requires considerable ingenuity. One soon learns how to hold a fixed tape taut, carry a clipboard and write measurements at the same time. With two overlapping six feet laths I can get round a room almost as fast as a team of three. Inevitably the solo worker must take several individual measurements; but measurements should preferably be 'running', that is the whole length of a wall measured from one end. With a series of individual measurements, an error can be cumulative, whereas with a running measurement it is possible to locate where the error occurred and correct it without returning to the building.

Drawing it up

Drawing should preferably be done by the surveyor as soon as possible whilst the memory is fresh. You will require the following equipment:

1 a drawing board. This is a flat smooth surface with at least one straight edge. Kitchen tables, surfaced block boards etc., have been used, but it is worth buying a small custom-built drawing board.
2 drawing paper (cheap in pads) and tracing paper (cheaper by the roll).
3 clips or masking tape to hold the paper.
4 a T square.
5 at least one set-square.
6 a hard pencil (4H or 6H).
7 a scale ruler with 1/8th, 1/4 etc., for feet and inches, or 1/10th etc. for metric.
8 a pair of compasses.
9 a draughtsman's pen with interchangeable nibs—0.2 and 0.5 are sufficient. (The expense of the pen and a 40 inch roll of tracing paper can be justified for other reasons. Maps are essential for the local historian, and from one tracing you can run off any number of cheap dyeline copies—enormous scope for the study of tithe, enclosure or estate maps.)

When drawing, the paper should be clipped or taped to the board; pins ruin the board, as can continuous drawing without a backing sheet. Sharpen the pencil to a fine point (I use sandpaper stuck to a piece of stripwood); remember, a line has length but no breadth! With the T square placed with its head over the left hand edge of the board, the long arm will slide up and down the board to give parallel lines. Plans have the main front towards the bottom of the sheet; thus a horizontal line along the long arm of the T square will represent the front wall of the building. Lines should always be drawn longer than the final line required: if you want to extend it later you will find it difficult to do so exactly. Sliding the T square down the board, place the set-square firmly at right angles against the T square and draw a vertical line for one gable wall of the building. The scale length and depth of the building can then be measured along these two lines, marking the two points with dots (a dot has no dimensions!). Using T square and set-square as before, draw lines through these two dots. The outline of a rectangular building is now drawn. The rest of the drawing can be filled in using the same methods. It is advisable to work up the drawing at different points rather than draw all the details of one room. In this way anomalies in the building (or your measurements) will become apparent at an early stage. Do not be disheartened to find measurement errors; honest professionals will admit to at least one in every survey.

So far all lines are at right angles. Such buildings do not exist. But unless there is a major deviation, it is acceptable on a drawing: we are making an historical record for interpretation, not surveying the building for re-erection. If deviation from right angles is required, the compasses can be used to produce two intersecting arcs from two fixed points; or the off-sets on the field survey may be reproduced to scale on the drawing. When you have mastered these simple two-dimensional techniques, you may want to produce 'three-dimensional' (isometric) drawings. To do this, the set-square should be turned round on the T square and the plan drawn at 45° to the T square. Then verticals may be drawn from this plan.

When all the field measurements have been transferred to the scale drawing, it should be inked in with the 0.2 nib, using the T square and set-square (3.3a). If the drawing is complicated, it is useful to pencil through lines which are not to be inked. When you are satisfied with the scale outline, you can proceed to a final drawing (3.3b). On tracing paper fastened over the outline, ink in the plan. From this point no mistakes are allowed; if they do occur, the tracing cannot be amended and must be thrown away. It is advisable to shade solid walls for clarity. It is possible to blacken them or to use dry transfer shading; I prefer cross-shading and dots. This is clearer and it enables features such as straight joints to be emphasized; but the original reason was because our photocopying machine could not deal with solid black areas! A useful way to cross-shade is to place the traced drawing over graph paper, positioning the building at 45° to the graph lines with a set-square. Then with a thicker pen (0.5 nib), the walls can be shaded along the graph lines. The tracing now requires lettering, a compass point and a scale. Unless you are exceptionally neat, hand lettering can ruin a drawing. Dry transfer lettering is available commercially to give a professional finish. The tracing may be repositioned along the graph lines, the best position for the title chosen and it may then be rubbed on using the graph lines as a guide. The compass point and scale can similarly be added in a suitable place; both are also available in dry transfers. Scales should not be written in words since reproduction, particularly for publication, often involves reduction in size. My own method is to draw a scale on a sheet of paper with a variety of vertical and horizontal lines around the scale. The latter lines enable parallel location of the scale to other features when the scale sheet is overlaid by the tracing.

A drawing cannot speak for itself, and a written description should always be added. My own descriptions are in note form, following a regular sequence as suggested above for preliminary surveys. The temptation to ignore an inexplicable feature must be resisted: you or your successors may see a significance later which may prove crucial. For example, the 1938 manuscript surveys of the Royal Commission on Historical Monuments for Dorset volume I (1952) describe many principal rafters as having 'curved feet'. On re-examination, these all prove to be jointed crucks. Moreover they are of different forms. Descriptions of these are now being added to the surveys, since it appears that the various types have implications for dating. Even if this opinion is proved wrong either wholly or in part the additional factual information will be available for later workers. I usually make a photocopy of the drawing and written account for the occupant of the house and file the originals plus all field notes in a numbered envelope. A collection of filed surveys is an invaluable record—but to whom? Even if you proceed to a general account, much detail will have to be omitted. Therefore at some stage the originals or copies ought to be deposited for general use. Some sympathetic local institution should be approached for this purpose, a museum, library, county record office or county planning office.

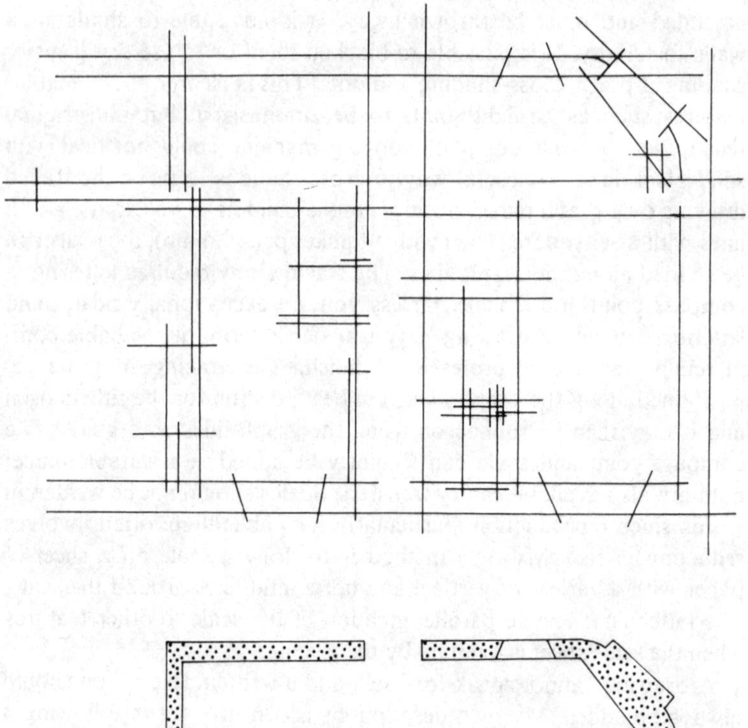

3.3 a (above) scale outline as it appears on drawing board
b (below) finished drawing of same

The Use of Detailed Surveys

So far we have done no more than collect data, factual knowledge without understanding. We can move from recording to architectural history by interpreting individual houses and comparing groups of similar houses. This is becoming a complicated subject which cannot be covered in a short essay. Methods may best be studied by a careful reading of some of the debates between experts. I recommend for a start the long-house controversy. This reached its climax in 1963 when P. Smith criticised I. C. Peate's conclusions on the distribution of the long-house in Wales, arguing that it was restricted to south Wales. In the same volume, J. T. Smith reviewed the evidence for the long-house in Fox and Raglan's *Monmouthshire Houses,* arguing that the majority of the houses were explicable only in terms of a theory of long-house development.[13] With S. R. Jones, he elaborated this theory in *Brycheiniog,*[7] whilst P. Smith re-stated his views in volume IV of *The Agrarian History of England and Wales.*[8] In 1970, S. R. Jones argued for the existence of long-houses in north Wales,[14] and J. T. Smith widened the geographical range of the debate to midland England.[15]

Having read all this, you may feel incapable or unwilling to study traditional buildings at this level. But it would be surprising if you do not feel tempted to interpret your own buildings. A start can be made by adding a separate interpretation to each individual survey, keeping an open mind and continually returning to make revisions. Most of my own filed surveys contain extra sheets giving better, alternative or amended interpretations with cross references to later surveys and articles which throw light upon the problems raised. You may eventually find this so absorbing that a publication on *The Traditional Buildings of . . .* shapes itself.

Such analysis of archaeological data is entertaining and provides intellectual satisfaction by itself. But archaeological data was not generated spontaneously and does not have an independent existence. Traditional buildings are not just houses: they were built as homes for living people to satisfy human needs. Until the study of 'vernacular architecture' is more closely related to history, it will remain a detached, quasi-theoretical piece of knowledge written by specialists for specialists. Documentary sources can be utilized. Wills, probate inventories and glebe terriers are well known, and deeds, building contracts and accounts are obvious specialized sources. But there remain a host of potentially useful sources known to the local historian but rarely considered from a building viewpoint—such as court rolls,

3.4 and 3.5. Number 3 The Green, Tolpuddle, Dorset (3.4) was listed as century originally an open-hall house of sixteenth-century date or earlier. Straight joints of a blocked doorway, visible beneath the sale notice, led to a cross-passage which was turned into a store in the eighteenth century. Some of the original roof structure has survived (3.5) with smoke blackened timbers and under-thatch wattling. The change in roof level should also be noted (3.4). The right-hand part was almost certainly the byre of a long-house

estate records and memoranda, surveys, leases, tax assessments and insurance records.[16] In fact, since house and home had an obvious central role in the life of our forefathers, practically the whole range of standard local history sources could play their part. There is great scope for local history groups, immersed in the documentary minutiae of a region, to incorporate or even focus their studies on buildings and demonstrate to the specialists the historical context of 'vernacular architecture'.

Some practical suggestions might be useful. Houses can be grouped according to a range of criteria, such as size, quality of finish, plan type or approximate date. Doing this for two Dorset villages I examined recently produced quite different results. Yetminster contains several notably large seventeenth century houses with dissimilar plans but all of high quality. Sydling St. Nicholas is a large village just over the hill but contains mainly small houses, unremarkable for their finish, similar in plan and mostly of eighteenth century date. This raises a large number of questions about the distribution of wealth, farm size, land ownership and tenure, types of farming and alternative employments in seventeenth century Yetminster and eighteenth-century Sydling. Why do so many seventeenth century buildings survive in Yetminster and apparently so few in Sydling? What happened, or perhaps failed to happen, in eighteenth century Yetminster and seventeenth century Sydling? As always, the documentary sources are inadequate. But combined with the archaeological evidence, we have some intriguing and well defined problems ranging from the late sixteenth to the nineteenth centuries. Old well-built houses represent increased wealth and a decision to invest some of that wealth in building rather than anything else. Wealth might increase for a number of reasons—through undervalued rents, enclosure, consolidation and/or engrossing of holdings, ability to respond to local market demands, or in other ways. Better houses might result from improved tenurial security, lack of alternative investment opportunities (for instance in land purchase), imitation of the example of a superior social group in the community or of social equals in adjacent areas, and so on. There is scope along these lines for telling an interesting story, focused upon the buildings of any settlement, using a wide range of sources. This would surely be much more interesting to general and specialist readers than the customary trudge through the standard chapter headings of the traditional local history book.

Notes and References

1 But *see* E. Mercer, 'The Houses of the Gentry', *Past and Present* 5 (1954), pp. 11–32 and chapter 1 in his *English Art 1553–1625* (1962).

2 The only general textbook on the subject is W. Harvey, *A History of Farm Buildings in England and Wales* (1970); the only detailed survey is J. E. C. Peters, *The Development of Farm Buildings in Western Lowland Staffordshire up to 1880* (1969).

3 W. A. Pantin, 'The Development of Domestic Architecture in Oxford', *Antiquaries Journal* 47 (1947) deserves careful study by anyone interested in urban houses: among recent studies D. Portman *Exeter Houses 1400–1700* (1966); V. Parker, *The Making of Kings Lynn* (1971), and M. Laithwait, 'The Buildings of Burford: a Cotswold Town in the Fourteenth to Nineteenth Centuries', in *Perspectives in English Urban History,* edited by A. Everitt (1973) are to be recommended.

4 For building materials, *see* A. Clifton-Taylor, *The Pattern of English Building* (2nd Edition, 1972); for an example of the study of stylistic features, *see* R. B. Wood-Jones, *Traditional Domestic Architecture of the Banbury Region* (1963) chapter 12.

5 N. W. Alcock, J. G. Braithwaite and M. W. Jeffs, 'Timber-Framed Buildings in Warwickshire: Stoneleigh Village', *Transactions of the Birmingham and Warwickshire Archaeological Society* 85 (1971–3) pp. 178–201.

6 P. Smith and C. E. V. Owen, 'Traditional and Renaissance Elements in some late Stuart and early Georgian half-Timbered houses in Arwystli', *Montgomeryshire Collections* 60 parts 2 (1958) pp. 101–124.

7 S. R. Jones and J. T. Smith, 'The Houses of Breconshire', *Brycheiniog* 9 (1963) and annually thereafter: one of the most stimulating series of articles I have yet read on the subject.

8 P. Smith, 'Rural Housing in Wales', chapter 11 of *The Agrarian History of England and Wales: volume IV, 1500–1640,* edited by J. Thirsk (1967), the first general survey of the principality since I. C. Peate, *The Welsh House* (2nd Edition, 1944); *see also* P. Smith, *Houses of the Welsh Countryside* (1975) Royal Commission on Ancient and Historical Monuments in Wales.

9 Sir Cyril Fox and Lord Raglan, *Monmouthshire Houses,* 3 vols (1951–4), an outstanding example of methodology. It must be among the first books you read, and it should be re-read at regular intervals.

10 W. G. Hoskins, *Fieldwork in Local History* (1967) p. 94; *The Midland Peasant* (1957) pp. 283–310.

11 Sir Robert de Z. Hall, 'Post-Medieval Land Tenure, Preston Plunckett', *Proceedings of the Somerset Archaeological and Natural History Society* 105 (1960).

12 R. W. Brunskill, 'A Systematic Procedure for Recording English Vernacular Architecture', *Transactions of the Ancient Monuments Society* 13 (1965–66).

13 P. Smith, 'The Long-House and Laithe-house: a study of the House and Byre Homestead in Wales and the West Riding', and J. T. Smith, 'The Long-house in Monmouthshire: a re-appraisal', both in *Culture and Environment:* Essays in Honour of Sir Cyril Fox, edited by I. Ll. Foster and L. Alcock (1963).

14 S. R. Jones, 'Cil-eos Isaf: a late medieval Montgomeryshire long house' *Montgomeryshire Collections* 61 (1969–70).

15 J. T. Smith, 'The Evolution of the English Peasant House to the late Seventeenth Century: the evidence of buildings', *Journal of the British Archaeological Association* 3rd series, 33 (1970) pp. 122–147; this is the best brief summary of the development of traditional house plans in print.

16 The best survey is J. H. Harvey, *Sources for the History of Houses* (1974).

4

The Hearth Tax and Other Records

ROGER FIELDHOUSE

There are two main approaches open to a local history group that wishes to engage in some project of local studies. Perhaps the most obvious is to select a theme such as religion, housing or local government concerning the area; a search can then be made for all the appropriate records relating to the chosen theme. But the other approach, equally useful, is to make a detailed study of one set of records, and it is this sort of approach which is discussed in this chapter. There are several sources which lend themselves to such an examination—wills, manor court rolls or census returns, some of which are discussed in other essays in this book. Of them all, the hearth tax records of the late seventeenth century have many advantages for local history groups. It is possible, for instance, to vary the area of study—a village, a town or a region. The records themselves are relatively easy to obtain and will not prove too difficult to read or to analyse; and they can be made to yield a lot of valuable information, especially if they are related to other near-contemporary sources. An approach to local studies based on one set of records needs to be supplemented from other material to be most useful; and in this respect too the advantages of the hearth tax records are clear. There are almost always plenty of other sources of information with which the taxation returns may be compared; and a number of recent studies have provided a basis for comparisons with other parts of the country.

The Records

The hearth tax (or chimney tax as it was sometimes called) was a revenue first granted by Parliament to Charles II in 1662 'for the better support of his . . . crown and dignity'. It was levied at the rate of two shillings per annum for every fire-hearth or stove, with certain exemptions on the grounds of poverty, and collected in two instalments, at Ladyday and Michaelmas each year. The tax was not popular and was widely evaded during the first two years, but in 1663 and 1664 Parliament passed new Acts, tightening up the administration and providing for the appointment of special tax collectors with powers to enter and search houses once a year, dispensing with the services of the unreliable local constables. Between 1666 and 1669 and again from 1674 to 1684, the tax was farmed out to private individuals and from 1684 until its abolition in 1689 it was controlled by salaried commissioners. Neither the farmers nor the commissioners were required to submit their returns to the Exchequer and so very few records have survived for those years. We are therefore left mainly with returns for the years 1662–6 and 1669–74 when the tax was administered directly by the Government.[1]

Apart from a few hearth tax records which may be found in private collections or county record offices, the surviving returns are amongst the Exchequer records (class E.179) at the Public Record Office in London. A list of all these records, arranged by counties, is shelved in the Round Room at the Public Record Office. It is a matter of only a few minutes' work to discover from this list what documents are available for any particular locality.

The records consist of the collectors' tax assessments; accounts of payments actually made; schedules of arrears of payments; receipts; and auditors' miscellanea. In practice, the assessments are the most useful record, normally consisting of more comprehensive and accurate lists than the returns of those who later actually paid the tax. Some seven or eight assessments were made for most areas during the years 1662–6 and 1669–74, and several of these are likely to have survived for each place. From these it is necessary to select the most comprehensive. Here however the question of exemptions raises a problem. The exempt fell into two categories: those who were too poor to pay rates and those who paid rates but obtained a certificate of exemption because the value of their property or income was below a certain level. Many, but by no means all, assessments list those who were exempt by certificate; a few record the paupers. To obtain the fullest possible record, it is necessary to choose the most comprehensive tax assessment which also includes a list of those discharged by certificate, and if possible, the paupers.[2] It is not possible to predict which of the surviving assessments will be the best for any one locality. The researcher will have to investigate all the returns for the village, town or wider area that he wishes to study. This is not a very arduous task as a fairly cursory glance will indicate which is the most comprehensive.

Table 2 **THE ASSESSMENT OF DOWNHOLME AND WALBURN IN THE WAPENTAKE OF HANGWEST IN THE NORTH RIDING OF YORKSHIRE (1673)[3]**

Mr Wm Frankland	4	Roger Harland	2	John Hodgson	3
Edw. Ellerton	2	Jo. Cooke	1	Barth. Lightfoot	1
Wm Loftus	1	Ann Cagill	1	George Lightfoot	1
Grace Dent	1	Edm. Jefferson	3	Hen. Hawe	1
Barth. Thompson	1	Fra. Ruswell	2	Fra. Nicholson	1
Tho. Dent	1	Fra. Loftus	1	Luce Jackson	1
Fra. Lonsdale	1	Hen. Gill sen.	1	Christ. Dent	1
Roger Beckwith Esq	15	Hen. Gill jun.	1	Jo. Fryer	1
Rd. Carter	2	Rd. Maltas	1	Jo. Alcocke	1
Jo. Pickersgill	1	Jo. Horne	1	Hen. Coultman	1
Wm Ridley	1	Fra. Lodge	1	*Total hearths*	57
Discharged					
George Hops	1	Hen. Ingram	1	Ja. Robinson	1
Luce Wiggin	1	Ja. Ingram	1	Eliz. Russell	1

For a small place, such as the township quoted in Table 2 above, it will be possible either to make a transcript of the return at the Public Record Office or obtain a photostat copy. But if it is intended to study a wider area, it will probably be necessary to obtain a microfilm copy from the Public Record Office (or a local library or Record Office), in which case the first task will be to transcribe the hearth tax list from the microfilm. It is not necessary to have a microfilm reader for this purpose: any slide projector which carries ordinary 35 mm film strips can be used to project microfilm onto a screen from which transcribing can be done very easily by a small group of students either in the classroom or at home. Alternatively, off-prints can be made from the microfilm quite cheaply, from which transcripts can more comfortably be made. It is generally advisable to transcribe the returns on to small record cards, one for each household, recording the name of the taxpayer and number of hearths at which he was assessed. The advantages of record cards are that they can be re-sorted into a different order later if necessary, and that extra information from other sources can be added on to the card below the hearth tax entry.

Population

Having selected the best tax list and transcribed it, the information obtained can be used in a number of ways, either by itself or in conjunction with other records. First, it might be used to estimate the size of the total population within the township, although this is problematic for two reasons. Unless the assessment includes those who were discharged by certificate and the paupers who were automatically exempt, it is extremely difficult to know how many people were excused from the tax (to say nothing of those who evaded it). And then we are faced with the further problem that the hearth tax consists only of a list of taxpayers; it is not a poll tax list of all the inhabitants. The number of householders has to be multiplied by the average number of inhabitants per house to obtain a population estimate. It is possible (but not advisable) to use a sliding-scale multiplier ranging from 3.7 for one-hearth houses to 30 for houses with over 20 hearths.[4] It is probably more reliable to adopt an average figure in the region of 4.5 for all households, although this is subject to local variations. By multiplying the number of households by this figure, an approximate estimate of the population may be obtained.[5]

A more useful demographic exercise is to study the pattern of population density by plotting the number of households, village by village, as was done, for example, by Margaret Spufford for Cambridgeshire.[6] This can best be presented as a distribution map (4.1). This does not give the population figures, but does illustrate the *relative* size of towns and villages within a locality. It can be compared with similar distribution maps drawn from other sources for earlier and later periods to discover how the pattern has changed. And the rate of increase or decrease in the number of households between, for example, a sixteenth century lay subsidy or the 1563 survey of households and the hearth tax, on the one hand, and between the hearth tax and an eighteenth century episcopal visitation return or early nineteenth century census on the other hand, can be calculated.[7] These sources list different groups, communicants, households or families, but the population growth-rates can be calculated in percentage terms and plotted on a series of maps without ever converting the totals into population estimates by the use of a dubious multiplier. The main difficulty to be overcome is how to compare sources which use different administrative boundaries. Whilst some may be listed by parishes, others will be by township, village, constabulary or ward. Here an intimate knowledge of the locality normally provides the key, but if it is not possible to marry all the administrative units, it may be necessary to leave some white patches on the map, indicating areas where the information is for some reason unreliable. Figure 4.2 illustrates the kind of map that can be drawn as a result of such comparisons of sources, although in this case it relates to an earlier date than the hearth tax.[8]

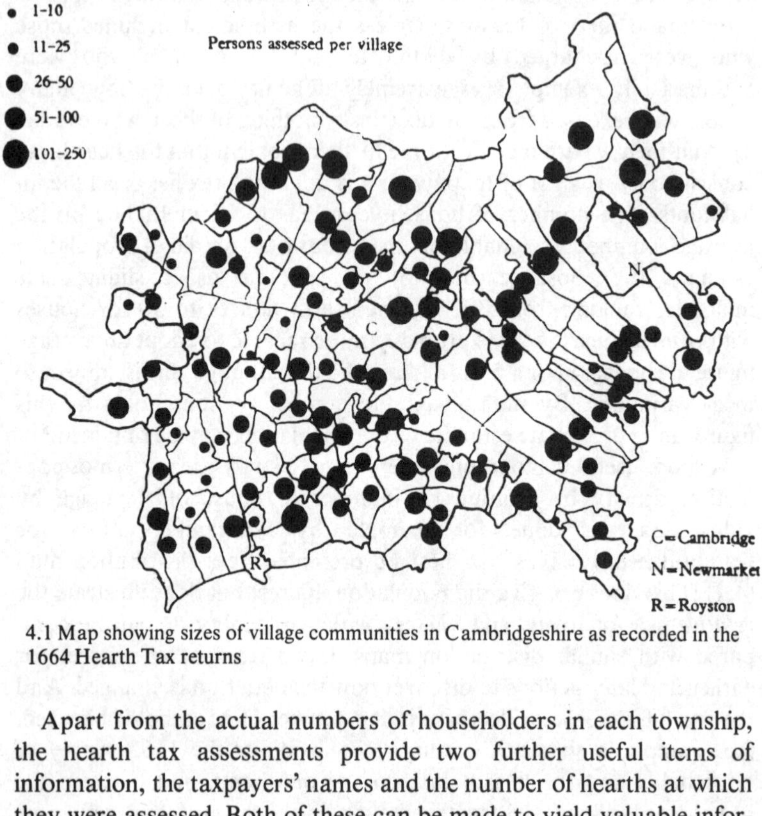

4.1 Map showing sizes of village communities in Cambridgeshire as recorded in the 1664 Hearth Tax returns

Apart from the actual numbers of householders in each township, the hearth tax assessments provide two further useful items of information, the taxpayers' names and the number of hearths at which they were assessed. Both of these can be made to yield valuable information, especially when compared with other records. Thus for instance, a comparison of the names recorded in the assessments with those in the protestation returns of 1642 may indicate something of the rate at which village families arrived or moved away.[9] Again, some returns contain the names of the parish officers at the foot of the assessments and these can be a useful guide to the personnel of local government. A correlation of the taxation records with parochial records,[10] where they survive, will add other dimensions to the study. Thus the parish registers may be used to point out the rate of illegitimacy related to house size and wealth, as indicated in the hearth tax, and where they record occupations, it will be possible to establish some sort of relationship between size of houses and occupations. Similarly, the poor law records, if they exist, may help to fill in some of the details of the households of those who were exempt.

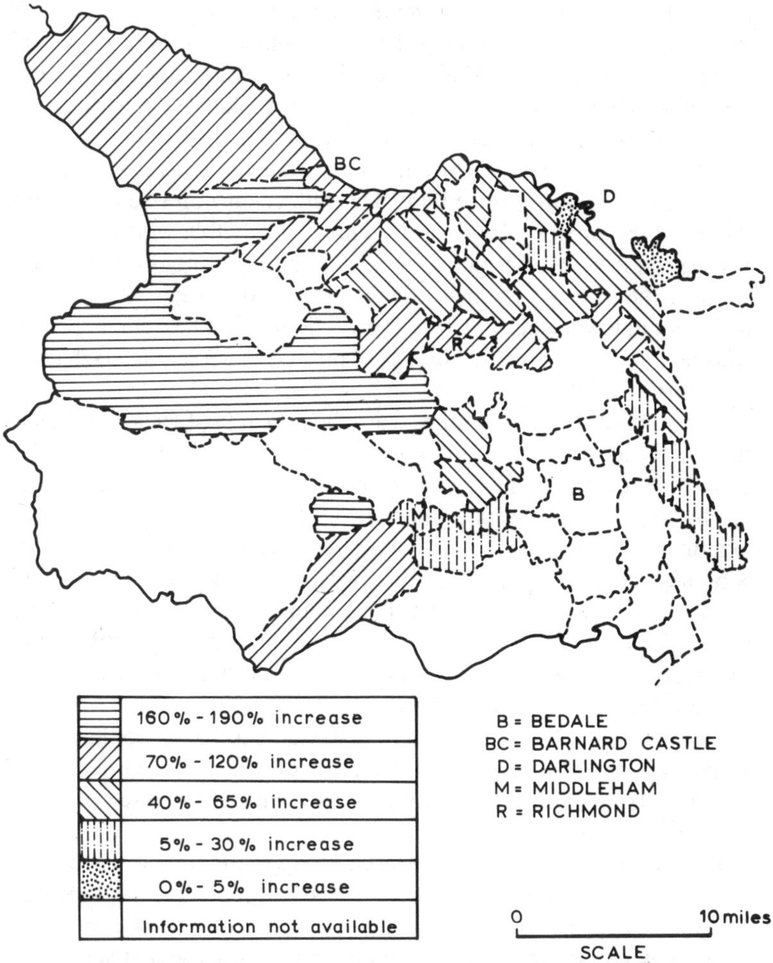

4.2 North West Yorkshire. Percentage population change 1377–1563. The population change for each parish is calculated as the average for that parish and all contiguous parishes for which reliable information is available

Social Structure

The hearths, too, as listed in the assessments, provide valuable information, although it must be remembered that ovens and forges (however these were defined) were exempt from the tax. If it can be shown that the varying number of hearths is a reliable indication of varying wealth and social status, then the tax can provide a guide to the social structure of the local community. The reliability of the tax assessments for this purpose can be tested by comparing them with the probate inventories of as many of the tax-payers as possible.[11] Probate inventories are among the most valuable and well known of all the sources for the local historian. They consist of a list and valuation of a man's moveable goods, drawn up by local assessors at the time of his death and filed with his will in the appropriate probate court.[12] They survive patchily however, ranging generally from the mid-sixteenth century to the mid-eighteenth century; for some villages there may be very few for the period immediately following the hearth tax assessments of the late seventeenth century. But where they do survive, they comprise an invaluable source of social history, their major limitation being that very few are found for the poorest people who had so few belongings that they did not make a will, so that no inventory was taken.

Armed with the list of names from the hearth tax (transcribed onto the record cards which can now be sorted into alphabetical order, for convenience), the researcher or research group can scour the records of the appropriate probate court[13] for the inventories of the local inhabitants. Obviously only a small percentage will have died very soon after the hearth tax assessment was made: therefore the probate records will have to be searched for a number of years after the date of the assessment. On the other hand, the longer the gap between the two records, the less reliable is any correlation between them. If the probate records are searched for a ten-year period from the date of the hearth tax, this would seem to be a reasonable compromise. Depending on how good the collection of probate records is, the search is likely to produce inventories for some eight to fifteen percent of the people listed in the hearth tax.

It may be possible for the research group to obtain photocopies of these inventories or it may be necessary to transcribe them where they are found. In either case, they will have to be transcribed eventually, either in summary form or, preferably, in full, because it is surprising how every item of an inventory can yield useful information. If a summary is made it will be useful to devise a standard form so that the summary can be made in the same way each time for ease of reference and comparison later; see the sample (4.3) which has been completed by a member of an adult education group to provide a brief 'summary of contents' of a full transcript.

The information in the inventories can then be compared with the

Information from Wills and Inventories

NAME Peter Bukton Date of will/inv. 15 March 1674, 10 June 1675.

1544 Lay Sub. assessment — 1673 Hearth Tax: No. of hearths 6 hearths

Occupation(s) Cordiner

Family Wife Jane. Sons: Matthew, William, Peter
Mother (Anne Buckton) Daughters: Margaret, Anne

Details of house(s) in Frenchgate. (7 rooms + shop)
Forehouse, Back Chamber, Further Chamber
Kitchen, Chamber over House, Shop.
Parlour, Chamber over Shop.

Land/other property 2 burgages in Frenchgate; Jolly Close
2 acres of arable in Low East Field; Pickering House (Frenchgate)
Acre of arable in Low East Field
Close of meadow in High East Field; Close near St. Nicholas.

Bequests (other than listed above)
£60 each to his 2 dtrs., Margaret and Anne.

Cash (Inv.). £13. 6. 8.

Farm or trade stock/tools etc. (Itemise interesting details)

Leather £17. 0. 0.
Shoes £18. 10. 2.
Farm stock £21. 0. 0.
} £56. 10. 2.

1 horse 4. 10. 0.
2 cows 8. 0. 0.
Corn. 7. 10. 0.
} £20.

Household goods, furniture, etc. (Itemise interesting details)

Furniture etc £19. 6. 8. → includes:
1 glass case.
2 standing beds with curtain valances + feather beds
1 seeing glass.
linen

Silver + pewter 6. 0. 0.
Brass. 2. 5. 0.

£45. 2. 6.

Total value of inv. £225. 7. 7 (excluding credits)

Credit £140. 2. 5. Debts £10. 3. 4.

Other information
Shoes in this inventory were valued as follows:
mens 3/- ; boys 1/6 ; boots 5/-
womens 2/- ; childrens 10d.

4.3 A standard form for summary of inventory transcription

hearth tax assessments, to see whether those people who were assessed at the highest number of hearths have more wealth (as expressed in higher total values to their inventories) or more and better household goods and furniture, or more work gear and equipment—the wherewithal to make more money. Conversely, those with small inventory totals may have a smaller number of hearths recorded in the assessments. To obtain this picture, it will be necessary first to group the inventories according to the number of hearths. Thus all the one-hearth inventories may be gathered together into one group, all two to three hearth inventories into another group, all four to five hearth inventories into another and the remainder into a fourth group. Because there were considerable local variations in the proportions of exemptions, depending on the inclination of individual J.Ps, ministers, churchwardens and overseers, some being more prone to issue certificates than others, it is safer to discount the fact that some men were exempt, and group them with the others according to the number of their hearths. The vast majority of those exempt will have only one hearth, although a few have two. It will then be necessary to work out the average or median values of the inventories in each group to discover whether they rise with the number of hearths. Unless the sample is very large, the median probably reflects a truer picture than the average, because it discounts the extremes which distort an average in a small sample. It is also probably true that the total value of household goods (excluding everything else) is a better guide than the total value of the inventory because the latter figure can arbitrarily include or exclude a number of the more uncommon items, such as the value of a lease or outstanding debts. The value of a man's furniture, on the other hand, reflects his real status, based on his 'life style'.

Having made these calculations from the monetary valuations of the inventories to discover whether the median values do rise with the number of hearths, it is also possible to make a more empirical evaluation of the quality of goods possessed by each group. For example, did the men with more hearths possess more silver plates and dishes (as opposed to wood or pewter), more chairs as opposed to forms to sit on, more hangings around their beds, more pictures, cushions, books and other luxury items?

Although there will be individual cases of rich men with apparently few hearths, this does not matter if the analysis shows that *in general* the more hearths a man had, the more *likely* he was to be of a higher social status and enjoy a more comfortable life style. If this proves to be the case, then the hearth tax can be accepted as a reasonably reliable guide to the social structure of the community. Then a social pyramid can be constructed, based on the evidence obtained from the correlation of the tax assessments and inventories. These pyramids can be used to compare the structure of societies of different communities, for example, a market town compared with its rural hinterland, or one town with another (4.4).[14] It may also be possible to

	No. of hearths	Social status
	Over 7	Gentry and squires
	4–7	Wealthy craft and tradesmen merchants and yeomen
	2–3	Most craft and tradesmen and yeomen
	1	Poor craftsmen, husbandmen and destitute and labouring poor

	% of households	
	RICHMOND	SWALEDALE
	2·5	0·25
	18·0	3·25
	32·5	19·5
	47·0	77·0

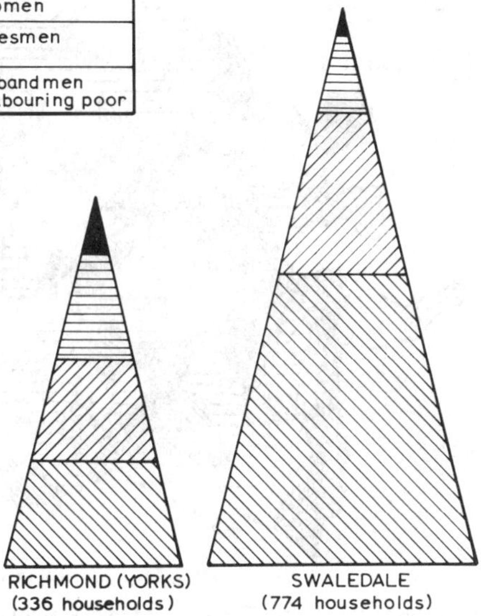

4.4 Social Structure from 1673 Hearth Tax

compare the social pyramid constructed from the hearth tax with another deriving from another source (the sixteenth-century lay subsidies or nineteenth-century censuses, for instance) so as to discover how the social structure of the local community had altered during the intervening period.

House Sizes

The number of hearths recorded in the hearth tax may seem to provide valuable information concerning the size of houses. Once more, however, it may be necessary to test the validity of this assumption, and here again the probate inventories prove useful. Inventories frequently list people's goods room by room, and if they survive in sufficient quantities, they can be used to test the reliability of the tax assessments in terms of house sizes,[15] as can other sources. Field surveys of surviving houses and comparisons with other records

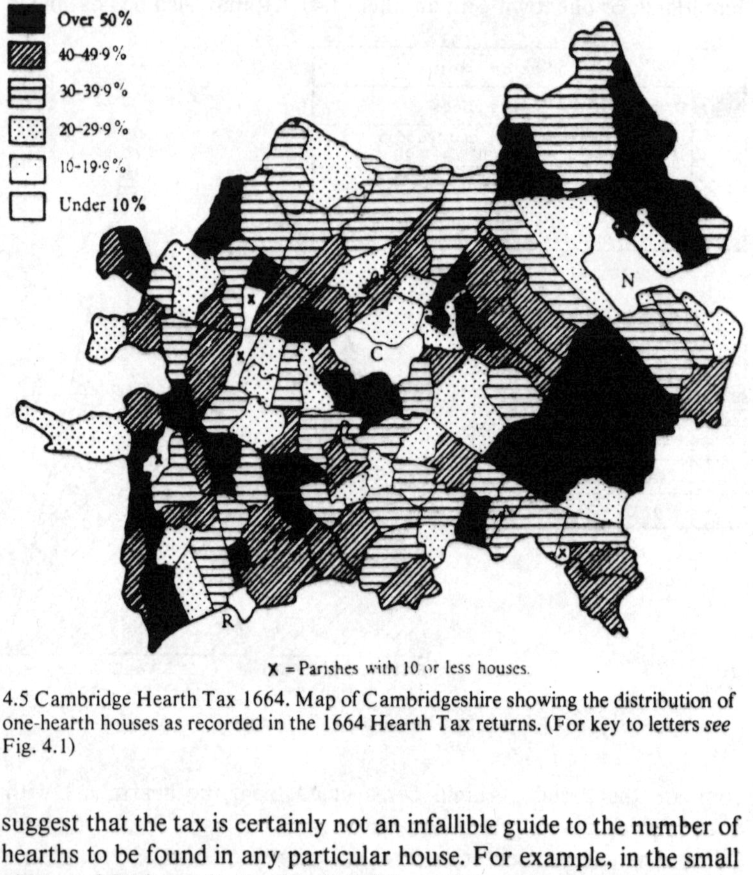

4.5 Cambridge Hearth Tax 1664. Map of Cambridgeshire showing the distribution of one-hearth houses as recorded in the 1664 Hearth Tax returns. (For key to letters *see* Fig. 4.1)

suggest that the tax is certainly not an infallible guide to the number of hearths to be found in any particular house. For example, in the small village of Stainton in the North Riding of Yorkshire, all the inhabitants were assessed at one hearth in 1673, but a manorial court roll clearly states that a number of the houses had two fires sixteen years earlier.[16] However, if a comparison of the hearth tax and inventories shows that *on average* the size of houses does increase with the number of hearths, then the tax assessment can be used to plot the distribution of different sized houses. This can be done either by parishes or villages, or by wards or constabularies within a town (4.5, 4.6, 4.7 and 4.8).[17]

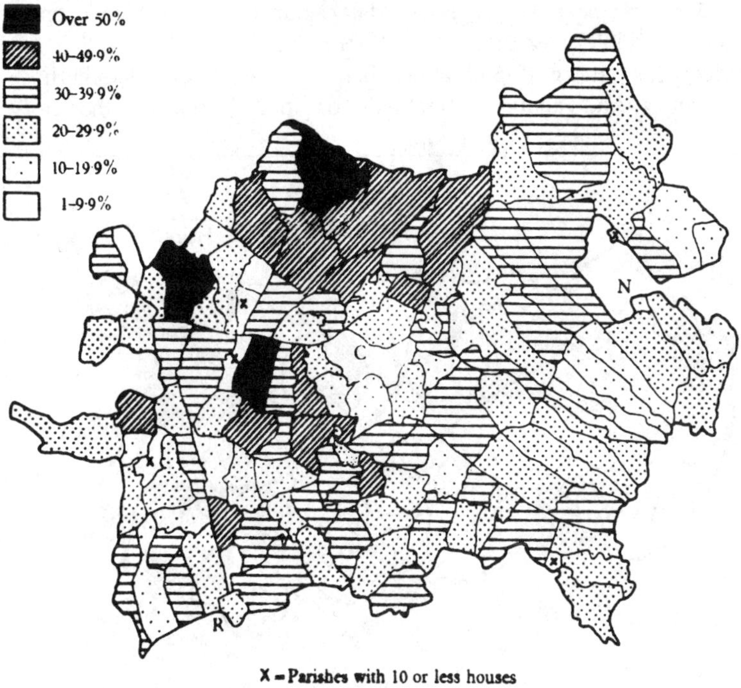

4.6 Cambridge Hearth Tax 1664. Map of Cambridgeshire showing the distribution of two-hearth houses as recorded in the 1664 Hearth Tax returns. (For key to letters *see* Fig. 4.1)

Further Studies

This distribution of houses can then be related to a whole variety of topographical, geographical and economic factors. For example, in Nidderdale, the largest houses are found at the lower (east) end of the area (4.7), where there was a greater quantity of good meadow and arable land; similarly, in Ripon they occupy the central commercial and ecclesiastical districts of the town (4.8), around the market place and minster. The central wards of Ripon also had the largest proportions of middle-sized houses, whilst the smallest were concentrated mostly on the outskirts. A comparison of the hearth tax with a list of burgage owners[18] compiled for electoral purposes proved difficult because the tax refers to *occupiers* rather than to owners. Nevertheless, it enabled the group to identify the exact location of a sufficient number of houses to confirm that the larger houses were situated mainly in the centre and the smaller ones concentrated on the outskirts of the town. In Nidderdale again (4.7), the high proportion of middle-sized houses in Dacre and Hartwith and Winsley reflects the pattern of land tenure there. The yeomen farmers in those townships had acquired freeholds or long leases by the early

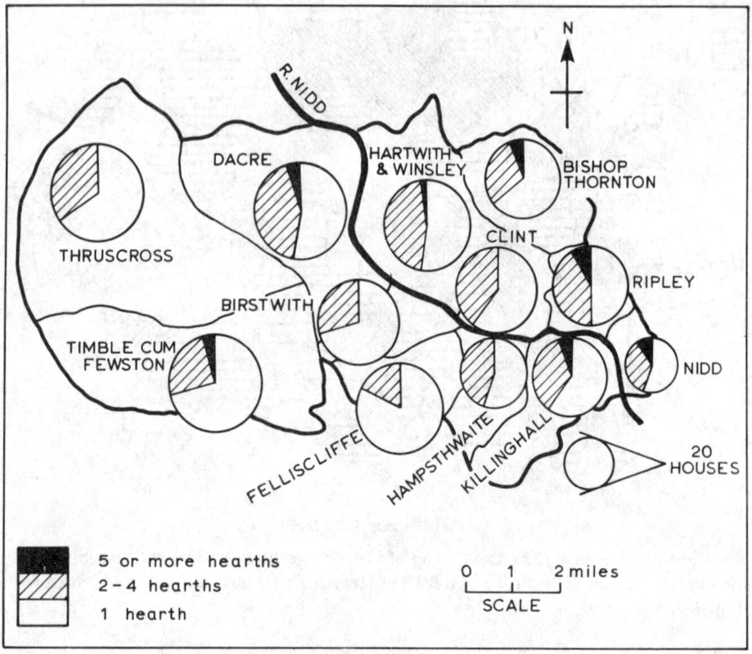

4.7 Nidderdale Hearth Tax (1672)

seventeenth century, which gave them a secure economic position. Their substantial houses were built as a result of their growing prosperity. But in the neighbouring Forest of Knaresborough township, the survival of copyhold tenure led increasingly to the sub-letting of smallholdings on short leases at rack rents to the growing population.[19] Hence the higher proportion of small houses in Felliscliffe, Birstwith, Timble-cum-Fewston and Thruscross townships.

The hearth tax assessments, thus, when used in conjunction with other sources, lend themselves to a number of research projects concerned with discovering the pattern of population distribution, social structure, and housing. Such a study may produce either a static picture of local society at the end of the seventeenth century or, when compared with other records, a chronological study spanning several

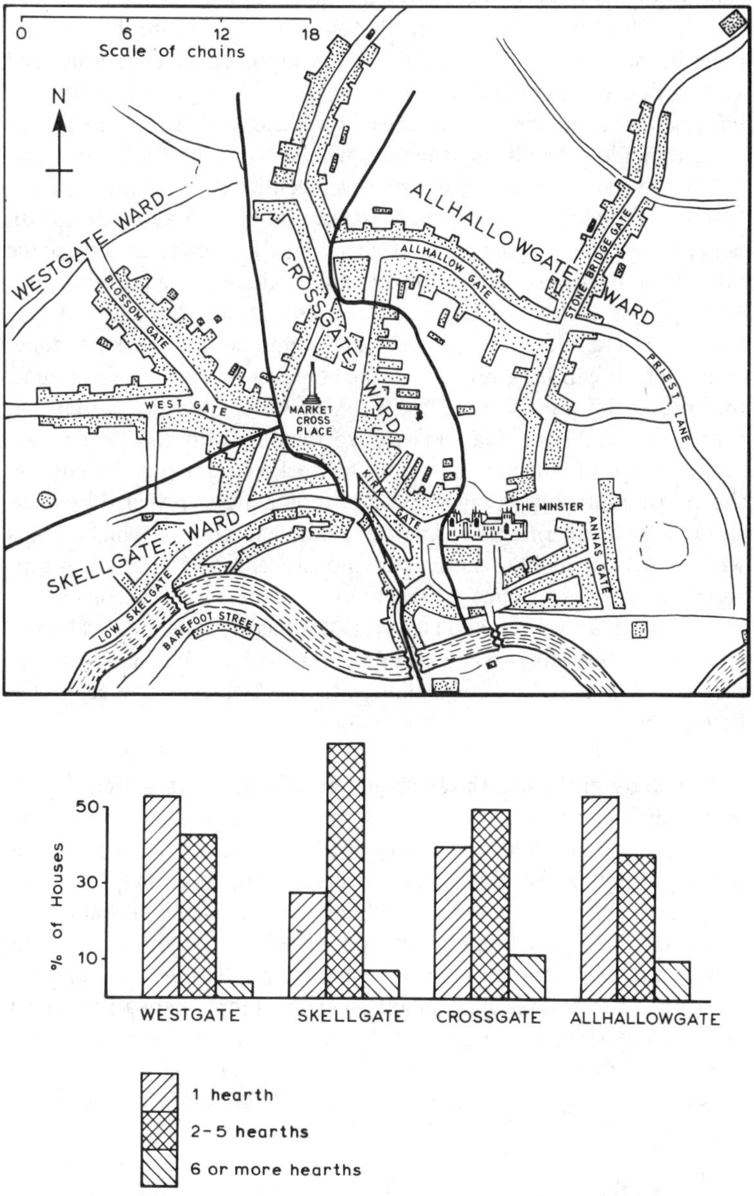

4.8 Ripon Hearth Tax (1672). A map of Ripon showing town wards, and (below) the main types of house recorded in the 1672 Hearth Tax returns. (re-drawn by Geoff King)

centuries. The records themselves are quite easy to handle by groups of adult students who can quickly learn how to transcribe and use them in the ways outlined above. The inventories, which can be used so beneficially in conjunction with the hearth tax by correlating the information from the two sources in a variety of ways, are a little more difficult to handle in groups. It will be necessary for the students to have a rather better grasp of seventeenth century palaeography before tackling these documents. It may be best to allow those students who show the greatest aptitude in this direction to undertake the task of transcribing whilst the others tackle some complementary work. Once transcribed, the inventories can be summarized; the transcript and the summary will then comprise the working documents which can be given out to the students to analyse. Of course, the inventories can be used for a much wider study of social and economic conditions than merely correlating with the hearth tax. Small groups of students can be set to work extracting and analysing the information concerning the standard of living as revealed by these records, or concerning housing (including the way in which rooms were used), agriculture and other industries.[20] These small groups should be able to produce general reports on the particular topics they have studied, as well as tabulated statistics based on the total values of inventories, the values of household goods and work equipment, and the size of houses, for correlation with the hearth tax as suggested here.

The study of the hearth tax should be seen as one research project in a wider scheme; it should not be isolated from other sources. As such it represents a useful source for group activity. On the other hand, presenting the conclusions in diagrammatic or map form, as suggested in this article, is essentially an individual task probably best undertaken by a small number of students with an inclination towards this kind of work (though it must be pointed out that the techniques of drawing a presentable map or diagram are simple enough for most people to master). Accuracy and clarity are essential: aesthetic purity is less important.

Notes and References

1 L. M. Marshall, 'The Levying of the Hearth Tax 1662–88', *Engl. Hist. Rev.*, vol. 51 (1936) pp. 628–46; C. A. F. Meeking, Introductions to *The Surrey Hearth Tax, 1664*, Surrey Record Society 17 (1940) and

Dorset Hearth Tax Assessments 1662–4 (1951); R. Howell, 'Hearth Tax Returns,' *History,* vol. 49 (1964) pp. 42–5; J. Patten, 'The Hearth Taxes 1662–89', *Local Population Studies* no. 7 (1971) pp. 14–27.

2 Patten, pp. 15–21.

3 PRO, E. 179/216/462.

4 This sliding-scale multiplier is based on the work of the seventeenth century demographer, Gregory King.

5 *See* Patten, pp. 22–4; R. S. Schofield, 'Estimates of population size: Hearth Tax', *Local Population Studies,* no. 1 (1968) pp. 33–4.

6 H. M. Spufford, 'The significance of the Cambridgeshire Hearth Tax', *Proceedings of the Camb. Antiq. Soc.,* vol. 55 (1962) p. 60.

7 For further information and guidance in the use and whereabouts of the sources for demographic history from the sixteenth to the eighteenth centuries *see* J. Thirsk, *Sources of Information on Population 1500–1760* (1965); W. B. Stephens, *Sources for the History of Population and their Uses* (University of Leeds Institute of Education paper no. 11, 1971 *passim*): M. W. Beresford, *Lay Subsidies and Poll Taxes* (1963); J. Cornwall, 'English population in the early sixteenth century', *Econ. Hist. Review,* 2nd series vol. 23 (1970) no. 1, pp. 32–44. J. Sheail, 'The distribution of taxable population and wealth in England during the early sixteenth century', *Transactions of the Institute of British Geographers,* vol. 55 (1972) pp. 111–126. There are many books and articles on nineteenth century censuses: those in *The Local Historian* vol. 5, no. 8 (by M. W. Beresford), vol. 8, no. 1 (by P. M. Tillott), vol. 9, no. 1 (by R. Smith) and vol. 10, no. 5 (by M. Barke) will be found useful. *See also* Census Reports of Great Britain, 1801–1931, *HMSO Guide to Official Sources,* no. 2 (1951); M. Drake, 'The Census 1801–1891', in E. A. Wrigley (ed.) *Nineteenth Century Society* (1972).

8 Reproduced from R. Fieldhouse, 'A Comment on population studies, with particular reference to North West Yorkshire, 1377–1563', *Cleveland and Teesside Local History Society Bulletin,* no. 12 (1971) p. 9.

9 For protestation returns, *see* F. West, 'Protestation Returns of 1642', *Bulletin of Local History, East Midlands Region,* VI (1971) pp. 50–54.

10 *See* W. E. Tate, *The Parish Chest,* and chapter 5 below.

11 Spufford *passim*; R. Fieldhouse, 'The Hearth Tax and Social Structure in the Borough of Richmond in 1673', *Cleveland and Teesside Local History Society Bulletin,* no. 14 (1971) pp. 9–17.

12 For a general introduction to inventories, *see* the introduction in F. W. Steer, *Farm and Cottage Inventories of Mid-Essex 1635–1749* (2nd edn., 1969) or M. A. Havinden, *Household and Farm Inventories in Oxfordshire 1550–1590* (1965).

13 For the best guide to the most likely whereabouts of probate records, *see* A. J. Camp, *Wills and their Whereabouts* (1974).

14 R. Fieldhouse, 'The Hearth Tax . . . Richmond in 1673' (1973); PRO, E. 179/216/461–2.

15 Spufford, *passim.*

16 PRO, E. 179/216/462; M. Y. Ashcroft and R. Fieldhouse, 'The population of Stainton in the middle of the seventeenth century', *Cleveland and Teesside Local History Society Bulletin,* no. 16 (1972) p. 26, and no. 18 (1972) p. 9.

17 Spufford, p. 61; PRO, E. 179/210/400.

18 Leeds City Archives, Vyner MSS/5408.

19 B. Jennings, *A History of Nidderdale* (1967) p. 129.

20 For examples of how inventories can be used in these ways, *see* Jennings, (1967), pp. 142–50, 162–81 and 352–60; J. Thirsk (ed), *The Agrarian History of England and Wales,* vol. IV (1967) pp. 412–29, 442–54 and 696–766; M. W. Barley, *The English Farmhouse and Cottage* (1961) *passim*; W. G. Hoskins, *The Midland Peasant* (1965) pp. 283–310.

5

Historical Demography: Games to Play with Parish Registers

CHRISTOPHER CHARLTON

Parish register analysis burst upon the local history scene some ten years ago. It followed the establishment of the Cambridge Group for the History of Population and Social Structure which, in 1964, had begun a systematic enquiry into English historical demography. This was from the beginning a sophisticated university-based project and in the normal course of events it could have been years before the implications of this new approach reached local historians. In fact, at an early stage in its life, the Group appealed to local historians for assistance in collecting data, and from all over the country there emerged individuals and groups who were prepared to extract information from the parish registers in their area to feed the Cambridge computer. The result was a unique partnership between professional and amateur historians.

To ensure that the work done by these untrained researchers would be accurate and uniform, the Cambridge Group devised carefully formulated 'idiot-proof' methods. These procedures were adapted from French experience and now, modified by years of practical application in this country, they form an excellent foundation for parish register analysis. The basic techniques are described in E. A. Wrigley, *An Introduction to English Historical Demography* (1966).[1]

It was not long before it became clear that many of the volunteers the Group had recruited for its specific and limited purpose wanted to continue their own, generally much less sophisticated, parish register research and looked to their mentors for guidance. This the Group provided through a Newsletter until the establishment of the magazine *Local Population Studies* in 1968.[2] Thus a group project in parish register analysis begins with the advantage of a well-tried methodology, a source of encouragement and advice through the Cambridge Group and *Local Population Studies,* and the prospect of undertaking work at a local level which in a variety of directions will be relevant nationally or regionally, or which will be immediately comparable with other work elsewhere.

The Sources

Of course, most local historians when they turn their attention to registers will be seeking answers to local historical questions rather than a chance to participate in a national enquiry. What they will find cannot be predicted. In rare cases parish registers survive from 1538, the year in which Thomas Cromwell's legislation established registration, but many more date from a century later.[3] Registers vary in continuity and in quality and it is always worth spending time examining them to find their defects before beginning even the simplest enquiry. Some, for instance, will cover several different villages within the parish area, making little or no distinction in the records between the various communities from which the persons listed came. Basically a register will record the date of a baptism or a burial and the name of the individual involved, but there is little consistency about the way this individual is defined in relation to parents or family. A child, for example, may be described as 'Ales daughter of Thomas Bown' or 'Ales daughter of Thomas and Elizabeth Bown'. Burial entries vary between a full family relationship, 'Jane Bown daughter of Thomas and Elizabeth Bown' and the meagre 'Jane Bown was buried'. Similarly marriage registers may record only the date and the names of the partners, although after Hardwick's Marriage Act which came into force in 1754 entries included the signatures of both partners and of witnesses. For genealogical investigations, or demographic analysis of the kind which depends on establishing family relationships, consistently detailed entries are essential. Enquiries into the number or pattern of events, the number of burials or the number of baptisms in a particular month or season of the year, or the changing size of the population, are less demanding and most registers approached correctly with patience and time can be made to yield an interesting harvest.

There are no quick returns, but parish registers do have advantages for inexperienced groups. It is inevitable that some parts of a register will be difficult to read but by comparison with other documentary sources registers present few problems. Entries follow a set formula which seldom varies and this makes it easier to cope with both the handwriting and the decayed state of some of the earlier registers. Also, as these complications will be limited to certain parts of a register, careful distribution of work between group members according to ability and experience makes it possible to overcome these difficulties. It is also an advantage that a register usually consists of several volumes and is therefore likely to be in units such as, for example, 'Burials 1703–1758', and these will provide a meaningful period for sections of two or three people within the group to handle; while overall the registers are likely to provide work for the entire group.

It should be possible to claim a further advantage for parish registers over most other local records available to the historian, in that so many of them having survived, parish register projects of some kind ought to be feasible in most parishes. Unfortunately, while the registers may have survived, it does not follow that they will be available for group use. Locating registers is usually fairly easy; they are to be found in the custody of the local incumbent or in the diocesan record office, or exceptionally, for instance during an interregnum or when parishes have been amalgamated, in the hands of churchwardens; or, where the rules have been ignored, deposited in some local record office or library other than the appropriate diocesan record office. The volumes of the National Index of Parish Registers as they appear will provide a comprehensive guide to the location of registers. However, in the meantime historians must rely on the guides produced by local societies and local record offices and an interim guide *Original Parish Registers in Record Offices and Libraries.*[4] Local lists will also indicate the registers which have been transcribed and printed, and in some parts of the country where a large number of registers have been published, it should be possible to conduct parish register projects with minimal use of the manuscript register.

Requirements and Rewards

Many registers have been studied and it is worth examining the section in *L.P.S.* known as 'Work in Progress' to see whether work has been done on the parishes in a particular area. At an early stage a group must decide what sort of work it wants to do; the interests and skills of the various members of the group, the quality of the registers and their availability, are all important considerations, and the decision is not made any easier because, like Tigger in A. A. Milne's *The House at Pooh Corner,* most groups don't know what they like or what they can do until they have tried it. Access often becomes the first question to be considered, if only because for obvious reasons incumbents and archivists have the habit of asking how long a project will last before committing themselves to supporting it. Parish register analysis is not feasible unless access to the registers is guaranteed over a comparatively long period and some of the problems of access are discussed in the Appendix to this chapter. If a full reconstitution study is to be attempted, even for the smallest parish for which the method is viable, it will require contact with the register for months, even years, particularly if work is confined to weekly meetings, and a copy of the register is virtually a necessity. The form of analysis involves the reconstruction, generation by generation, of the pattern of births, marriages and deaths of as large a number of families as can be documented. Aggregative studies, though ultimately less rewarding, have the advantage of requiring less time in contact with the registers than family reconstitution, and here copying may not be necessary. Excluding parishes of exceptional size, a group of eight–twelve people will complete the basic task of aggregation, that is of counting and recording the baptism, burial and marriage entries, in six or eight two-hour periods. This estimate does not include the time which may be needed to extract additional information which an individual register may contain. This could range from detailed occupational information, evidence of smallpox or some other epidemic or a list of inhabitants to scurrilous remarks about parishioners, or even poetry, which the group or some members of it may wish to study.

Parish register analysis in any form is thus unsuitable for short-term projects. In extra-mural class terms an aggregative study requires at least a sessional course of twenty-four meetings (thirty meetings for a large parish). This assumes that approximately half the time will be spent at work on the registers and half making calculations and discussing the project before and after information has been collected. Some groups have the confidence and courage at an early date to recognise that their work will extend over several years and the aggregative study becomes part of a larger piece of local history and is planned accordingly; more often groups stumble one step at a time, and how a group starts a career in parish register analysis is bound to depend on the background and ability of its members. For many groups the need to adopt systematic and statistical methods may be new and to some it will be alarming, and it is essential that a group should recognize the need for this sort of approach before embarking on it. Some tutors have found it helpful to let their students browse through the registers without direction to discover for themselves the limitations of the selective or anecdotal approach. In this way some students may come to recognize the need for quantification. Sometimes the discovery that local case studies can contribute to a national debate is a potent stimulus, and here an examination of the population explosion of the eighteenth century can provide an excellent starting point. Nowadays anyone who reads the newspapers or who watches television reckons to know something about why population has increased, and anyway, this was the period we all learned about at school; an elementary discussion of possible causes is thus not difficult to initiate. An examination of the basic demographic issues of the eighteenth century, why the population increased, when the process began and what course it followed, reveals the startling fact that nobody really knows.[5] The certainties of a few years ago have dissolved; then it was all a matter of 'the new cheap cotton clothing' and of medical progress reducing mortality! Now, though cheap clothing, soap consumption and hygiene are still in the race, the search is for evidence of a fluctuation in the age of marriage, for the practice of birth control, for changes in family size and for an accurate graph of the rate of population growth. The discovery that the demographic and economic history of the eighteenth century must be rewritten and that the new truth upon which it will be based may lie in their parish register is a mixture strong enough to hypnotise many groups. Fortunately this intoxication rarely survives acquaintance with the published research of the Cambridge Group. This is seen to be statistical and highly sophisticated and far beyond the competence of laymen.[6] The moral is simple; groups must limit their enquiries to material they can handle and methods they can understand.

A group tempted to embark on a reconstitution study in the form described by the Cambridge Group should first ensure that someone in the group who can be relied on to stay with the project until the end has a good grasp of statistics. The initial procedures in a reconstitution are time-consuming and tedious but they are not difficult, and it is not until the data collected from the register is ready for analysis that the problems begin. The group without statistical expertise could find itself stranded, possessing a huge bank of information without the skills to organize or process it. This can be scaled down to some extent by selecting part of the register on the basis of surnames. The reconstitution might cover all names from A to D for instance and in this way the sheer bulk of information would be reduced to manageable proportions. If reconstitution is attempted, the group is best advised to select a smallish parish and to confine itself to some of the comparatively simple measurements for different periods, such as the age of first marriage of men and women or a calculation of the intervals between births. These measures do not demand complicated procedures and can be compared easily with figures from other case studies.[7]

The greatest rewards of a reconstitution study for an amateur group however need not be strictly demographic. Instead of seeking more and more complex statistical information, the framework of the reconstitution can become the index in and around which all the conventional sources of information are correlated. The family reconstitution form (5.1) on which the information about each generation of the families identified from the register is set out are easily adapted to record additional information, so that a file can be assembled containing information about land-holding or social and occupational activities in the parish or between individual members of a family. This form of social analysis is likely to reveal inferences and associations which would be hard to spot if the sources were examined less systematically.[8] Wills and inventories, manorial rolls, rentals, deeds, overseers' accounts, census enumerators' books, tithe information and any documents which contain personal names can be fed into this system. Such a study would take a very long time and few groups are likely to muster the loyalty, perseverance and longevity to sustain work on this scale.[9] For most groups parish register analysis will mean some sort of aggregative study and this form of enquiry provides many of the same opportunities as reconstitution. Case studies can be related equally well to the wider national and regional picture.

Counting Heads

Whatever is to be done finally, analysis must begin with a count of all the information contained in the registers by month and year, and there is no better way of doing this than on the forms devised by the Cambridge Group and reproduced here. Such forms are available from the Cambridge Group who also supply instructions for their use (5.2). These forms are ideal for use by groups and teams working in pairs or, if it is a register in which baptism, burial and marriage entries are interspersed, in a team of four, one reading the register, the other three entering the number of baptisms, burials and marriages on the appropriate forms.

Before embarking on any calculations, however, it is advisable to check the register against the copy of the register which may be available in the diocesan record office. This copy, known as the Bishop's Transcript, may contain important additional information

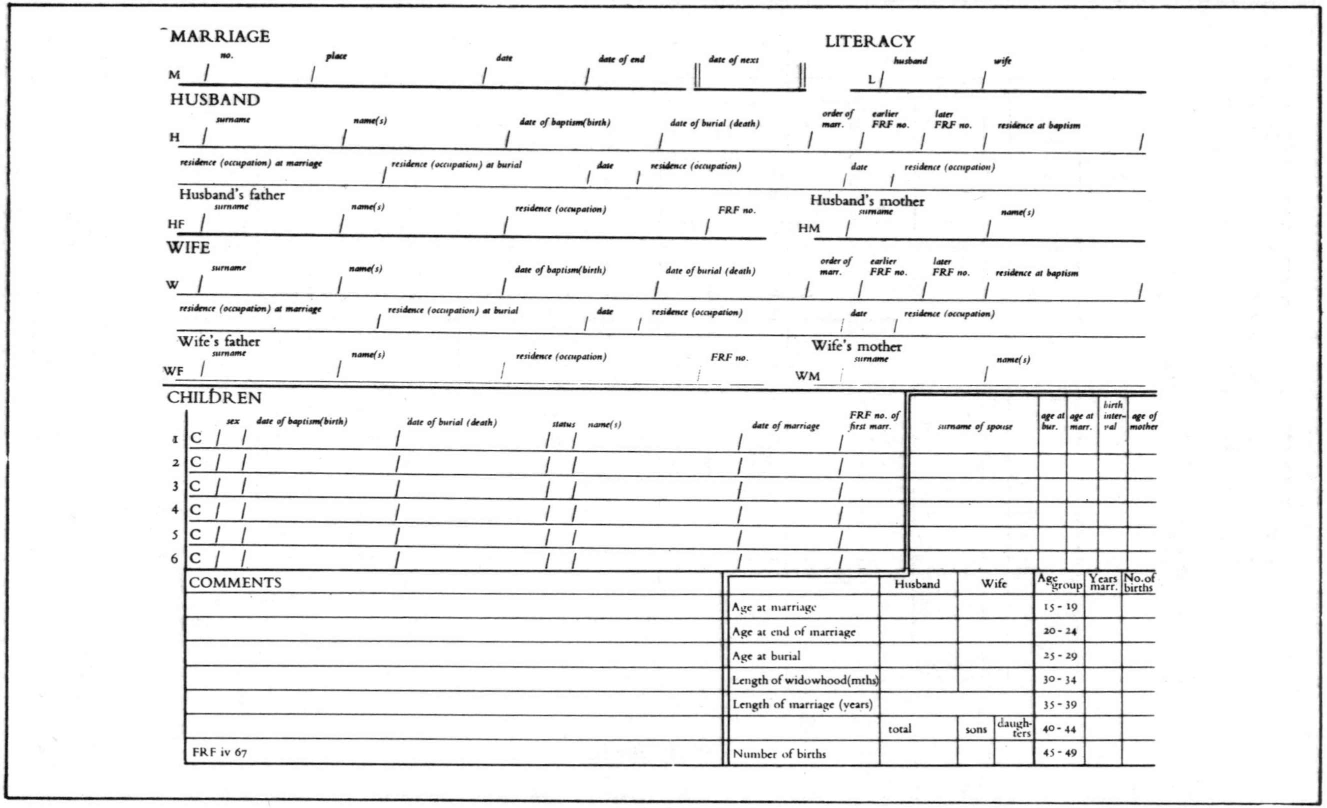

MARRIAGE
M / no. / place / date / date of end / date of next

LITERACY
L / husband / wife

HUSBAND
H / surname / name(s) / date of baptism(birth) / date of burial (death) / order of marr. / earlier FRF no. / later FRF no. / residence at baptism
residence (occupation) at marriage / residence (occupation) at burial / date / residence (occupation) / date / residence (occupation)

Husband's father
HF / surname / name(s) / residence (occupation) / FRF no.

Husband's mother
HM / surname / name(s)

WIFE
W / surname / name(s) / date of baptism(birth) / date of burial (death) / order of marr. / earlier FRF no. / later FRF no. / residence at baptism
residence (occupation) at marriage / residence (occupation) at burial / date / residence (occupation) / date / residence (occupation)

Wife's father
WF / surname / name(s) / residence (occupation) / FRF no.

Wife's mother
WM / surname / name(s)

CHILDREN

		sex	date of baptism(birth)	date of burial (death)	status	name(s)	date of marriage	FRF no. of first marr.	surname of spouse	age at bur.	age at marr.	birth inter-val	age of mother
1	C												
2	C												
3	C												
4	C												
5	C												
6	C												

COMMENTS

	Husband	Wife		Age group	Years marr.	No. of births
Age at marriage				15 - 19		
Age at end of marriage				20 - 24		
Age at burial				25 - 29		
Length of widowhood(mths)				30 - 34		
Length of marriage (years)				35 - 39		
	total	sons	daugh-ters	40 - 44		
Number of births				45 - 49		

FRF iv 67

5.1 Family Reconstitution Form as devised by the SSRC Cambridge Group. Please note that this form has been abridged. The original has provision for sixteen children

P.E.F. I

BAPTISMS

PARISH: County:

YEARS:

YEAR	MONTH OF CONCEPTION Apr. / MONTH OF BAPTISM Jan.	May / Feb.	June / Mar.	July / Apr.	Aug. / May	Sept. / June	Oct. / July	Nov. / Aug.	Dec. / Sept.	Jan. / Oct.	Feb. / Nov.	Mar. / Dec.	Baptisms by Civil Year (totals)	Conceptions Jan.-Apr.	Conceptions May-Dec.	Concep-tions by Harvest Year (totals)	Bastards	Comments
TOTAL																		

5.2 Baptisms: one of the recording forms issued by SSRC Cambridge Group

and give the impression of providing a better record than the parish copy, or it may be incomplete or in some other way inferior. The chances are that both the parish register and the Bishop's Transcript are copies from a third source (very often some sort of notebook), now lost, and so there is no guarantee that throughout the period either the parish or the diocesan copy will contain the more accurate or detailed version.

At some stage it will be worth looking at the local nonconformist registers if they have survived, and gathering whatever information is available from them and from any other source about the strength of non-conformist groups, for certain nonconformists would not use Anglican baptism rites and thus would not appear in the baptism register, with the result that calculations based on that register could become seriously inaccurate. This is especially true in the later years of the eighteenth century and early nineteenth century when Methodism was spreading rapidly.[10] A large number of nonconformist registers are to be found in the Public Record Office (RG4 and 5). In finding registers for a particular locality it is important to realize that nonconformist registers were not organized on a parish basis and sometimes serve a wide area, so that the entries for the parish you want may appear in a register bearing the name of a neighbouring place. The late seventeenth and eighteenth century Anglican visitation returns are an important source of information about the extent of nonconformity in any locality. They have been printed for many areas; the originals are usually in the Diocesan Record Office.

Once the figures have been extracted, various forms of analysis are possible. It is helpful to plot the annual totals of baptisms, burials and marriages on a graph, and because in many parishes there will have been periods of considerable fluctuation, a second graph is usually added which smoothes out these short-term differences in order to reveal longer-term trends. This is achieved by means of a nine- or seven-year moving average. This is calculated by adding up the totals for nine consecutive years, dividing by nine and then attributing the figure which results to the middle year of its period, i.e. the fifth year in this case (Table 3) or the fourth year in the case of a seven-year moving average.[11] Such trends become especially interesting when a graph is constructed showing the comparison of one parish with another or a group of parishes (5.3).

This exercise is possibly the quickest way to demonstrate the fascination and difficulty of making valid generalizations about the demographic history of an area. Further comparison can be made by the simple technique known as the natural increase curve. This

Table 3 NINE-YEAR MOVING AVERAGES—BAPTISMS

	1	*2*	*3*
1666	23		
7	24		
8	13		
9	23		
1670	17	*187*	21
1	19	187	21
2	22	185	21
3	23	192	21
4	23	196	22
5	23	194	22
6	22	189	21
7	20	181	20
8	19	180	20
9	23	177	20
1680	14	174	19
1	14	185	21
2	22	182	20
3	20	190	21
4	20	196	22
5	33	202	22

Col 1—annual total
Col 2—9-year total attributed to the middle year
Col 3—9-year average

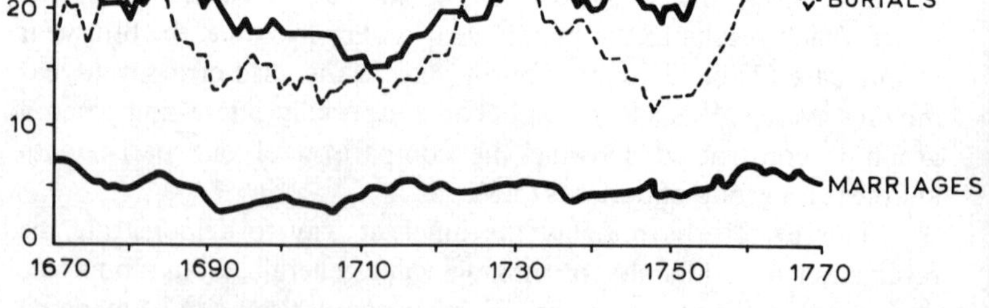

5.3 Nine Year Moving Averages: Gedling. Graph showing register totals in nine year averages for the parish of Gedling (Notts)

assumes each parish to be a desert island, unaffected by migration, and by adding year by year the excess of baptisms over burials or subtracting if the burials exceed the baptisms, it is possible to indicate the increase or decrease in the population in a given period (Table 4).

Table 4 CUMULATIVE NATURAL INCREASES 1640–1740

	1	*2*	*3*	*4*
1671	19	16	3	3
2	22	17	5	8
3	23	16	7	15
4	23	20	3	18
5	23	33	– 10	8
6	22	14	8	16
7	20	10	10	26
8	19	11	8	34
9	23	18	5	39
1680	14	35	– 21	18
1	14	37	– 23	– 5
2	22	15	7	2
3	20	16	4	6
4	20	23	– 3	3
5	33	18	15	18

etc.

Col 1—baptisms
Col 1—burials
Col 3—excess of baptisms over burials (from cols 1 & 2)
i.e. Natural Increase
Col 4—cumulative Natural Increase

The natural increase curve is easily calculated and enables the profiles of several parishes to be compared on a single piece of paper. This method has obvious defects but it has the advantage of dealing in actual figures rather than averages, so that the impact of particular events such as a period of heavy mortality can be examined and compared parish by parish (5.4). In some cases, where for instance parishes of very different size are being compared, this device can be refined by expressing the surplus of baptisms over burials as a percentage of the number of baptisms.

It has also been suggested that a form of fertility rate can be derived by dividing the number of baptisms by the number of marriages. This can be done either by relating the number of baptisms for a particular year to the marriages for the same year, or the periods may be staggered to reflect the fact that the marriages in one year contribute

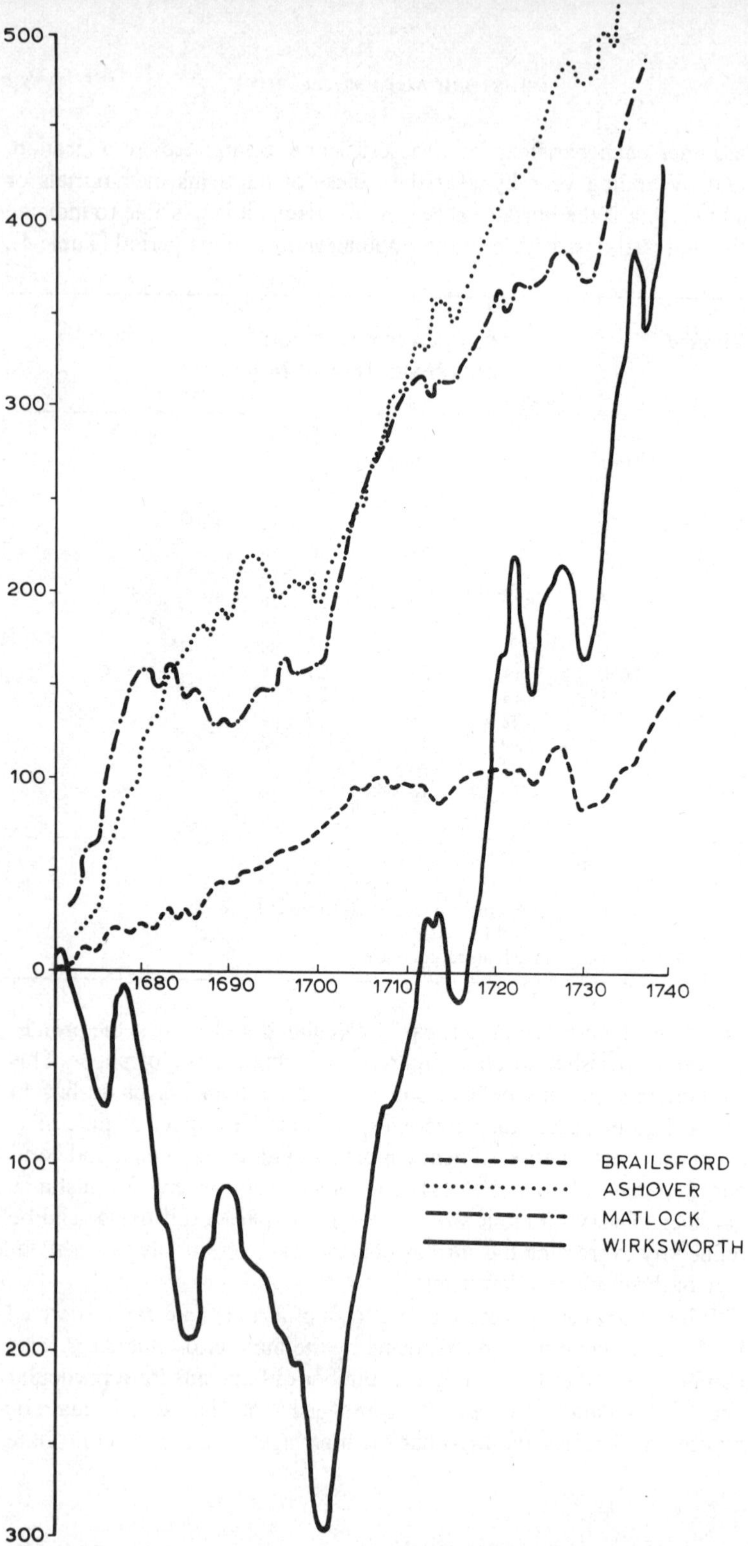

5.4 Graph showing cumulative natural increase for four Derbyshire parishes, 1670–1740

to baptism totals over a period of years. This can be a valuable diagnostic tool in analysing aggregated data of a parish but care must be taken not to rely too blindly on the results.[12] If the ratio rises to a very high level, say six or eight, there is a strong probability that the data is faulty. Such results could well have been caused by the under-registration of marriages. This is often found in the seventeenth century and it seems likely that common law marriage, unblessed by the Church and therefore unrecorded in its registers, was widespread then and that it continued well into the eighteenth century.

In most groups long before these experiments have begun, someone will have been set to work estimating the population of the parish. This is the question local historians expect local historical demographers to answer and it is no good trying to evade the issue. In fact the use of parish registers to estimate a local population is very much more speculative than sometimes has been suggested and it is more realistic to think in terms of plotting population movement than estimating an actual figure at any point in time. The well known rule of thumb method of assuming baptisms to have been at the rate of between thirty and forty per thousand or a similar calculation based on assumptions about the burial rate will not necessarily produce a reliable figure, and it is important to compare results with other measures. It is possible in many cases to compile a dossier from a number of sources of information which may contain details from which population can be estimated and then for comparative purposes to plot the estimates on a graph (5.5). For the seventeenth century there are various taxation documents such as Hearth Tax or Poll Tax and the Compton Census, and for the eighteenth century the returns made to diocesan enquiries which very often asked the size of the parish, though not always in the same terms. Thus the replies may refer to families, households, communicants or farms and cottages, so that in each case an appropriate multiplier has to be selected to translate the terms used in the reply into a total population. Clearly the result can be only an estimate and is best recorded as a range rather than a single, almost certainly spurious, figure. At best the outcome will be a series of population limits which can be linked to the early nineteenth century census information.[13]

Analysis

Once the basic calculations have been made and the information from the registers is available in a series of graphs and tables showing crude annual and monthly totals, the same figures as moving averages and possibly a natural increase curve, it is time to pause and take stock. It should be possible to use the information that has been collected to answer certain basic questions, such as when the population began to increase consistently, when the periods of difficulty were and when there were any notable fluctuations. If the work has been based on a number of parishes, it is likely that differences between parishes will become apparent and that these differences will require explanation. It will be interesting to compare results with those that have been obtained elsewhere.[14]

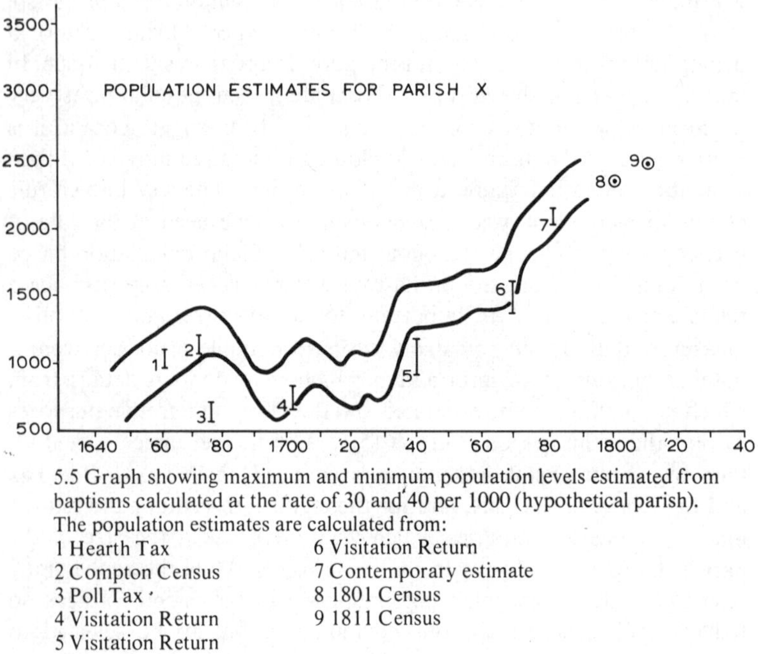

5.5 Graph showing maximum and minimum population levels estimated from baptisms calculated at the rate of 30 and 40 per 1000 (hypothetical parish). The population estimates are calculated from:

1 Hearth Tax	6 Visitation Return
2 Compton Census	7 Contemporary estimate
3 Poll Tax	8 1801 Census
4 Visitation Return	9 1811 Census
5 Visitation Return	

It is important at this stage to analyse carefully each step that is taken and to ensure that group momentum is not mistaken for a sense of direction—a problem common to all group projects in local history. Much of the group's work will be done in research units of two or three people and these will rapidly acquire their own horizons. The group members working on the eighteenth century burial register and avidly pursuing this study may not want to spend time in a general discussion of over-all strategy which they will resent as an interruption and a delay in the important business of collecting data.

But by the time they themselves recognize the need, it may be too late to prevent permanent fragmentation. It is a fine balance. A group cannot be for ever pulling up its roots to see how they are, but if there is no planned timetable for the analysis of objectives, ultimately the group will lose its way and founder.

Some groups have found it helpful to establish a system of written reports whereby each unit agrees to make a presentation to the whole group in six weeks' time, or by the end of the term. These submissions can then be duplicated and distributed, discussed and amended, and ultimately incorporated into a single report. This document might be suitable for circulation outside the group and even for publication but its importance is as a working document, securing the past, outlining the future and binding the group together. Such a device is necessary to confront group members with their responsibility as historians to explain and interpret what they have found. Interpreting the evidence will not be easy. The aggregative study will not present a tidy historical scenario and is likely to expose five new questions for every one that is answered. Whatever happens, a group must retain its footing in local historical studies and not attempt to follow the experts into the complex statistical jungle which is now the world of the professional historical demographer. Professor Chambers' pioneer study of the Vale of Trent provides a useful model in demonstrating what can be achieved by simple methods and how it is possible to integrate demographic data with information from a range of other sources, though of course his work is on a scale few groups could emulate.

Questions: Burials

What a group decides to do next will depend on various local factors. Occasionally there will be those working on registers which are of sufficient quality and where there are no problems of access who will attempt a full reconstitution. Space does not permit this form of analysis to be described here but a full account of it will be found in Wrigley (1966), chapter 4. Other queries will receive attention if they are directed to *Local Population Studies*. For the group which does not want to plunge so deep, there is no shortage of things to do. If the parish has outstanding characteristics in its demographic history or in its location or the register contains unusually detailed information, selecting priorities is not difficult and in any case, working in a group with a need to keep everyone employed, a number of enquiries can be conducted simultaneously. The pages of *Local Population Studies* contain numerous examples of the work individuals or teams of two or three people might engage in and it might be helpful to describe some of these in detail.

For many people the burial register has a particular fascination. Burial registers frequently present an impression of vivid and marked fluctuation which captures the layman's eye but in reality the analysis of mortality will usually require more complicated methods than a group has at its disposal to yield significant results. There are however exceptional registers in which the age at death is recorded consistently and from an early date, and sometimes even the cause of death. In such cases it is not difficult to describe and analyse mortality by age and relate this to cause, and enquire whether a disease has seasonal characteristics or is common to a particular age group.[15]

More often work will focus on the seasonal distribution of burials and the examination of outstanding or crisis years. An approach to seasonality enquiries has been outlined by Leslie Bradley in a series of three articles published in *LPS* nos 4, 5 and 6. He suggests that analysis of burial registers over long periods should proceed on a time unit of ten years. This has been chosen to avoid the effect of accidental variations to which any single year might be subject, on the one hand and the risk of obscuring real and significant events by averaging on the other. The process is not complicated though it may take a long time. First decadal totals of burials are calculated for each month of the year. Each month total is then reduced to a percentage of the total number of burials for the decade. These percentages are most easily compared if they are presented in the form of graphs and it is then possible to identify seasonal patterns. The interest of such studies is enhanced if the burial information for a number of parishes is compared. An alternative and simpler method has been demonstrated by Margaret Massey (*LPS* 8). A comparison of the two methods is attempted in Table 5 and 5.6 using information from the registers of the parish of Burton Joyce (Notts). The more detailed approach has an advantage in cases where the pattern becomes complicated but for most purposes the simple presentation will suffice.

The examination of crisis years is also preferably a multi-parish project. Once a definition of crisis has been accepted (and it has been suggested that this should be simple, perhaps as simple as each year in which mortality exceeds twice the average annual number of burials), this sort of enquiry is quite straightforward.[16] It is probable that an increasing number of these studies will be finding their way into print over the next few years, and comparisons will be easily made.[17]

Table 5 PEAK MONTHS FOR BURIALS IN DECADES

J	F	M	A	M	J	J	A	S	O	N	D	
X												1581–90
X	X											1591–1600
										X		1601–10
								X				11–20
											X	21–30
			X		X							31–40
X												41–50
										X		51–60
	X									X		61–70
										X		71–80
		X										81–90
	X											91–1700
	X								X			1701–10
	X											11–20
			X									21–30
											X	31–40
										X	X	41–50
											X	51–60
		X	X									61–70
											X	71–80
X												81–90
			X									91–1800
										X		1801–10
			X	X								11–20
				X								21–30

In certain areas it may be possible to relate evidence of named epidemics or of periods of high mortality from the burial register to other sources. For obvious reasons these should be local or regional in origin. They may be diaries or notes in account books which describe the weather, the economic situation or the nature of the epidemic itself which will lead to a more complex diagnosis. The work of John Huxham, 1692–1768, a medical practitioner in Plymouth, who attempted to keep a record of prevailing disease in Plymouth and Devonport between 1728 and 1762, has attracted attention recently, and the work of Thomas Short, based primarily on Sheffield and Derbyshire, is well known already;[18] but if for example it is thought likely that it is a subsistence crisis that is under review, all sorts of local information about prices and market conditions can be valuable. Registers which contain detailed information about one of the notorious diseases such as plague or smallpox are not common, but where they exist they open a new area of study for part of the group.

Reconstitution on a limited scale may be necessary to unravel the strands of the infant and adult mortality or study the transmission of disease amongst households, but once again this is an area which has been fought over extensively and one in which case studies are likely to be the only way of proving the issue one way or another.[19]

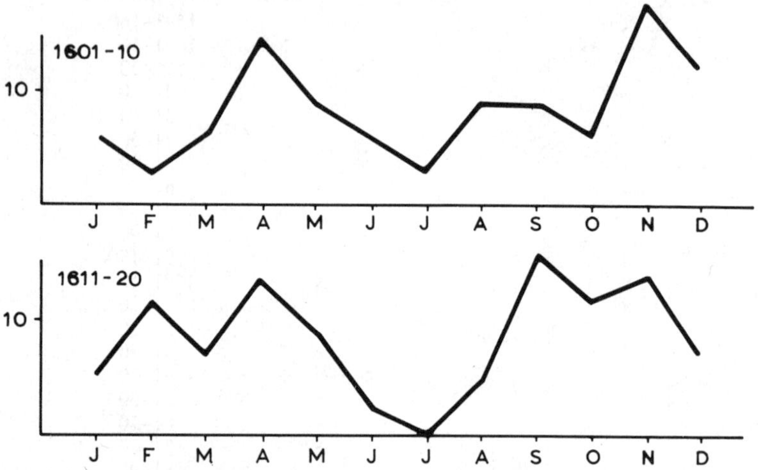

5.6 Seasonality: Burials, Burton Joyce (Notts). Table 5 shows a simple method to identify peaks. These two graphs show the same information for the period 1601–1610 and 1611–1620 used in a more sophisticated way

If detailed analysis is precluded by the imperfections of the register, it is still possible to do useful work by examining a number of parishes for evidence of plague or smallpox. In the case of smallpox in the eighteenth century to seek out evidence of inoculation from the local press or from records such as overseers' accounts and estate papers, and so contribute to the smallpox controversy. This centres around the claims made by Dr Razzell that the population increase in the eighteenth century could be explained in terms of the reduction of smallpox mortality which followed the widespread adoption of inoculation. Only local research is likely to reveal whether smallpox was ever a major killing disease and how far the practice of inoculation was widespread.

Questions: Baptisms

The baptism register offers similar opportunities for group studies. Like burial registers, baptism registers repay examination for seasonal trends. The methodology here is substantially the same as for burial registers but in the case of baptisms the analysis can proceed on two fronts. The baptisms themselves exhibit interesting seasonal characteristics but they also provide evidence of birth and conception patterns. A study of seasonality in six Derbyshire and six Nottinghamshire parishes revealed an interesting phenomenon in the latter part of the eighteenth century—the concentration into one particular month of the year of a high proportion of the total baptisms for the decade. The month in which the peak occurred varied between parishes.[20] Similar studies elsewhere could not be guaranteed to produce such striking results but the prospects are good and the explanation for such events must be sought in other areas of local enquiry such as church or local village customs, superstition and the practice of private baptism soon after birth.[21] This is an area of research a local group may be well qualified to undertake since it demands an intimate local knowledge of both sources and customs. It requires attention since it is only by understanding the intricacies of christening customs that the baptism registers can be used with confidence for demographic purposes.

The question of birth-baptism intervals is more complicated. It has been demonstrated that even for quite early periods the convention that baptism should take place within a few days of birth, as the Prayer Book instructs, was not followed, and that there was considerable variation from parish to parish and possibly between regions. Thus in some parishes the pattern of baptisms might follow closely the pattern of births and so the baptisms with minor adjustments can be used to calculate demographic trends. In others lengthy delay or the practice of saving up baptisms and concentrating them at one point in the calendar has weakened the validity of baptism information as a guide to birth or to conceptions. It is interesting and important to try to form some impression of the birth-baptism interval in a parish. This is easy if the register gives the date of birth as well as the date of baptism for a considerable length of time, but few registers do, and in this area uncertainties usually remain unresolved. Where the information is available, the seasonality of births and of conceptions can be established, and these in turn will demand explanation. This is unlikely to be forthcoming! But the clear identification of the pattern of events is in itself valuable and will provide the basis for testing hypotheses. It is possible there may be evidence of abstinence from intercourse during Lent or during the strenuous harvest period, or of more intercourse taking place in the long winter evenings. This enquiry leads easily into the evidence provided by the marriage register, since if marriages were celebrated at one time of the year rather than another, it is reasonable to assume in a society without effective means of birth control that a bulge in the pattern of births would follow approximately nine months after the peak period for marriage. Unfortunately this relationship is generally masked by the baptism register's failure to distinguish between a couple's first and subsequent children, although it would be possible to uncover this information in a reconstitution study.

Questions: Marriages

Marriage registers do however repay study in other ways. The seasonal pattern of marriages is no less interesting than that of baptisms or burials and once again there are certain features to look for and comparisons to be made. It may be worth examining the extent to which the periods in which the Church discouraged marriage were observed and comparing the results with other areas. Again local

	Both of This Parish				Both from Other Parishes				Man T.P. Woman O.P.				Woman T.P. Man O.P.				Names of Other Parishes
Year	ss	Man s	Wom. s	Both xx	ss	Man s	Wom. s	Both xx	ss	Man s	Wom. s	Both xx	ss	Man s	Wom. s	Both xx	

5.7 Form to record parishes of origin of Marriage Partners, and literacy (s = signature, x = cross)

customs or attitudes or the attitude or availability of the incumbent may be revealed as a potent force influencing the seasonal distribution of marriages and even the overall total. This is especially noticeable in those parishes which have more than their share of marriages and are clearly drawing people from other parishes.

A more usual form of analysis for marriage registers makes use of their information about residence and, after 1754, a person's ability to sign his name. Mobility studies are possible for single parishes but are more interesting when registers are available for a number of contiguous parishes. Such investigations are laborious but comparatively straightforward. All that has to be done is to abstract the details of entries in which at least one of the partners is recorded as resident in another parish and then to plot the results on a map or in a table, set out in appropriate categories, as distances from a chosen point.[22] Clearly the value of such studies will depend on the extent to which an enquiry of this kind can relate its findings to the significant geographic and economic influence of the area.

Literacy studies based on a count of the number of people able to sign their names in the marriage register also gain from being spread over a number of parishes, although the study of a single parish may yield interesting results. An example of a form used in an enquiry of this kind is set out below (5.7), and the result of a study for the parish of Matlock (5.8). Once again this is an area in which considerable research has been done, making available to a group the opportunity for comparison.[23]

Other Questions

There are numerous other forms of enquiry based on register analysis which individuals within a group or small teams of two or three people might choose to follow up. For example, in the early nineteenth century use can be made of the baptism register's record of occupations and, if it is intended to move on to census studies, these can provide a source of information for a period when there is seldom anything better. Registers can be used in conjunction with the records of nonconformist churches, and some fascinating inter-relationships emerge. A comparison between the seventeenth century Quaker records and the parish register reveals the agonizing decisions made by Quakers supplementing or being forced to supplement their own marriage ceremony with a Church ceremony and facing expulsion from the Society for having done so. A study has been made of the frequency with which Catholics registered their baptisms, marriages and burials during the seventeenth century and it is clear that the study of registration during the Commonwealth and of the impact of other legislation affecting registration will provide further areas of study.[24] There is not space here to extend the list further but some reference should be made both to surname analysis and to occupational analysis. By a quite simple study of surnames over a long period it is possible to form an impression of the turnover of the population and this is especially interesting in those cases where this information can be related to a listing of inhabitants which will serve as a dating line against which to measure turnover. Occupational analysis is effectively limited to parishes fortunate enough to have a listing, though occasionally a register may provide sufficient information to justify an enquiry. The analysis of listings is a whole subject in itself but there are useful examples which suggest how this can be done.[25]

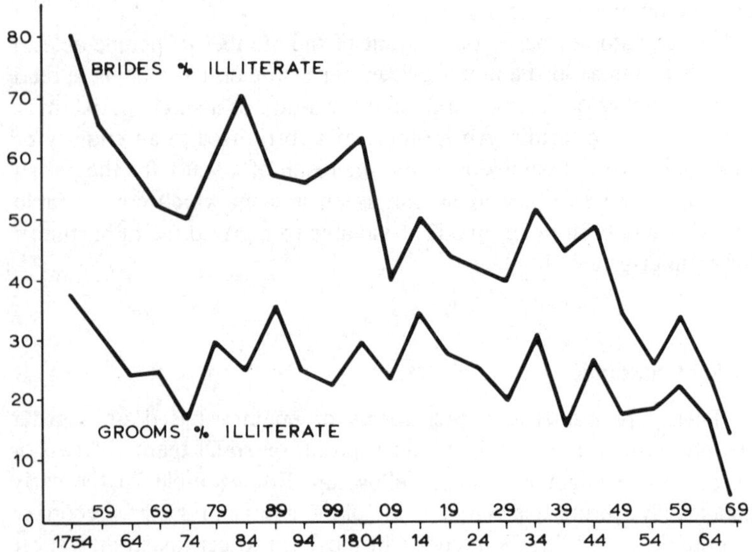

5.8 Graph showing literacy figures, five yearly averages for Matlock (Derbyshire) parish 1754–1870

Projects in parish register analysis demand considerable investment of time and effort before they yield results, and this and the unfamiliar and daunting prospect of having to do some arithmetic and produce tables and graphs will deter some groups from entering this field. But for those who do there are many advantages. On an organizational level there are usually simple and complex tasks to be performed so that people of extremely varied ability can take part and the work tends to divide conveniently into units which can be handled by groups of two or three. Much of the work is demonstrably important and can be related to national research and to other case studies, and through the inter-relationship between registers and other local sources it is sometimes possible to provide a new slant on old problems.

Appendix: Access, Fees and Copying Costs

The public has a right of access to registers. This is seldom disputed but, as groups up and down the country have discovered, there is considerable variation from parish to parish, diocese to diocese and among record offices in interpreting the regulations which govern their use. Many incumbents favour historical research and have been prepared to allow groups a free hand to work on the registers without their supervision provided the safety of the registers is ensured. More often than not in such cases the fees which the law entitles an incumbent to collect are waived or commuted to a single modest payment. But there are other parishes in which access is tied to personal supervision by the incumbent or in which fees are charged in full. Sometimes photocopying is allowed, sometimes it is forbidden. Some incumbents prefer it to be their own parishioners using the registers rather than outsiders, frequently it is the other way round. Amongst record offices the principal variation is between those which charge fees for demographic enquiry and those which do not.

There is no doubt that for most groups the ideal arrangement includes unrestricted access, reasonable payment and the right to microfilm or photocopy the registers, so that contact time with them in manuscript form is kept to a minimum. But in trying to negotiate these terms with an incumbent it is important to recognize that on two crucial points, the right to make lengthy unsupervised searches and photocopying, the law, strictly interpreted, may not favour historical research. The position has been stated recently in an appendix to a report presented to the General Synod of the Church of England (the report is known as GS.114/C). This makes it clear that an incumbent must allow searches to be made of the baptism, marriage and burial registers at all reasonable times and suggests that this means in practice business hours at a time compatible with the incumbent's other parochial commitments and after adequate notice has been given of the desire for an appointment. Clearly, the definition of search is important here and the interpretation goes on to explain that while search probably includes the right to make extracts, these must not take an unreasonable time to make and the register must remain within the control of the person responsible for its custody while they are being made. On the question of photocopying and microfilming the report is definite. These rights are not included in the right of search, although the printing and reproduction of registers can be permitted with the authority of the Bishop to whom application should be made and who may order the temporary deposit of a register in the diocesan record office where copying may take place.

The proposed Parochial Registers and Records Measure which should soon come into effect will simplify and improve the situation. Under its provisions it will be illegal for registers to be retained in parochial custody except under the most favourable circumstances. Thus most groups embarking on register studies will have to negotiate with record offices rather than incumbents. There can be no doubt of the Measure's importance, and as soon as its final form is settled and copies are published, anyone interested in parish register research should obtain a copy.

The fees to be paid for searches are laid down by the Parochial Fees Order 1972 and while a distinction is made between fees for certified copies of register entries and fees for searching registers, no distinction is made between searches made by the incumbent personally and searches made by researchers themselves. By a strict interpretation of the regulations, charging at the rate of 30p for the first year and 15p for every subsequent year, an incumbent could claim sums of money which would be beyond the means of the average group and so prevent their enquiry from taking place. These fees are currently under review and there is a proposal to charge fees for general searches at an hourly rate and a scale of £1 for the first hour and 50p for each subsequent hour has been suggested (GS.114/C, section VI). This would reduce costs, though not to a level many groups could afford. However, it is some comfort to learn from the same source that there is no legal reason why an incumbent should not waive his right to fees and allow facilities for searchers to make copies of entries by photocopying and that these copies, once made, are the property of the person who has made them and may be published if he wishes. The implication of all this for the local research group is plain. A project is unlikely to succeed unless the local incumbent wishes to cooperate, at least to the extent of commuting fees and probably in agreeing to photocopying. There is no prospect that reminding him of his legal obligations will persuade him to change his mind!

If the registers in question are in the diocesan record office, the position over fees and copying will depend on the policy agreed between the diocese and the record office, and once again on the attitude of the incumbent who may still insist on the payment of fees.

In practice the majority of record offices do not charge fees where registers are used for historical rather than genealogical research, but if the record office is twenty miles away and not open at a time of day convenient to the group, this liberality is of little consequence. In such a case it is possible for the incumbent who deposited the register to have it returned to the parish. If this will enable it to be studied under suitable conditions, there is nothing improper about this procedure, but clearly it may put the registers at risk and for this reason it is not encouraged by archivists.

Photocopying remains the best solution. The cost of copying and the ease with which arrangements can be made to have it done will depend on local circumstances. A record office, library or university may have microfilming equipment and be prepared to offer favourable terms. Even this transaction may become unexpectedly complicated in some dioceses where movement of registers, especially across diocesan boundaries, is strictly controlled and in at least one case it was this, rather than any opposition to photocopying or lack of money, which led to the abandonment of the project.

Once a register has been microfilmed, the information it contains can be made available in the form which suits the needs of the group. A microfilm can be projected through a microfilm projector such as a Microgen Monitor which will produce a large image on a screen, so that several people can study the information at the same time; or less satisfactorily through an ordinary microfilm reader or even a film strip projector. Often it is more convenient to have prints made from the microfilm so that in effect the register can be cut up and distributed amongst members of the group or taken home and worked on at will. Making prints could be expensive but experience has shown that a substantial saving can be made by reducing them to postcard size and reading them through a magnifying glass or, more conveniently, through a plastic reading bar. Two pages of a register, even if it has large pages, can be reduced to this size and still be clearly legible. The cost of all this will depend on circumstances so varied that prediction is impossible, but a recent enquiry suggested that a cost of between 3p and 5p a frame is to be expected. The cost may very well represent a substantial investment and before plans are made to microfilm a register, it will be wise to examine it in detail and discuss the form analysis will take.

Notes and References

1 For work in schools and colleges, *see* D. Turner, *Historical Demography in Schools* (Historical Association, 1971); K. S. Duffy, 'An Approach to Parish Register and Census Work', *LPS* 5, 1970 pp. 44–60; D. J. Steel and L. Taylor, *Family History in Schools* (1973); C. Barham, *Social Problems Arising from the Industrial Revolution,* Longman Secondary History Packs, Pack 6, *Population,* and J. A. Williams, 'A Local Population Study at a College of Education', *LPS* 11, 1973 pp. 23–39.

2 *Local Population Studies* (*LPS*) is published twice a year and is obtainable from Mrs M. H. Charlton, 9 Lisburne Square, Torquay, Devon. All back numbers are available. LPS has also published *A Glossary for Local Population Studies* (*1971*) by L. Bradley, designed to introduce the amateur to some of the basic techniques and terminology in current use by historical demographers. The LPS Society runs a book club which provides members with books on demography, local history and more general historical themes, at considerably reduced prices.

3 A detailed account of the history and development of parish registers will be found in J. C. Cox, *The Parish Registers of England* (1910, recently reprinted by E.P.); W. E. Tate, *The Parish Chest* (3rd edition, 1969). A list of parishes with the dates of the earliest known registers will be found in A. M. Burke, *Key to the Ancient Parish Registers of England and Wales* (1908).

4 *National Index of Parish Registers,* edited by D. J. Steel, Vol. 1 *Sources of Births, Marriages and Deaths before 1837,* Part 1; Vol. 2 *Sources for Nonconformist Genealogy*; Vol. 3 *Sources for Roman Catholic and Jewish Genealogy*; Vol. 5 *South Midlands and Welsh Border*; Vol. 12 *Sources for Scottish Genealogy. Original Parish Registers in Record Offices and Libraries, LPS* Supplement (1974). This lists all the original registers in England and Wales which have been deposited in record offices or libraries and the registers' earliest and latest dates; and *A First Supplement to Original Parish Registers in Record Offices and Libraries, LPS* (1976) gives additional information on deposited registers.

5 An excellent analysis of this situation is provided by M. W. Flinn, *British Population Growth 1700–1850,* (Studies in Economic History, 1970). For recent contributions to the debate on why the population in the eighteenth and nineteenth centuries increased, *see* McKeown and R. G. Brown, 'An interpretation of the Modern Rise of Population in Europe', *Population Studies* 27 (1972); McKeown, Brown and Record, 'An Interpretation of the Modern Rise in Population', *Population Studies* 26 (1970); 'An Interpretation of the Modern Rise of Population in Europe—a Critiqué', *Population Studies* 28 (1974); and J. D. Chambers, *Population, Ecomomy and Society in Pre-Industrial England* (1972).

6 *See* for example, the following works by E. A. Wrigley: 'Family Limitation in Pre-Industrial England', *Economic History Review* 2nd series, XIX no. 1 (1966), and particularly *Daedalus* (Spring 1968), since reprinted in *Population and Social Change,* ed. D. V. Glass and R. Revelle (1972); for an easier passage through some of the material, *see Population and History* (1969), and *Some Problems of Family Reconstitution using English Parish Registers: the Example of Colyton in Identifying People in the Past* (1973).

7 *See* E. A. Wrigley, (1966) Chapter 4.

8 W. Newman Brown, 'Wider Reconstitution', *LPS* 7, 1971, p. 44, describes work which goes some way along this line.

9 As an example of the use of parish register information and other sources of population history and their interpretation in a wide context, *see* David G. Hey, *An English Rural Community: Myddle under the Tudors and Stuarts* (1974).

10 The debate about under-registration continues and some authorities argue that registration had collapsed by the late eighteenth century. *See* J. T. Krause, 'The Changing Adequacy of English Registration 1690–1837' and P. E. Razzell. 'The Evaluation of Baptism as a Form of Birth Registration through Cross-Matching Census and Parish Register Data', *Population Studies* 26, no. 1 (March 1972) pp. 121–146.

11 A detailed description of the use and calculation of moving averages is to be found in Bradley, *A Glossary for Local Population Studies,* an *LPS* supplement (1971).

12 D. Turner, 'The Effective Family', *LPS* 2, p. 47.

13 For a discussion on the use of multipliers in constructing population estimates from Hearth Tax, *see LPS* 1, 1968, p. 30, and Lionel Munby, *Hertfordshire Population Statistics 1563–1801,* Hertfordshire Local History Council (1964) and C. A. F. Meekings, *Surrey Hearth Tax,* Surrey Records Society 17 (1940).

14 'The Population of Stepney in the Early Seventeenth Century', *LPS* 3, p. 39, and notably J. D. Chambers, *The Vale of Trent, 1670–1800, Economic History Review* Supplement no. 3.

15 Work of this kind was attempted by a WEA class in Colne, using exceptionally detailed registers and published with a transcript of the registers as *The Parochial Chapelry of Colne Burial Register 1790–1812,* edited by Wilfred M. Spencer (1968).

16 R. S. Schofield, ' "Crisis" Mortality', *LPS* 9 1972, p. 10 and D. Turner, 'Crisis Mortality in Nine Sussex Parishes', *LPS* 11, 1973, p. 40.

17 A. Gooder, 'The Population Crisis of 1727–30 in Warwickshire', *Midland History* (Autumn 1972); J. A. Johnstone, 'The Impact of Epidemics of 1727–30 in South-West Worcestershire', *Medical History* 15 (1971) and D. E. C. Eversley, 'A Survey of Population in an Area of Worcestershire from 1660 to 1850 on the Basis of Parish Registers', *Population in History* (1965).

18 N. F. J. Pounds, 'John Huxham's Medical Diary', *LPS* 12, 1974, p. 34; T. Short, *Comparative History of the Increase and Decrease of Mankind* (1767, reprinted 1974); and T. Short, *New Observations on City, Town and County Bills of Mortality* (1750, reprinted 1974).

19 On plague, *see* J. F. D. Shrewsbury, *A History of Bubonic Plague in the British Isles* (1970) and *The Plague Reconsidered; A New Look at its Origins and Effects in Sixteenth and Seventeenth Century England,* an *LPS* supplement. On smallpox, *see* Razzell, *Economic History Review* 2nd Series XVIII no. 2 (August 1965).

20 Leslie Bradley, 'An Enquiry into Seasonality in Baptisms, Marriages and Burials', *LPS* 5, 1950, pp. 18–35.

21 Dennis R. Mills, 'The Christening Custom at Melbourn, Cambs.', *LPS* 11, 1973 pp. 11–23, and R. W. Ambler, 'Baptism and Christening Custom and Practice in Nineteenth Century Lincolnshire', *LPS* 12, 1974, pp. 25–28. On the question of the interval between births and baptisms, *see* B. M. Berry and R. S. Schofield, 'Age of Baptism in Pre-Industrial England', *Population Studies* 25 (1971).

22 Bessie Maltby, 'Parish Registers and the Problem of Mobility', *LPS* 6, 1971 pp. 32–44, and 'Easingwold Marriage Horizons', *LPS* 2, 1969, pp. 36–40.

23 R. S. Schofield, 'Dimensions of Illiteracy in England 1750–1850', *Explorations in Economic History; Literacy and the Development of the West,* ed. Carlo M. Cipolla (1969); *Literacy in Traditional Societies,* ed. Jack Goody (1968); Laurence Stone, 'Literacy and Education in England 1640–1900', *Past and Present* no. 42 (1969).

24 V. T. J. Arkell, 'An Enquiry into the Frequency of Parochial Registration of Catholics in a Seventeenth Century Warwickshire Parish', *LPS* 9, 1972 pp. 23–33, and Donald Woodward, 'The Impact of the Commonwealth Act on Yorkshire Parish Registers', *LPS* 14, 1975, pp. 15–32.

25 *See* D. Baker, *The Inhabitants of Cardington in 1782,* Bedfordshire Historical Record Society, vol. 52 (1973), and Valerie Smith, 'The Analysis of Census-Type Documents', *LPS* 2, 1969, pp. 12–25.

I wish to record my thanks to Mr. Richard Wall of the SSRC Cambridge Group, Mrs. Young and Mr. Leslie Bradley of the Matlock Local Population Studies Group for their advice and assistance in the preparation of this article and for permission to reproduce graphs, diagrams and other material.

6

Local Nonconformist History

DENIS STUART

Forming the Group

There is no lack of expert guidance for the individual local historian or the class student in what sort of records exist for the study of local nonconformist history and where in general they are located. The topic has been dealt with in a number of books which have appeared over the last three or four years. But few local history societies or adult classes have been organized to study the subject, and it is usually relegated in the general local histories that are produced to part of a chapter on 'Church, Chapel and School', or some similar title, and treated very summarily. The main reasons for this are perhaps twofold: difficulties of access to source materials and a lack of imagination in the teaching approach to the subject. On the latter point, the contrast between the help given to school teachers and the lack of it for adult class teachers can be illustrated by reference to D. J. Steel and L. Taylor, *Family History in Schools* (1973) which might be taken, with suitable adaptation, as a model for the adult class tutor who wishes to make his teaching humane and comprehensive. Adults deserve, but rarely receive, as good teaching as children. Contrary to popular belief, adults are docile and habit-ridden students and they will sit through an excruciatingly dull series of lectures in the hope of enlightenment. What is needed, particularly in local nonconformist history, is a lively and imaginative approach to the subject which will provide a new interest for the established student of local history and also attract other adults who would not normally engage in such studies. Many types of project are possible in the field of local nonconformist history which can be adapted to the needs, interests and abilities of the particular class. This essay describes some which have been undertaken in the North Staffordshire/Potteries area with encouraging results.

The first problem usually encountered is that of recruiting a group of persons who wish to know more about or to research on the subject. Although some local history societies have shown a considerable interest in this area, on the whole established groups may show a resistance to a subject which in their experience has usually been narrow and dull. It is the task of the would-be leader of such a group to show the exciting possibilities of the subject, and this will involve him in the preliminary organisation and meetings. The usual publicity issued by local societies or by Extra-Mural Departments of Universities and W.E.A. Districts will probably not reach or make impact upon those members of the public whom it is desirable to recruit—local nonconformist church members themselves. Pre-session organizing is essential. Bodies such as the Methodist Church guilds and fellowships draw up their programmes of winter activities soon after Easter, and local ministers and secretaries can be visited, the research or class project explained, the help and approval of responsible persons obtained and the names of possible students noted. The offer to talk at one of the meetings of the religious body concerned—they are usually grateful to receive such an offer—will often get a return in the form of official co-operation for a project. Such co-operation is essential in any case if access to locally-held archives is to be facilitated.

The adult class tutor, whether full-time or part-time, should not expect therefore that there are groups already organized and ready and waiting for his ministrations. He must be prepared to go out and find them for himself. Nor should this be thought of as below the dignity of, or irrelevant to, the functions of the academic. This kind of field-work is an important part of research into recent local nonconformist history. Not enough attention is paid to twentieth century history by local historians, yet it is in the present century that many of the nonconformist churches have undergone or are undergoing their greatest changes. The local manifestations of these changes are more promising subjects for study than the usually well-trodden ground of earlier periods. For example, the arrival of a Primitive Methodist preacher in a locality for the first time—not infrequently greeted by a shower of rotten eggs—is inevitably quoted, but the visit of a revivalist preacher in the early part of this century is ignored. The historian of local nonconformity will pay as much attention to the later developments in his subject as to its origins. And to do this it is important to meet people as well as to study documents. Moreover such contacts are likely to throw up fresh documentary material not found in the official archives.

An example of such an approach is provided by a recent project undertaken by the Department of Adult Education of the University of Keele in the Stoke-on-Trent area. Six local Methodist groups agreed to devote two of their meetings during the winter session to participating in a study project. The aim was to encourage Methodists to take a fresh interest in their own local church history, to undertake some research, however elementary, using their own local records, and to start collecting new material, especially oral information. The response was encouraging. Once people had got over their surprise at not being lectured at and their diffidence over their ability to contribute to research, they became enthusiastic students. They asked for meetings in addition to those which had been officially arranged; new written materials on local history came to light, oral information was tape-recorded, and in one case students began to produce their own chapel history in instalments in the circuit quarterly news-letter. The detailed results of the project cannot be catalogued here, but it became clear that the keen local history society member or adult tutor, provided he is willing and able to devote the necessary time and energy to the project, can act as a sort of catalyst among nonconformist church groups to produce in them a new interest and excitement over their history, and then can act as guide, director and co-ordinator of the amateur research groups that emerge.

Background Material

A group studying or researching into local nonconformity should have a box of books available if possible. These may be supplied by the University Extra-Mural Department or W.E.A. District which is sponsoring the course, or sometimes arrangements can be made with local public libraries for members of a local history society to have books on extended loan. In compiling a list of titles for possible use during the study, the tutor should refrain from parading his own scholarship and cite only a few books which he knows to be essential or useful or which cover topics which he knows to be among the interests of his students. Where the group is undertaking research, books may be listed under three headings:

1 those which list general sources for the study of nonconformist history. Among the most recent, Alan Rogers in chapter VII of *Approaches to Local History* (1977) opens up the history of English

dissent in a brief but wide-ranging manner and discusses sources with some reproductions of actual documents; David Iredale's *Enjoying Archives* (1974) deals with local history sources from the point of view of types of repository and also offers useful hints on research methods and palaeography, while W. B. Stephens' *Sources for English Local History* (1973) provides one of the fullest treatments of the subject of nonconformist records of these general books. Of works devoted to nonconformity exclusively, the most useful is D. J. Steel's *Sources for Nonconformist Genealogy and Family History* (National Index of Parish Registers, vol. ii, 1973), which is much wider than its title suggests; it is valuable to others than genealogists for it discusses the lesser nonconformist bodies, such as Plymouth Brethren and Sandemanians, often omitted in histories of local nonconformity. These books also refer to a number of useful articles in journals such as *The Local Historian* and its predecessor, and there is no point in listing these again in this essay. But there are two booklets that deserve special mention because they offer some guidance on local nonconformist research themes and methods as well as on sources of information: W. F. Swift, *How to Write a Local History of Methodism* (revised by T. Shaw, Wesley Historical Society, 1964), and B. R. White, *Writing Baptist History* (Living Issues Booklets, Baptist Union). Other works are cited in the notes to this chapter.

2 books which deal with the history of English nonconformity generally and with the history of particular denominations. Tutors should use the bibliographies of the books mentioned in this essay, particularly in those by Rogers and Steel. A basic list, to be added to according to local circumstances, might include H. Davies, *The English Free Churches,* W. O. Chadwick, *The Victorian Church* and R. Davies, *Methodism.*

3 any books which deal with or ostensibly cover local nonconformist history. Tutors should make full use of the catalogue of the 'local collection' in the nearest large public library and enlist the help and interest of the local librarian. Using the catalogue of a large local library to its maximum advantage is not such a simple task as it may seem, and the tutor can profitably have one meeting with his class in the library on this task. Nor is the catalogue an infallible and exhaustive guide to holdings—it cannot be—and there is no substitute for a browse through the shelves of the local collection, where one may find information about local nonconformist history in the most unlikely places. Most often the local collection is behind glass-fronted cupboards and under lock and key. Librarians may not welcome a large

group having access to their shelves, and the tutor may have to bring in individual students one or two at a time. Again the assistance and full cooperation of the librarian is essential. An offer to provide the librarian with any references or information found which are not catalogued will help to ensure this.

In recent years there has been a phenomenal growth in the number of local history research groups. They usually have the objective of producing a general history of the locality. While this is desirable, it normally results in local nonconformity being given a brief and—it must be frankly admitted—usually dull treatment because of considerations of space. It may not be feasible to do much more when commercial publication is being considered. But an alternative format, for example a series of essays, typewritten and duplicated, which examines local nonconformist history in depth and which can be clipped together into a plastic binder, is just as useful and far more stimulating. Copies can be sold cheaply to local libraries and other institutions and public access to the results of the research is thus ensured. Where such an approach is adopted, it means that the usual type of nonconformist history production, consisting of a chronology of the chapels and Sunday schools, can be greatly expanded. A general summary history of the local development of nonconformity is obviously necessary and desirable, but from the beginning of the nineteenth century or even earlier in some cases, each denomination —perhaps even each chapel—deserves more detailed and separate treatment, with a leisurely tempo and extensive approach.

Sources: Documents

Such an approach involves the use of sources that are listed fully in the books mentioned above. Details of the earlier Dissenting conventicles can be culled easily from G. Lyon Turner, *Original Records of Nonconformity,* but generally little use is made of Anglican diocesan episcopal visitation records which can sometimes provide hints on early Puritanism in the area. Here is one example from the Lichfield Diocesan Records concerning Archbishop Laud's Visitation in 1635, relating to the wife of Ambrose Grey, esquire of Enville:

> *Uxor* Ambrosii Grey *armiger* for absentinge her self from our parish church upon Sondaies in the afternoone, and for goeinge to Alveley within the jurisdiction of Bridgnorth to heare Mr. Thomas Wynnall a lecturer there, whome the Lorde Bishop of this diocese silenced; and also for goeinge to heare Mr. Crosse a lecturer att Kinver upon Sondaies in the afternoone

Equally neglected are the episcopal returns and visitations of the mid- and later eighteenth century, by which time Methodism had sometimes appeared, to the dismay of one local Staffordshire incumbent making his return to the bishop:

> I don't know if we have any sectaries in ye Parish except two Presbyterian familys, who frequent one of ye Meeting houses at Birmingham and one Methodist Farmer, who receives ye Sacrament with us, but preaches often, not in my Parish but at Birm., Wedgebury and Dudley . . . Tis hard to say, who is, or who is not a Methodist; We have perhaps an Itinerant Preacher once or twice in a Sumer, holding forth upon ye Comon, who, like other Mountebanks never fails to get a Crowd about him.[1]

With some exceptions, county and borough quarter sessions records are also untouched, largely because of the time involved in searching through them at the local record office. Nor are registrations of meeting houses under the 1689 Toleration Act used as much as they should be, again because of the time required for a search, unless, as in the case of Staffordshire, the students are fortunate enough to have a local record society publication which has done the job for them.[2] This involves using the returns made to the Registrar General at Somerset House in 1852 and checking these from local records of registrations (which sometimes provide more details than those made to the Registrar General). Thus for example, one entry in the Staffordshire volume reads:

> 229 A room at UTTOXETER, registered for Protestant Dissenters by Thomas Key, on 20 June 1809.
>
> (This registration occurs in Bishop's Register E, 488, where it is described as a large room in the Old Star Inn occupied by Mrs. Grace Bates and registered by Thomas Key, Thomas Salt and Thomas Wright for Methodists).

Where a local record office is involved, the problems of obtaining group access are not insoluble. Some actually hold evening classes at times when the office is normally shut, although this requires the attendance of an archivist. And it is generally possible for the tutor to get one or two of the students in the research group to come with him by car to the record office or diocesan registry during the day time for the few visits that may be necessary.

The visit to the Public Record Office or other repository in London to consult enrolled nonconformist trust deeds (Class C.54) is another matter. Unfortunately, these documents are little used, although they often provide much information on congregations, doctrinal beliefs and other matters, as well as details of lands and buildings. Nonconformist (non-parochial) registers at Somerset House are rather better known these days, thanks to the current interest in genealogy. So also are the returns made for the religious census of 1851—Staffordshire again being fortunate in that the local Victoria County History editors have produced a volume dealing with the religious history of the county and reproducing the attendance figures for the chapels dealt with.[3] But in general central government records, including various Parliamentary Papers, are not used by adult research groups as much as they should be. The difficulty, apart from ignorance, is usually one of time and access. Groups in the provinces can hardly be expected to go to the Public Record Office or elsewhere in London to gain the information. But the difficulty is not insuperable. A letter to the Public Record Office asking whether there is a return for a particular locality on a specific topic will usually receive a helpful and informative reply. Given notice, the Public Record Office will supply a photocopy of the document/s concerned. If the information is in the form of a printed Parliamentary Paper, the local Public Library will normally be able to borrow a copy. Most libraries are now building up their stock of local history source materials and librarians will be glad of the reference to a local return and may even pay for the photocopying themselves.

Where members of local nonconformist bodies are part of a research group, difficulties of obtaining access to locally held records are usually much less. The person officially in charge of archives, for example, the Superintendent Minister of a Methodist circuit, will be more willing to make the special arrangements necessary for the group to consult the documents in his circuit safe. Ensuring such sustained and regular access to the archive is usually the chief difficulty encountered in researching into local nonconformist history. If the group meets weekly there may be problems of space, lighting, heating, caretaker's costs and so on, and special financial arrangements may have to be made. Local official cooperation is essential. In the case of the Methodist Church this body has now appointed archivists for many of their districts. The name and address of the district archivist can be found by application to the local circuit superintendent or from the Methodist Archives and Research Centre, 23–25 City Road, London, E.C.1. Of the other Protestant nonconformist denominations, the Society of Friends is best organized in respect of the care of its records, which are usually a joy to the historian. Most General Meetings now have an official Clerk or Clerks of the Records. If there is no working Quaker Meeting House locally, information about the location of archives can be obtained from the Librarian, Friends' House, Euston Road, London, N.W.1. It can sometimes happen that special arrangements can be made for the temporary deposit of nonconformist archives in a local library or record office—they may of course be there already—in which case problems of group research are in some respects eased.

But wherever the records are located, much careful prior planning of the research by the tutor, the assignment of individual tasks, the preparation of suitable proforma sheets for the quick recording of information and so on are essential. It is highly undesirable for the tutor to have his first sight of the local material only when he brings his research group with him. He should make a careful list of the material for himself beforehand, and most important, know exactly what he wants to do in the usually limited amount of time he and his group will have for working on the documents. It is impossible and unwise to try to lay down general principles of guidance on group research on a local deposit of nonconformist historical material. Much depends on the nature of the material and the interests of the tutor and the group. But a useful and compromise solution of the problem of what to do with a mass of varied material is first to extract the basic chronological, statistical and other information required for the usual orthodox account of the development of the particular institution it deals with—individual chapel or meeting house, circuit or other larger unit of organization—and confirm dates derived from secondary sources. Then the material should be exploited for any special interest it contains on particular topics or periods.

Here, for example, is a list of the contents of a North Staffordshire Methodist Church circuit safe taken in 1969—Wolstanton and Audley Circuit. It may be regarded as not untypical of the range and nature of material found in a circuit safe.

Minute Books

- Brunswick Chapel Sunday School Teachers' Meeting 1892–1903
- Brunswick St. Wesleyan Church Leaders' Meetings 1895–1908
- Local Preachers' Meetings, Brunswick and Audley Circuit 1954–1965
- Trustees' Meetings, Brunswick Church 1944–
- Combined Leaders and Church Council 1946–
- Trustees of Brunswick Chapel and Sunday School 1880–1910
- Leaders' Meetings 1908–1915
- Trustees of Basford New Connexion Methodist Church 1877–1913

	Quarterly Meeting of Newcastle Circuit 1879–1893
Registers etc.	Register of Baptisms in Parish of Stoke-on-Trent Basford Church Methodist New Connexion 1878–1916 Register of Marriages do. 1879–1906 Admission Book, Sunday School 1878–1883
Account Books etc.	Circuit Trusts Account Book Statistical Summary 1860–1879 Newcastle Quarterly Meetings Account Book
Deeds	Various bundles of deeds
Circuit Plans	Framed plan of Wesleyan Methodist Itinerant and Local Preachers in Newcastle Circuit 1814–15 and 1825

Miscellaneous Printed Books and Pamphlets
includes Official Handbook of Grand Victorian Bazaar 1897.

Faced with the problem of how to extract the maximum of information in the minimum of time from this collection, the tutor might assign students in pairs to summarize the Brunswick Chapel and the Basford New Connexion material, omitting the very recent years. In deciding what to copy and summarize, the interests of individuals in the group will be a determining factor, but where no specific interests have yet emerged the tutor should be prepared to give a strong lead. Perhaps three sample years of the circuit accounts might be copied out fully, comparative figures of baptisms, marriages and Sunday School admissions compiled, deeds glanced at to confirm early dates and the names of pioneers, and the attendances and nature of the business conducted at quarterly meetings noted. But having obtained such basic information the tutor would do well to make a full copy of the circuit plans and of the 1897 Bazaar Handbook. The most useful piece of equipment he can have is a small manual photocopying machine, which is transportable in the boot of a car and can be plugged into the electric power supply (a variety of plugs of different amperage and a long length of cable being also necessary). This can copy foolscap-size pages at the cost of about 5p a sheet, and is thus an expensive tool but a tremendous time-saver. A tape-recorder is now virtually standard equipment for the local historian and a photocopier should be similarly readily available. The plans and the handbook in the list above might both be copied by this method at relatively small financial cost.

The experienced historian of local nonconformity will not rest content with the records officially deposited at local level. In the course of time, as minister has succeeded minister or trustee has succeeded trustee, some of the material will have found its way into private hands. Another great leakage occurs when chapels and circuits are amalgamated or closed. Individual Methodist chapels will often have material which pertains to their own history rather than to that of the circuits to which they belong, and the stewards and the Trustees of the local chapel as well as the minister should be contacted. This applies to other nonconformist denominations equally. A canvass among the older members and officials of a nonconformist church will often produce records other than those officially in the care of the local minister or another responsible person. But having traced as far as possible all the official records, the historian of local nonconformity will then seek for other kinds of historical material like the Handbook of the Bazaar of 1897 found among the contents of the circuit safe listed above. Bazaars were favourite money-raising devices of the Victorian and Edwardian periods, and the souvenir booklet is likely to tell the historian more about the life and nature of a nonconformist organization than the official minute books.

Most often there is a mine of such material about the locality in the possession of individuals, and one way of revealing the existence of this is to organise an exhibition of local nonconformist history. The exhibition can cover one denomination only or all the denominations in an area. The appropriate local ministers or officers will be approached, their approval and co-operation gained and individual congregations asked to mount one stall. The organization of such an exhibition can prompt an adult class, where one is involved, to considerable activity and research, acting as an executive committee, preparing diagrams and summaries which will provide an historical perspective on each denomination contributing, listing and copying all the material produced and so on. Usually such local exhibitions are organized by Women's Institutes or similar organizations, but there is no cause for the academic to look down his nose at such activities. Properly approached they can be more educationally rewarding and stimulating than any number of lectures. Libraries and county record offices will usually be pleased to co-operate. But one of the chief values of such an exhibition is the revelation of the wealth of primary material of immense social interest that still survives. Methodist circuit plans (6.1) may come to light to fill in the gaps in an official series; and from other material—souvenir programmes of past events, membership cards, temperance pledges, photographs of chapels long since demolished, revivalist hymn books, pictures of the Victorian Sunday School outing (a brewer's dray full of solemn little boys and girls in their best suits and dresses, the poorer children provided for by the special clothing fund)—the past comes to life in a vivid way (6.2). Such an exhibition used at the beginning of a class in local nonconformist history can do much to show the depth and richness of social history in the subject that are so often missed in the usual academic approach.

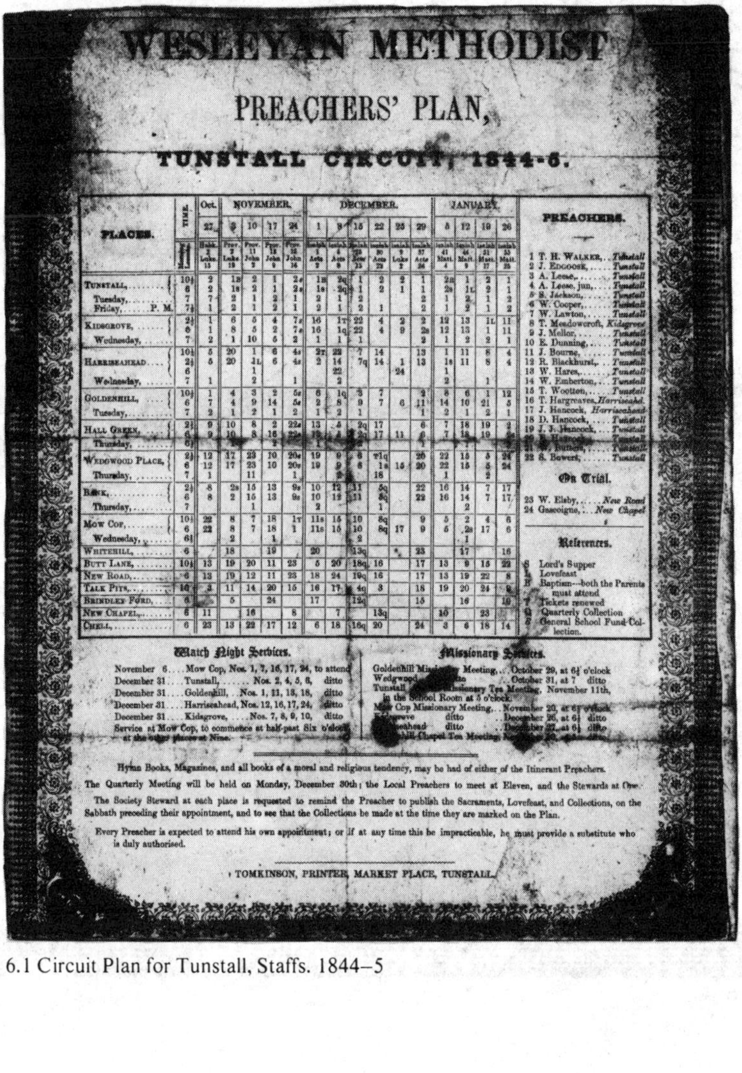
WESLEYAN METHODIST

PREACHERS' PLAN,

TUNSTALL CIRCUIT, 1844-5.

PREACHERS.

1 T. H. Walker, . . Tunstall
2 J. Edgoose, ... Tunstall
3 A. Leese, ... Tunstall
4 A. Leese, jun, . . . Tunstall
5 S. Jackson, ... Tunstall
6 W. Cooper, ... Tunstall
7 W. Lawton, ... Tunstall
8 T. Meadowcroft, Kidsgrove
9 J. Mellor, ... Tunstall
10 E. Dunning, ... Tunstall
11 J. Bourne, ... Tunstall
12 R. Blackhurst, . . Tunstall
13 W. Hares, ... Tunstall
14 W. Emberton, . . . Tunstall
15 T. Wootton, ... Tunstall
16 T. Hargreaves, Harriseahd.
17 J. Hancock, Harriseahead
18 D. Hancock, ... Tunstall
19 J. J. Hancock, . . . Tunstall
22 S. Bowers, ... Tunstall

On Trial.

23 W. Elsby, ... New Road
24 Gascoigne, . . . New Chapel

References.

S Lord's Supper
L Lovefeast
B Baptism—both the Parents must attend
T Tickets renewed
Q Quarterly Collection
S General School Fund Collection.

Watch Night Services.

November 6 . . . Mow Cop, Nos. 1, 7, 16, 17, 24, to attend
December 31 . . . Tunstall, ... Nos. 2, 4, 5, 6, ditto
December 31 . . . Goldenhill, . . Nos. 1, 11, 13, 18, ditto
December 31 . . . Harriseahead, Nos. 12, 16, 17, 24, ditto
December 31 . . . Kidsgrove, ... Nos. 7, 8, 9, 10, ditto
Service at Mow Cop, to commence at half-past Six o'clock at the other places at Nine.

Missionary Services.

Goldenhill Missionary Meeting, . . October 29, at 6½ o'clock
Wedgwood . . . ditto . . October 31, at 7 ditto
Tunstall . . . Missionary Tea Meeting, November 11th, in the School Room at 5 o'clock.
Mow Cop Missionary Meeting, . . November 20, at 6½ o'clock
Kidsgrove ditto . . December 26, at 6½ ditto
. . . head ditto . . December 27, at 6½ ditto

Hymn Books, Magazines, and all books of a moral and religious tendency, may be had of either of the Itinerant Preachers.

The Quarterly Meeting will be held on Monday, December 30th; the Local Preachers to meet at Eleven, and the Stewards at One.

The Society Steward at each place is requested to remind the Preacher to publish the Sacraments, Lovefeast, and Collections, on the Sabbath preceding their appointment, and to see that the Collections be made at the time they are marked on the Plan.

Every Preacher is expected to attend his own appointment; or if at any time this be impracticable, he must provide a substitute who is duly authorised.

TOMKINSON, PRINTER, MARKET PLACE, TUNSTALL.

6.1 Circuit Plan for Tunstall, Staffs. 1844–5

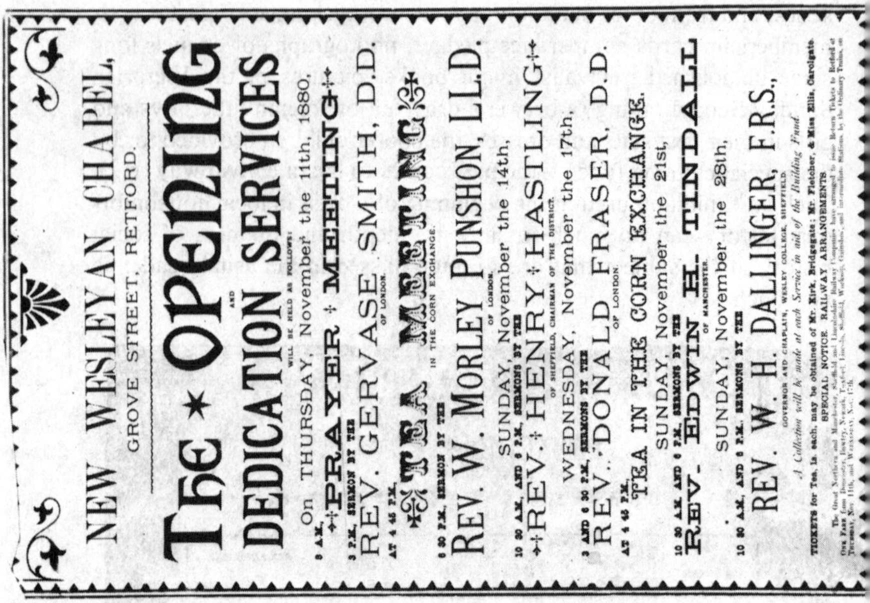

NEW WESLEYAN CHAPEL,
GROVE STREET, RETFORD.
THE ★ OPENING AND DEDICATION SERVICES
WILL BE HELD AS FOLLOWS:
On THURSDAY, November the 11th, 1880,
8 A.M. PRAYER MEETING
3 P.M. SERMON BY THE REV. GERVASE SMITH, D.D. OF LONDON.
AT 4 45 P.M. TEA MEETING IN THE CORN EXCHANGE.
6 30 P.M. SERMON BY THE REV. W. MORLEY PUNSHON, LL.D. OF LONDON.
SUNDAY, November the 14th,
10 30 A.M. AND 6 P.M. SERMONS BY THE REV. HENRY HASTLING OF SHEFFIELD, CHAIRMAN OF THE DISTRICT.
WEDNESDAY, November the 17th,
3 AND 6 30 P.M. SERMONS BY THE REV. DONALD FRASER, D.D. OF LONDON.
AT 4 45 P.M. TEA IN THE CORN EXCHANGE.
SUNDAY, November the 21st,
10 30 A.M. AND 6 P.M. SERMONS BY THE REV. EDWIN H. TINDALL OF MANCHESTER.
SUNDAY, November the 28th,
10 30 A.M. AND 6 P.M. SERMONS BY THE REV. W. H. DALLINGER, F.R.S., GOVERNOR AND CHAPLAIN, WESLEY COLLEGE, SHEFFIELD.
A Collection will be made at each Service in aid of the Building Fund.
TICKETS for Tea, 1s. each, may be obtained of Mr. Kirk, Bridgegate; Mr. Fletcher, & Miss Ellis, Carolgate.
SPECIAL NOTICE. RAILWAY ARRANGEMENTS.
The Great Northern and Manchester, Sheffield and Lincolnshire Railway Companies have arranged to issue Return Tickets to Retford at One Fare from Doncaster, Bawtry, Newark, Tuxford, Lincoln, Sheffield, Worksop, Gainsboro', and intermediate Stations, by the Ordinary Trains, on Thursday, Nov 11th, and Wednesday, Nov. 17th.

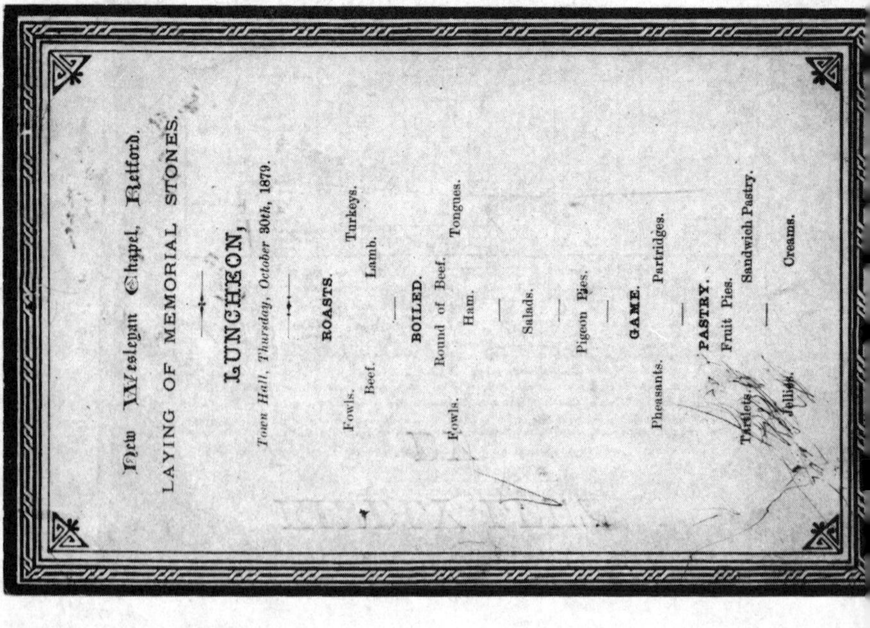

New Wesleyan Chapel, Retford.
LAYING OF MEMORIAL STONES.
LUNCHEON,
Town Hall, Thursday, October 30th, 1879.
ROASTS.
Fowls. Turkeys.
Beef. Lamb.
BOILED.
Fowls. Round of Beef. Tongues.
Ham.
Salads.
Pigeon Pies.
GAME.
Pheasants. Partridges.
PASTRY.
Fruit Pies.
Tartlets. Sandwich Pastry.
Jellies. Creams.

Sources: Oral Tradition

Of the new material that can be found for a study of recent nonconformist history, none is more rewarding than personal reminiscence and information. The value of oral history is now recognized by most local historians, even if A. J. P. Taylor still distrusts the 'droolings of old men'. A pioneer of the technique of oral history was George Ewart Evans, whose books on the East Anglian farming community have given a new dimension to this topic. Since the later 1950s, the use of oral information for the study of recent history has become more widespread. In the field of national history it is being used for the study of twentieth century Labour history and of particular industries like coal mining. An Oral History Society[4] now exists which publishes an occasional news-sheet of much interest and value. But generally in the study of local history, oral information tends to be used as illustration rather than as a major source which can throw fresh light on the recent past. Much more can be done using this technique to investigate particular subjects in depth and intensively, rather than for general local history extensively.

That oral history is suitable for adult class work and for the study of local nonconformist history has recently been demonstrated by an experimental course organized by the Adult Education Department of the University of Keele. The course was entitled 'Living Archives: the oral history of local Methodism in North Staffordshire'. Two meetings were used to help students to acquire a basic skill in the use of the portable UHER tape recorder (the BBC local radio station education producer taking these sessions) and dealing with the technical side generally. The next few meetings were devoted to the discussion and practice of interviewing technique in general, with brief lectures on national and local Methodist history, followed by guidance and hints on interviewing for Methodist history specifically. Students were then sent out to get their interviews with persons from a list previously prepared and also asked to find new informants. Their interviews were played back to the whole class for comment and criticism. About twenty hours of oral information was recorded in all, much of it centred on a very small number of Methodist chapels in the Potteries. The recordings were then systematically indexed by topics, informants and place, although they were not transcribed. It is intended that they should become part of an archive of local oral history of the area, if and when this can be established.

The utility of the project for the adult students themselves was readily apparent. In addition to acquiring a new and specialized skill, the students were exposed to a wide range and variety of information on local Methodism in all its aspects, as a social phenomenon as well as a religious movement. The index headings for just one chapel indicate the wealth and range of the material collected: Boys' Brigade, Class Meetings, Harvest Festivals, Local Preachers and their Training, Revivals and Revivalists, Social Distinctions in the Chapel, Temperance Activities, etc.; and there was of course much information about particular individuals. The year 1932 was taken as the effective terminal date for research, although information on even later years was taken if the informant proffered it. But interviews were sought particularly with people who could recall the pre-1914 period. The occasional gem of information that reached deep back into the nineteenth century was forthcoming, like that of the old lady who could recall in some detail her grandmother telling her how she had once washed Hugh Bourne's feet after he had walked miles to preach at their chapel (Bourne died in 1852). And most interviewers had some minor classic piece of recording such as that with the old lady who could recall word for word the way in which the revivalist of the late nineteenth century, Gipsy Smith, preached and glossed on Psalm 23. But students were encouraged to seek the humdrum rather than the sensational, to elicit information on the daily or weekly routine of Victorian or Edwardian Methodists rather than on headline events of the past. The result was a revelation of the extent of material on local Methodism that exists in people's memories and is nowhere written down.

This experiment dealt with only a few dozen people, belonging to one denomination. A similar determined team attack to collect information on other Methodist chapels and on other nonconformist denominations would produce a vast corpus of material, much of it fresh and able to supplement the written records, to personalize and individualize nonconformist history, to record the individual emotion and reaction to events, that would refresh if not revolutionize the study of the subject locally. The value of oral information for the study of the history of denominations other than Methodism can be illustrated from an interview with an ex-Secretary of a Salvation Army Corps in Burton-on-Trent. A fire at the local Citadel had destroyed all the local records, and Salvation Army headquarters in London lost all theirs in the blitz on London during World War 2. But the informant was able to supply the names of most of the local officers from about 1900 and much other information that helped to overcome the loss of written records. In addition he was able to bring the Salvation Army and its activities before 1914 back to life in very vivid fashion, as the following transcript of part of the interview shows:

'Dad was captain of the roughs—three or four men who protected the women officers. He was originally a maltster from Oxfordshire and a bit of a fighter who was converted. And he really turned. He signed the pledge. Open Air was in the Market Place on a Saturday night. I don't think there were all that many drunks. When we did get them it was the drum that attracted them.

'I've heard my Dad say "Well, have a bang", and after that they'd be all right . . . On Sundays we started with knee drill at the Citadel at seven o'clock. Then we had Open Air at ten, and again in the afternoon, and at night it was a general meeting. We didn't confine our attention to the town, but covered the whole of the Corps area as far as Alrewas and Tutbury. I've seen the whole Band bike it to Repton for Open Air on a Wednesday night, after a full day's work. The hymns I remember singing included, "I found a pearl of greatest price", "O happy day that fixed my choice", and "Hold the fort". They would throw their pennies on the drum when we reached the top note . . . We've had converts: I've seen them kneeling by the drum at Open Air in the Market Place on a Saturday night, begging for mercy . . .'

Sources: Physical Remains

One of the first tasks of the researcher will be to make a careful physical survey of all the nonconformist buildings, both inside as well as outside, in his area. The tutor of a group can quickly encourage and train his students to recognize and to draw tentative conclusions about architectural styles and local fashions. Provided there is a sufficient number of chapels in the neighbourhood to study, changing tastes will soon become apparent to the group; they can learn to see the struggle between classical and Gothic revival of the nineteenth century in its local manifestations; they can be prompted to take note of what is so familiar as to be unremarked, for example, a local use of blue or yellow brick for decorative purposes, perhaps even a distinctive style of a fashionable local architect like William Sugden and his son at Leek. Nonconformist architecture with some exceptions is generally undistinguished from an aesthetic point of view, and this accounts for the relative lack of books on the subject. But there are a few useful works, and the class book box ought to contain some of the most important of these, like Dolbey's *Architectural Expression of Methodism,* Kenneth Clark's *Gothic Revival* and particularly stimulating and pleasant to read, John Betjeman's *First and Last Loves.*[5] Pevsner in his series *The Buildings Of England* can only occasionally find a nonconformist chapel or meeting house worthy of mention. But he looks at buildings with the eye of the architectural critic; the local historian will find plenty of interest in any building if he looks at it as a document illustrative of social history rather than as an object of aesthetic judgement.

He will approach the locally-held records of a particular chapel not merely to confirm dates of buildings, so often the only use to which the records are put, but to find answers to such questions as why and how did it come to be built? Was the land given to them by some local nonconformist benefactor? How strong was the local congregation at the time of first building, of rebuilding, of the addition of the Sunday School? The building of a chapel was for most congregations in the nineteenth century a gamble based on an act of faith. They put themselves heavily into debt with a large mortgage, and trusted that by subscriptions, gifts and special fund-raising efforts they would be able to pay it off. The chapel or circuit treasurer's accounts, provided they have survived, will tell the story in figures. Primitive Methodists relied much on the annual anniversary collection. Usually some eminent Methodist of national reputation was invited to preach on the occasion; there was some competition between chapels for the services of the best money-spinners, people like the Reverend Joseph Hocking, the novelist of the early twentieth century. It was a matter of conscience that the collection at a special anniversary should equal or exceed that of the previous year. If it did not, Primitive Methodists resorted to the practice of 'sweating': the congregation sat there until first one then another member promised a few more pence or shillings until the desired total was reached—they sweated the money out of themselves.

Where the denomination was growing fast and attracting wealthier tradesmen and manufacturers into its congregations, the task was easier. Hints of this can be gathered from the names on foundation stones. In these days when chapels are being rapidly demolished a careful inventory of a threatened building is essential. The local planning authority or conservation society may be persuaded to take photographs, but they will seldom go to the length of recording the foundation stones. Yet sometimes these are the only evidences that have survived. Chapel interiors are equally important to survey and record. Unlike Anglican churches they are usually kept locked, and prior contact with the caretaker is necessary to obtain access (caretakers themselves are often useful sources of information and if possible should be involved in the survey). The chapel will sometimes contain a number of monuments of past worthies and pillars of the church and rolls of honour of those who served or were killed in war. But the rooms behind the chapel are frequently as full of interest to the local historian as the chapel itself, the walls hung with pictures and photographs, perhaps a framed copy of the earliest local circuit plan (if it is a Methodist chapel), a reproduction of Holman Hunt's 'Light of the World' to indicate mid-Victorian taste, and evidences of previous systems of heating and lighting. A rusty Victorian gas bracket can not only be evocative of the past but a useful prompt to a flow of reminiscence from an informant. The local historian will approach the whole of the building with his historical antennae extended as it were, sensitive to the depth of social history behind the material objects he examines. He is thus more likely to come across some unexpected gem of information—the minister whose picture appears on the wall got into trouble with his congregation for appearing too frequently on Liberal Party platforms before 1914; the stained glass window of 1911 vintage was made by William Morris and Company (how many other nonconformist chapels in the area have Morris glass?); a leaflet rescued from the bottom of a cupboard advertises an early twentieth century revival meeting, with a picture of the revivalist, 'Owd Mo' before and after his conversion from a life of sin and intemperance to one of vigorous but respectable Christian evangelism: such material widens the historical horizon.

Another relatively neglected aspect of nonconformity is the graveyard that may still be, or was formerly attached to the chapel or meeting house. In many cases they have been lost in rebuilding in the later nineteenth century or in urban redevelopment in the twentieth century. But a few survive, like that of Bethesda Chapel (formerly Methodist New Connexion), Hanley, Stoke-on-Trent (6.3), and many others can be traced. A number of counties have local history societies that have undertaken Anglican churchyard surveys, but little has been done for nonconformist graveyards. To survey and trace these over an area would be a useful task for an adult education research group. Detective work with documents and pleasant rambles in town and countryside in summer can be usefully combined. A listing and survey of burial grounds belonging to the Society of Friends provide an example of this kind of project. In Staffordshire alone there are fifteen such burial grounds.[6] They are not distinguished by gravestones. Friends found anything but the simplest and plainest of gravestones objectionable, and some Meetings refused to allow them at all. Thus the burial ground attached to the Quaker Meeting House in Uttoxeter, Staffordshire, has only two gravestones, but the records show over sixty burials there in the nineteenth century alone.

The large town chapels of the nineteenth century will attract the immediate attention of the local history researcher. But the humble

6.3 Methodist Graveyard, Stoke on Trent, from a sketch made in 1971

'tin church', meeting room or wooden hut should not be neglected for the non-conformist classical temple or Gothic cathedral. Some of them have had careers as the homes of a succession of religious denominations—Anglican mission church, Primitive Methodist Chapel, Salvation Army Citadel—and perhaps still survive today as a place of worship as a Pentecostal church for a largely coloured congregation. Sometimes these smaller religious denominations attracted to membership a well-to-do local businessman or executive whose wealth and influence could considerably help its progress. Such was the case with one of the four meetings belonging to the Plymouth Brethren (or more strictly, 'Christian brethren', with no capital 'b') in Burton-on-Trent, amongst whose members was a local brewery managing director. Research on such less well-known religious bodies is as important and necessary as on the large organizations; their documentation may not be so readily available, and more reliance may have to be placed on oral information.

New Projects with Old Documents

The bare chronology of the institution which usually passes for local nonconformist history may be all that commercial publication considerations allow, but the local history group untrammelled by such considerations need not so restrict itself. It can also aim at producing essays, articles or pamphlets and engaging in other forms of activity than the writing of straightforward narrative history. Recently adult groups in Staffordshire have been producing semi-dramatized documentaries for local radio. Here the bare chronological recital of events is enlivened and illustrated by extracts from contemporary minute books, letters, memoirs, sermons, almost anything written. Such sources can be used to provide dramatic dialogue without injury to historical accuracy, at the same time serving to stimulate the historical imagination and evoke the feel of the past. Nothing need be invented, just a minimum of linking words to provide any necessary dramatic continuity. The tutor can act as historical consultant and final editor. Someone in the group may have technical expertise in handling tape recorders, and the local radio station education producer will usually only be too pleased to help and advise, and even provide professional assistance and studio facilities. He is interested in the educational aspects of such a project and if the programmes produced are good enough will broadcast them.

To illustrate what can be done here is a short extract from one such programme in Methodist history broadcast by BBC Radio Stoke-on-Trent. Background music was provided by a local Methodist choir.

Methodist Hymn No. 507 'Give to the Wind thy Fears'

NARRATOR It is believed that John Wesley first came to Cheadle in Staffordshire in the year 1785, on his way from Ashbourne to Newcastle under Lyme. Tradition holds that he preached here, standing on a horse block under a tree opposite the present Royal Oak Hotel. Wesley does not mention Cheadle in his *Journal,* but he says that the area generally was responding to the efforts of Methodists.

VOICE OF WESLEY (*a man of 82, rather tired with age but still forceful and cultivated*)

I preached in the new preaching-house at Henley-Green; but this was far too small to hold the congregation. Indeed this country is all on fire, and the flame is spreading from village to village. The preaching-house at Newcastle just held the congregation, many being kept away by the election, especially the gentry; but still the poor heard the Gospel preached and received it with all readiness of mind.

NARRATOR Cheadle at this time was attached to Burslem Circuit, but probably only as a preaching place, together with

Dilhorne and Cockin. But then in the early years of the 19th century Primitive Methodism came to the area. Hugh Bourne had a personal connection with Cheadle through his mother Ellen Steele, who was the daughter of a farmer from Hatchley. In 1807 Bourne, holding his Camp Meetings on Mow Cop and elsewhere in defiance of the Methodist authorities, came to Kingsley and preached in the open air, strong in the conviction that this was the work he had been called upon to do.

VOICE OF BOURNE (*he speaks with a strong Potteries accent, but the voice is firm and well-informed*)
I was necessitated to have no other head but Christ, and I felt like a solitary being. I did not, however, lose respect to my old friends, although they laboured to set people against me. My wish was to labour for the conversion of souls. The decree of the Lord was gone forth to bring forward open-air worship and the converting work afresh . . .

NARRATOR Cheadle became part of Ramsor Primitive Methodist Circuit and was served by two travelling preachers. These preachers were the nucleus around which each little congregation gathered. If they had to, they slept rough, in a haystack or hedgeside. They got £24 a year—which had to be raised by the local circuit, and had to preach at least eight sermons a week and after each preaching hold a prayer meeting. In theory the circuit provided them with a lodging. In practice this was often a miserable hovel. William Clowes's son-in-law, who became a travelling preacher, found at one circuit that the preacher's house had been given up and what furniture was to be found was stored away under the circuit steward's bed. Another minister personally transported the circuit furniture to another house which had been found—in a wheelbarrow. One of the early 19th century travelling preachers in the area, Samuel Heath, kept a diary. It's clear from this that he measured his success not in miles walked but in souls saved.
(*Outside broadcast effects of wind and rain and the sound of footsteps on a gravelly road in between each reference.*)

HEATH February 3rd. Onecote, and the Lord was there. February 5th preached at Waterhouses, there was a shaking amongst the dry bones.

> Sunday March 9th. Cheadle Common, afterwards Tean. Great hungering and thirsting after righteousness . . . .

In the writing of these scripts Methodist circuit plans (6.1) are particularly useful and their value as a source of information and as a general teaching aid is very considerable. The circuit plan lists all the preachers in the local circuit (consisting of perhaps a dozen or more chapels) with the places, dates and times of preaching appointments for a quarter or perhaps fifteen weeks. All save one or two of the persons listed, who are the paid professionals and whose names are usually printed in capital letters at the head of the list, are local preachers, that is laymen competent and authorized to conduct services. Each preacher, as the example provided above shows, is indicated by a number in the appropriate column. Methodist circuit plans date back to the eighteenth century, although it is rare to find any earlier than 1810. The Society of Cirplanologists has listed the whereabouts of a great many circuit plans up to 1860, and these are held in official Methodist hands, at the local Methodist circuit level, and by private individuals who have made collections. Some have found their way into County Record Offices and Public Libraries. Circuit plans show not only the growth or contraction of a circuit but are evidence of the kind of religious provision afforded. Thus in the example shown, Tunstall Wesleyan Circuit provided a baptismal service once a month but at Tunstall only. All the chapels or preaching places had quarterly collections but not all celebrated the Lord's Supper or held Lovefeasts. On the last point it is interesting to try to trace when the last Lovefeast was held in a circuit—they became rarer in the country generally in the early twentieth century and had almost disappeared by 1939.

But it is the role and importance of the local preacher that shows up most clearly on circuit plans. There would have been much less expansion, both geographically and in membership, in the Methodist Church without the work of these laymen. They provided the bulk of the preaching workforce. From the circuit plan the itinerary of individual local preachers can be plotted and compared with that of others. With the aid of a map the number of miles walked per quarter can be worked out. Comparisons can be made between the local preachers' stints at, say thirty year intervals starting with the earliest circuit plan available and coming up to the present. It is noticeable that the last seven places listed on the Tunstall Plan, presumably only preaching places, are not served by either of the two (paid) itinerant preachers. Comparison of the 1844/1845 plan with that of the same circuit in 1854/1855 shows ten of the earlier preachers still in the circuit, which now required the services of thirty-two preachers rather than twenty-four. There are neither watch night services nor missionary services listed as there were ten years previously. Morning lessons are taken only six times from the Book of Isaiah instead of ten times. The possibilities of historical analysis in a series of circuit plans are many.

Local Methodism because of its nature and the wealth of its records offers perhaps the best subject for the adult class tutor who wishes to widen and vary his approach to the teaching of local nonconformist history. But the other denominations also offer interesting and fruitful fields for class study and activity. Quaker records, for example, where easy and regular access can be obtained, provide opportunities for numerous sorts of project. One such is the biographical index of Friends within a Monthly or Quarterly Meeting, compiled from local sources helped out by reference to the registers at Friends House in London. These go back to the mid- and later seventeenth century, and an index compiled for Staffordshire now has about 3,000 names, most with dates of birth, marriage, death and other details.

These projects mostly have an aim which is other than that of the concise narrative history. They do not have to provide a comprehensive coverage of the subject to be useful pieces of historical research or to be educationally valuable. If time and energy permit, it is obviously desirable to produce a total rather than a partial picture. But the importance of chronology should not be allowed to obscure the value of, say, producing the portrait of nonconformity at a particular period. And a compromise can sometimes be reached by offering a history of nonconformity in a locality at different points in time, for example, 1750, 1850 and 1950. This provides not a complete history but a moving picture of an important aspect of the life of a local community. Local history is one of the last do-it-yourself subjects in an increasingly packaged and professionalized world, and local nonconformist history is a rich and still largely unexplored field of study.

Notes and References

1 Lichfield Diocesan Records B/V/1/52, quoted in D. A. Johnson and D. G. Vaisey, *Staffordshire and the Great Rebellion* (Staffs. County Council, 1964); Lichfield Diocesan Records B/V/5, Visitation of 1772.

2 *Collections for a History of Staffordshire,* Fourth Series vol. III (Staffordshire Record Society, 1960).
3 V. C. H. *History of the County of Stafford,* vol. III (ed. M. W. Greenslade, 1970).
4 Oral History Society, c/o Department of Sociology, the University of Essex, Wivenhoe Park, Colchester.
5 G. W. Dolbey, *The Architectural Expression of Methodism* (1964); K. Clark, *The Gothic Revival* (3rd edition, 1962); J. Betjeman, *First and Last Loves* (1952).
6 D. G. Stuart, 'The Burial Grounds of the Society of Friends in Staffordshire' in *Transactions of South Staffs. Arch. and Hist. Soc.,* vol. xii.

7

Parliamentary Enclosure

REX C. RUSSELL

Preparing the Ground

It is understandable that any group undertaking its first venture into local historical research wishes to see quick and worthwhile results from such work. Such an immediate outcome is heartening and can give confidence to the members to embark on longer-term research into more complex fields. For this reason an admirable topic to choose for beginning group work in local history is the parliamentary enclosure of a single parish. The number of documentary sources which the group has to master is small: it is possible to achieve good results by using three sources only, the local enclosure Act (the printed document which authorized and legalized the enclosure of the parish (7.1), the enclosure Award (the permanent legal record of the enclosure) and the local landscape. The total time necessary for work on this subject need be little more than one full winter session—provided that some 'homework' is undertaken between class sessions—and the total cost of publication of the result of this group work is limited.

If the first essential for any group considering work on parliamentary enclosure is enthusiasm, then the second essential is a limited, but guaranteed, sum of money to spend on photocopying and perhaps duplicating. Resources must be available for photocopying a selection of source material to enable the group to work purposefully as a group. If the group is constituted as an adult education class, then the body responsible for providing the course may be willing and able to give some financial help; in addition to this support (or in the absence of it) the members of the group, perhaps backed by a grant from their

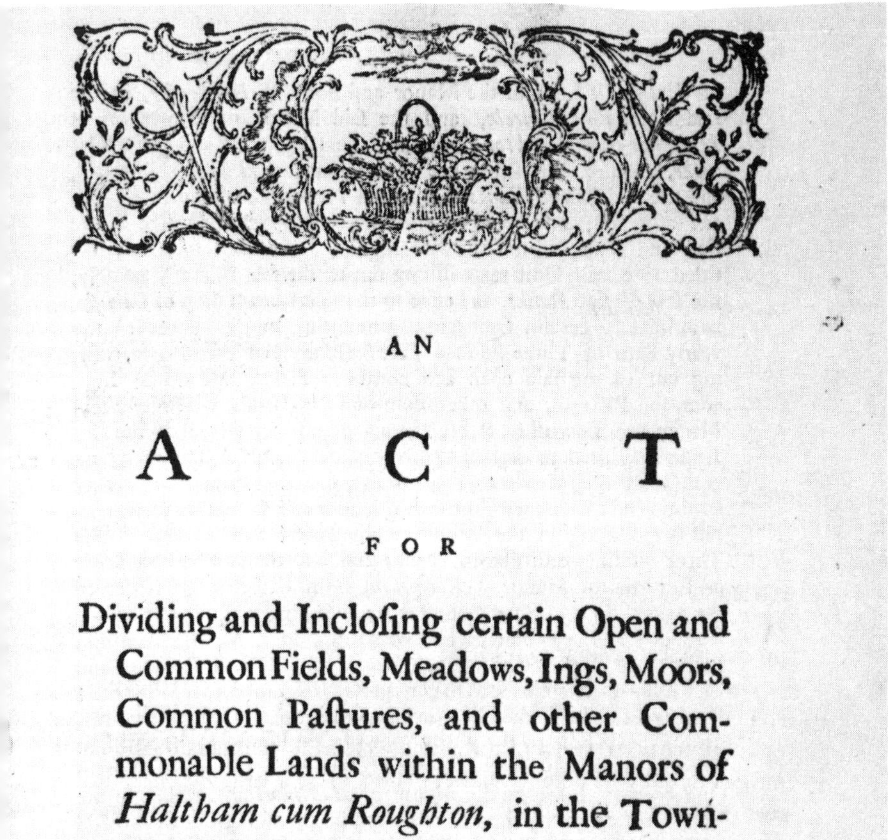

AN

ACT

FOR

Dividing and Incloſing certain Open and Common Fields, Meadows, Ings, Moors, Common Paſtures, and other Commonable Lands within the Manors of *Haltham cum Roughton*, in the Townſhips of *Haltham* and *Roughton*, in the County of *Lincoln*.

WHEREAS there are within the Manors of *Haltham cum Roughton*, in the Townſhips of *Haltham* and *Roughton*, in the County of *Lincoln*, certain open and common Fields, Meadows, Ings, Moors, common Paſtures, and other commonable Lands, containing Two thouſand Acres or thereabouts: Preamble.

And whereas *Joſeph Banks*, Eſquire, by virtue of a Leaſe for Three Lives from the Lord Biſhop of *Carliſle*, in Right of his See

A of

7.1 Enclosure Act, a copy of the first page

local history society or W.E.A. branch, must be prepared to contribute money themselves. One pound each from a group of fifteen people would finance the necessary research: costs of possible publication are a separate matter which will be discussed towards the close of this chapter. It is important to make this point initially, otherwise the frustration arising within a group which attempts such research without some financial resources will largely cancel out the undoubted advantages of group research.

Much of this expenditure will be incurred, not at the start of the project but as it progresses. And this is true of the third essential requirement for the study, a knowledge of the background to the nature and process of parliamentary enclosure. It is necessary for the particular local study to be put into the general framework of the enclosure movement; and some generalized acquantance with the chronology, the processes and the results of the enclosure of open fields into farms held in severalty will itself suggest questions to ask and methods of work for the particular enclosure now under review. For this purpose, some reading in the general works on the history of agriculture, together with such publications as deal with other enclosures in the county and region, should be done as the project proceeds (see Bibliography).

Once the subject has been chosen and the ground prepared, how should the group begin work? Simply, but essentially, by discussing and writing down a list of questions which the members of the group may eventually be able to answer. These in their turn will raise further relevant queries such as: what range of sources do we need in order to begin to find answers to our questions? Where are these sources likely to be located? How can we use these sources most profitably as a group? How can we present the results of our group work? We will deal with these two stages in sequence.

The Questions the Group is Asking

No attempt is made here to list more than a selection of the initial questions which the group should discuss *and write down*. No group is likely to frame all the relevant questions as a result of one full discussion; further queries are bound to arise as the work progresses and such additional questions should be added to the first list compiled. The list will however form an invaluable outline guide to direct the group work.

Some essential guiding queries will be: What did the parish look like immediately before enclosure?[1] How did the landscape and the road network differ from the post-enclosure pattern? How was the arrangement of farms different from the post-enclosure system and are there any features of post-enclosure farm-layout which take into account the logic of the open-field system? Who wanted enclosure? Did any owners of land or common-rights object to the intended enclosure? Why did this local enclosure take place (for example) in 1793–96 rather than in 1769–71 or in 1824–28? How were the local enclosure commissioners selected and who helped to determine the local choice of commissioners (and surveyor)?[2] Are the main hedging species the same throughout the parish or do some hedges contain markedly different species?[3] Are there now some hedgerows the courses of which were clearly planned on a surveyor's drawing board and others which follow an irregular course? Why do a number of chalk, stone, gravel or sand-pits abut onto several of the roads in our parish? What can local farmers and farm-workers tell us about soil variation within the parish? What are their land-drainage problems and which areas present the greater drainage problems?

It is suggested that the compilation of such a list of initial questions will help direct attention to the sources the group will need to study.

The Range of Sources

The most accessible source is also one of the most essential: the modern landscape itself. But to make fully profitable use of the landscape the group will need other relevant material—air photographs (7.2) (the vertical photos taken by the R.A.F. are most useful, while some local newspapers may also have such photographs) and maps. The most valuable maps are those of the Ordnance Survey, on the 6″ scale to cover the whole parish, and on the 25″ scale to cover the area of the heart of the parish, the village (or town) and its adjoining old enclosures. Some of these maps (the earlier editions) are now out of copyright: it is very much cheaper to obtain *several* photocopies of these maps than to purchase *one* copy of the most recent and the most expensive edition. The group needs several copies to use and there may well be positive advantages in working with such older maps—hedges which have since been uprooted will often be depicted on the earlier editions.

These three sources, the landscape, maps and aerial photographs, used together may tell us much of value which would not be apparent if the sources were used separately. The air-photographs (7.2) may reveal features not apparent in the modern landscape. Two things especially should be noted: areas of ridge and furrow (possibly running

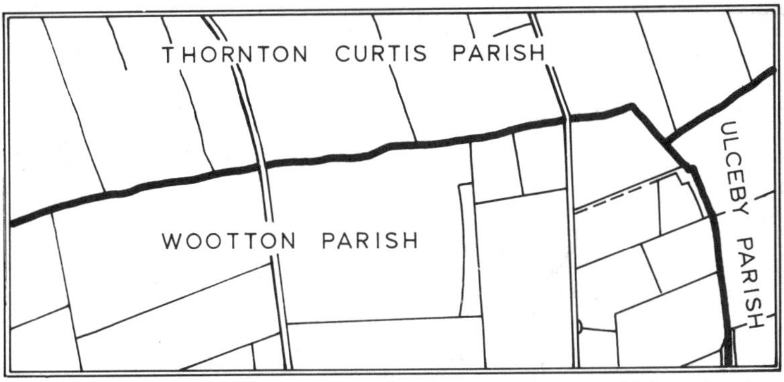

7.3 Map showing a typical change of alignment of roads at a parish boundary in north Lincolnshire; note too that no hedge crosses this boundary

through several modern hedges and across modern roads or railway tracks) may indicate something of the furlong pattern of the obliterated open-field system, while the courses of former roads may be clearly evident from the air although not visible on the ground. Such features should then be marked in on the copies of the Ordnance Survey maps. The maps themselves enable the group members to view the parish as a unit. It is advantageous if the map sheets cover parts of adjacent parishes, for each parish was (normally) enclosed at a different date, and the visible results of enclosure are different in many cases on each side of the parish boundaries.[4] Few modern hedges cross parish boundaries; in very many cases the courses of roads change direction at the parish boundaries (7.3). Thus, once these boundaries have been established on the map, their nature is worth investigation on the ground. There may be a distinct boundary bank, or the field-level may be markedly higher on one side of the boundary than on the other; the hedgerow on the boundary may contain many more species of bushes and trees than those hedges set after enclosure. All such matters should be recorded for further investigation. Irregularly-shaped closes which abut onto the parish boundaries need attention; they may be areas of old enclosure created by the taking in of parcels of land from the waste for arable use or for grazing. Boundaries such as that shown (7.4) are worthy of particular investigation: if the air-photographs reveal signs of ridge and furrow on each side of such a boundary, this may be evidence that two adjoining parishes have, before the boundary was finalized, competed for good arable land in this area.

Maps and aerial photographs are two items in our range of sources. Two further essential sources are the enclosure Act and the enclosure

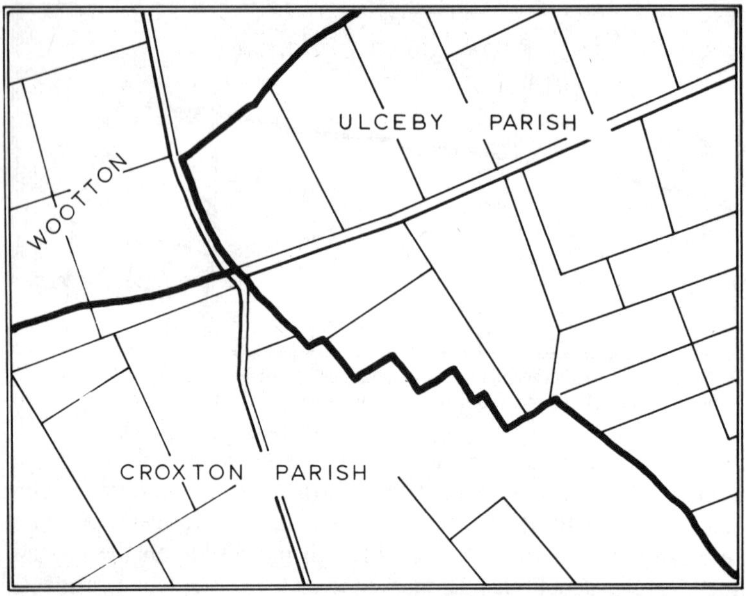

7.4 Parish Boundaries in North Lincolnshire. The series of squared ends suggests that the medieval farmers of Croxton and Ulceby competed for good arable land

Award (the permanent legal record of enclosure). The Minutes and Accounts of the enclosure commissioners together with any associated letters, lists of proprietors' claims and solicitors' letters and papers will prove invaluable, if they still exist. An additional source of considerable value can normally be found (after 1770) in the files of the relevant local newspaper. In the public notice columns of the county press appear the notices relating both to the intended enclosure of a parish and to the commissioners' meetings during the process and progress of enclosure. Once a group has established the date of passing of their enclosure Act[5] (for example 1793) and also the date of the execution of their enclosure Award, given in the final paragraph of the award (for example 1796), it is not an uninteresting task to search the public notice columns of the newspaper between these dates to locate these notices inserted by the commissioners or their clerk. They will reveal a 'time-table of enclosure': when and where the commissioners will hold their various meetings, together with the purpose of such meetings. Other relevant and significant information may also be found during such a search: advertisements for the sale of farmland whilst enclosure is in progress, and notices inviting contractors to submit estimates for hedging and fencing the tithe-allotments, for the construction and metalling of new enclosure roads or for the building of bridges over new drains and tunnels to carry water under roads and paths. In the absence of commissioners' minutes and associated papers, such newspaper notices can fill many important gaps in the group's researches.

The Location of Sources

Where should the group look for these various documentary sources? The enclosure Award may still be where it was deposited immediately after the work of enclosure was completed, in the parish chest within the parish church, in the custody of the incumbent. It may have been transferred into the custody of the clerk to the parish council: it is possible that the County Council may have it and also possible that it has been deposited with the County Archives or in the county Record Office. There are some local awards in the Public Record Office and others (originals as well as copies) in the offices of local firms of solicitors. The enclosure Act may likewise be located in any of these places, but since many copies of local enclosure Acts were printed, it is normally easier to locate at least one copy of these: several libraries have extensive collections of such Acts, and they are cheap to photocopy.

The Minutes and Accounts kept and prepared for the enclosure commissioners are relatively rare documents. Enquiry for these should be made at all the places already mentioned. Several remain among the papers of major estates or in the offices of local solicitors who have acquired the business of eighteenth century attorneys together with the documents and papers prepared and used by such attorneys. Because enclosure awards are the permanent legal records of enclosure, several local solicitors made verbatim copies of these documents (written in a hand often more easy to read than the original award itself and in a far less cumbersome form than many original awards). Where such a copy exists, this is a document much more suitable for photocopying than an original award.

There is, at present, no complete published guide to the whereabouts of enclosure documents for all counties which experienced parliamentary enclosure, though for some counties such guides have been published. One good example is the handlist for the East Riding of Yorkshire.[6] The invaluable, comprehensive bibliography published in 1972 by the British Agricultural History

Society, *Enclosure and the Open Fields* by J. G. Brewer, should be purchased and used thoroughly by any group working on enclosure.

There is one way in which a group undertaking a study of a particular parliamentary enclosure has a natural advantage over an individual researcher—it has more local contacts than the individual research worker. It has been proved (by Bernard Jennings working in the North and West Ridings of Yorkshire and by the experience of the present writer working with local groups in Lincolnshire among others) that persistent enquiries made by such groups can unearth documents which are now in private hands. It is certainly worthwhile for any group to let the local newspapers know of the research they are undertaking, for such publicity may help to discover the whereabouts of 'lost' parish documents. (Where the clerkship of a parish council has remained in the hands of one family over many years, the documents in their custody may come to be regarded as family property and carefully guarded as such!)

The Use of Sources for Group Work

When the essential documentary sources have been located the problems of the use of these sources for group work must be considered. Any research work undertaken by individual members of a group or carried out by sub-groups should be discussed by the group as a whole. Such discussion has two main purposes: it keeps all group members fully aware of the results of all research undertaken, and secondly it leads to the posing of new questions to promote further investigation. One sub-group can check and extend the results of work undertaken by another sub-group. It is desirable then for the same documents (or summaries of such documents) to be available to more than one sub-group. The question (and the cost) of photocopying arises; the group must consider what has to be done with each source for the most productive use to be made of each.

(a) *The Landscape as a source*

The landscape can only be used effectively if the permission of the owner and occupier has first been obtained to walk over his land—an obvious point to make, but one worth making because it is well worthwhile to enlist the help of local farmers who know their land and the variations in their lands better than any outside enquirer. The group may ask questions of the landscape which few farmers might ask, but the question, once asked, may be answered better by the farmer(s) than by the unaided group members. Group work, at its most effective, should aim from the start at enlisting the help of people (such as farmers and farm-workers) who are not formally members of the researching group. Some of the questions to ask of the landscape evidence have already been indicated: add to these the questions of your enlisted helpers and attempt to enlarge the number of these invaluable allies by recruiting the help of those people who live in houses which were formerly farm-houses. Some further questions to ask will include these: When did some farms move out of the village (or town) into the newly-awarded enclosed lands? How many such farms (or barns and farmsteads) appear on the first edition of the Ordnance Survey map for your area? Of what materials were these buildings made; has any use been made of specifically local material—chalk in the wold areas, limestone in limestone areas? Is there any local evidence that farms which now exist furthest away from the village centre were the first outlying farms to be built after enclosure? What became of the farms within the village old enclosures, to what use were they put, and how many can now be identified with certainty? Did enclosure make some land available for use other than farming—for quarrying or brickmaking?

(b) *The Local Enclosure Act*

At least two complete photocopies of this document (7.1) should be obtained and each member of the group should read it. Summarize its main provisions by answering such questions as the following: What field and common names appear in the Act (sometimes these differ from those used in the Award)? What reasons for the desirability of enclosure are given in the Act? Which land-owners are named in it? Who is the Lord of the Manor (or who are the Lords of the Manors); who are the tithe-owners? What provision, if any, is made for awarding land or corn-rents in lieu of future tithes? Are tithes to remain on any part of the parish? What is to happen to farm leases—are farmers to be compensated for the ending of unexpired leases? Who are the Commissioners and the Surveyor(s) named in the Act? What powers are they given; what fees are they to receive? Who can appoint successors to commissioners who may die during enclosure or who may refuse to act; and does the answer to this last query help us to understand who had a major voice in appointing the original commissioners? Does the Act contain any clauses relating to the keeping and periodical inspection of the accounts of enclosure? Are provisions made to deal with cases of landowners who fail to meet their proportions of the costs of enclosure? Is there any legal appeal against the decisions of the commissioners under this Act?

This is not a full list of the questions which need consideration. Most useful information is likely to be obtained from the Act if several members of the group each work independently on the text and then report their findings and questions to the whole group for thorough discussion. Although enclosure Acts are normally fairly straightforward documents, several group members working on their own are very likely to note different points as important, to consider as especially revealing different clauses or paragraphs in the same Act. After discussion by the whole group, a summary should be made of the main points—and a discussion of this summary is quite likely to throw up new questions which may necessitate further work on the Act.

It could be profitable to look at two or three other enclosure Acts for the nearby parishes. Enclosure Acts follow a fairly common pattern, so that provisions found in one Act and not in another may raise helpful questions about the particular enclosure under study.

(c) *The Local Enclosure Award*

First make a tracing of the award map; this should be done whether or not a complete photocopy of the original map is made. Since several members of the group will need to work on this map, several copies are desirable, and it is cheaper to have multiple copies made (by a commercial drawing office or perhaps by a co-operative local government architect's department) of an accurate tracing than to have several photocopies of the original map. The tracing must be accurate, made on good quality heavy tracing paper, and preferably drawn in black ink for good copies to be made. The areas of old enclosures must be distinguished from those of the parliamentary enclosures; the number and acreage of each of the awarded plots should be indicated, together with the name of the owner, and the courses of new roads be shown.

What essential information is needed from the text of the award? The group will need to know how the appearance of the open-field parish was transformed, what new features were created by enclosure, and what old features were obliterated. This information may be summarized from the main body of the award. Among the changes to be listed, the number and the courses of the newly laid-out roads (with their widths) and of the newly constructed drains (with their dimensions), and the locations of old roads, the use of which is to cease at enclosure, should be included. The names of all owners awarded land, the acreage which each owner was awarded and the location of each of the owners' plots are all to be found in the award. This information can best be recorded in tabular form:

Names of Owners	Number of Plot	Acreage of Plot Acres.	Roods.	Perches.	Location of Plot
e.g. Charles Anderson Pelham	20	110.	3.	37.	in West Field
	35	57.	1.	29.	in the Ings
	71	3.	0.	12.	in East Common

Details of the exchanges and purchase of land during enclosure should also be noted: the number of land-owners could increase or decrease during enclosure. Any other information relating to the changes wrought in the parish by enclosure should first be summarized (accurately) and then discussed by the whole group to evaluate the value and meaning of the facts recorded and to ascertain whether further facts need to be elicited from the award.

How can a group best approach work on the Award? Normally the Award will have to be studied in its place of custody, in the Record Office search room, in the church vestry (preferably in warm weather, for vestries are rarely adequately heated) or in the local government offices. If a solicitors' copy can be located and if money for photocopying is available, this should be copied: it would normally be too costly to photocopy an original Award. The summarizing of an Award can, and should, be undertaken by several members of the group, working in pairs; but it is vital that each pair of workers works to an agreed common pattern. The great advantage of two people working together is that one can read whilst dictating notes for the other to write down: words difficult to decipher can be looked at by both people. Awards can be very large and cumbersome documents; each line of text can be very long, and if the person who is reading alone is also making notes it is easy to lose one's place and waste hours. Two people working together can do much more than twice the work of each working alone.

After the location of each plot has been recorded (in the West Field, in the Ings, in East Common, in the Cowpasture, and so on), it is possible to reconstruct the open-field appearance of the parish as it was immediately before enclosure, although it must be stressed that there is no certainty that this pattern would have been the same one hundred or four hundred years previously. This can be done by

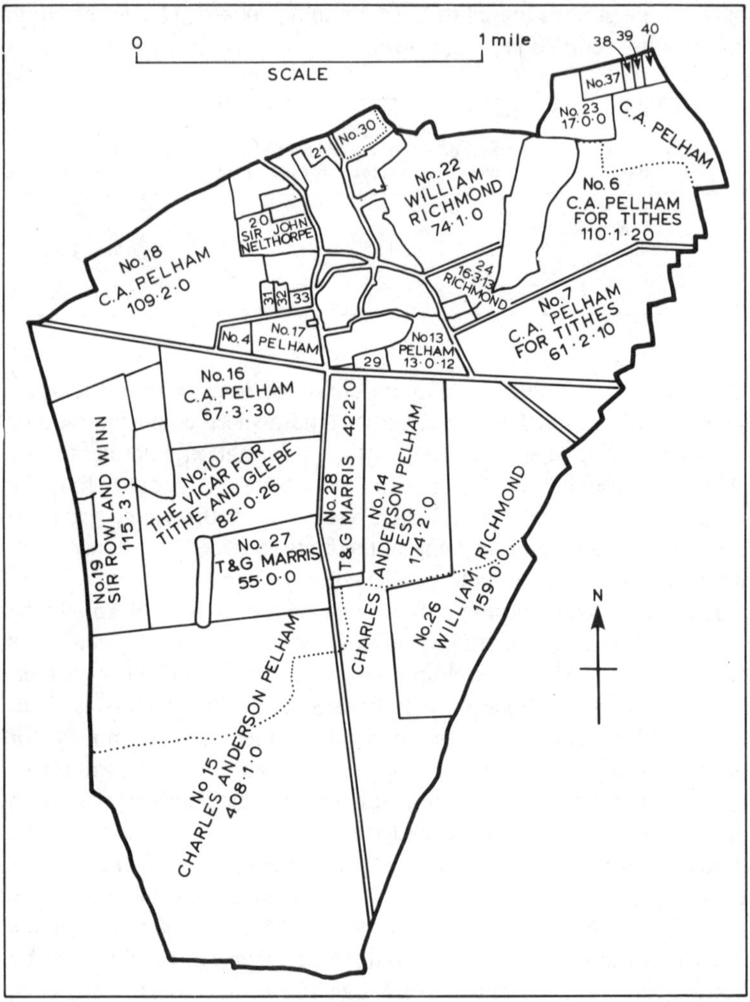

7.5 Kirmington (Lincs). A redrawing of the surveyor's map in the Enclosure Award of 1778, depicting the location of newly-awarded plots of land, their ownership and acreage. The text of the Award records where each plot was located in the former open field system (old enclosures are shaded)

writing the location of each plot (as given in the Award) on a copy of the Award map. When each plot has been thus located, it is possible to ring round in colour all the plots lying in (for instance) the West Field, all the plots lying in the Cowpasture, all the plots lying in East Field, and the open-field layout of the parish stands revealed (7.5 and 7.6). A minority of Awards do not contain such information on the

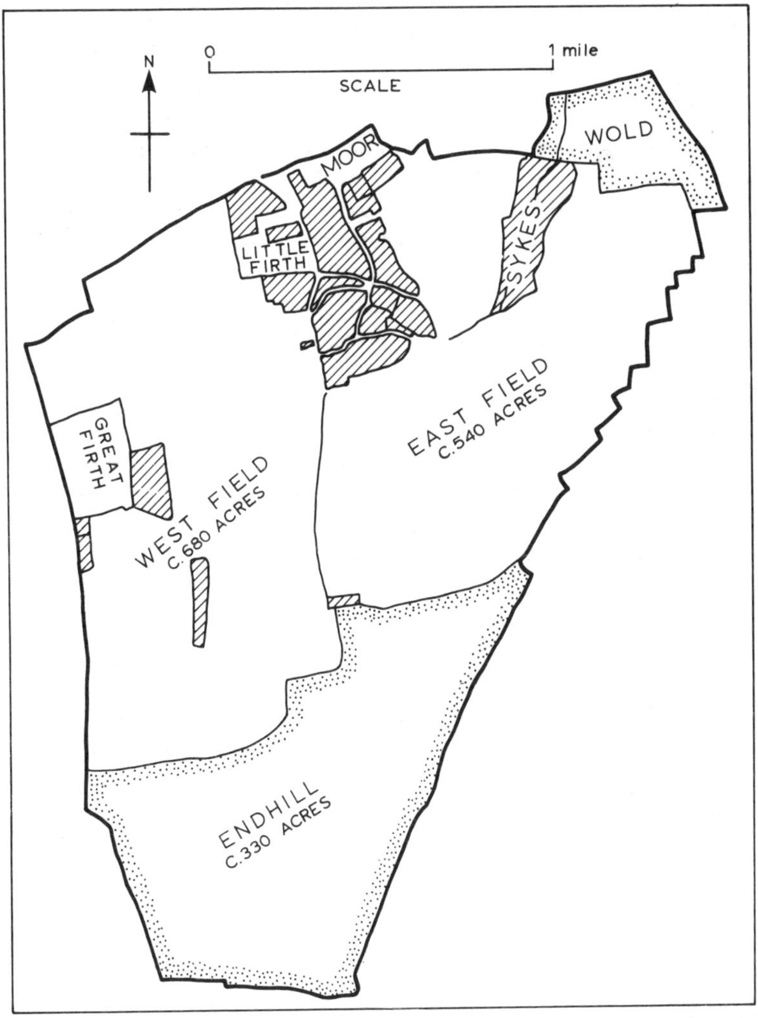

7.6 Kirmington (Lincs). The open field system reconstructed from the surveyor's map and the text of the Award

location of each individual plot, and in such cases it is not possible to reconstruct a pre-enclosure map with any real accuracy unless the surveyor for the enclosure has been especially helpful. On some surveyor's maps the boundaries of the open fields are shown in colour and occasionally these areas are named on his map. Most surveyor's maps distinguish the old enclosures from the newly-awarded lands by colouring the former green or by using a different type of lettering and numbering to reveal such distinction. Several Awards describe some plots as lying in two fields, in other words across the boundaries of the former common fields; the use of aerial photographs and a walk over the fields in question can sometimes determine the exact boundary.

If the costs of enclosure are stated in the Award (by no means a usual practice) these obviously should be written out. They may well reveal the cost-per-acre to owners of different acreages and this in turn can prompt further questions for the group to explore. It would be valuable to see whether the higher costs-per-acre were borne by the smaller or the larger owners. Further important work can be done on copies of the Award map. Using different colours to block in the lands awarded to different owners, the group can ascertain whether many (or any) of the lands of individual owners lie within areas which can be ring-fenced. If such ring-fencing is clearly impossible, why have the commissioners awarded dispersed lands? Examples of such dispersal in the parish today may be located and the farmers asked why (or whether) they consider such dispersal was necessary. It is profitable and essential to go from documents to landscape and back from landscape to written evidence once more.

(*d*) *Other documents*

A discussion of the use to which commissioners' minutes, accounts and associated papers can be put has been left until last, because these are the most rare of enclosure sources. Should they exist for your enclosure they may well prove both rewarding and frustrating: the minutes for example are rewarding in that they record the commissioners' decisions, but they are frustrating since they rarely reveal the reasons for such decisions. However, the group will discover from them the stage-by-stage process by which the enclosure progressed, the sequence in which different aspects of the work occurred, the dates upon which owners could enter upon their awarded lands in the different fields and commons, the dates on which 'rates' were to be paid to meet enclosure expenses, and when and with whom contracts for stoning and gravelling the newly awarded roads were made. Amongst the associated documents may be minutes of the meetings called to discuss the expediency of the intended enclosure, the decisions reached (to petition Parliament for leave to bring in an enclosure Bill or to postpone such a procedure until a more expedient time) and the numbers and names of owners present at such meetings. And one question to ask here would be whether these owners represented a majority of the owners of land or simply a majority of the land owned.

Discussions relating to the abolition of tithes by granting land in lieu of future tithes may also be minuted. This may enable the group to decide on what basis the value of the land to be awarded was decided, and whether there was agreement or dispute over this. Did the rector and the vicar, if both existed, see eye to eye over this compensation? If the claims of the proprietors to ownership of land and common-rights survive, it will be possible to determine which claims the commissioners accepted and which they amended or rejected. A comparison between the claims accepted and the lands allotted (as shown in the award) will reveal what compensation in acres was given for certain rights of pasture and common grazing (some Awards are specific on this; others are quite unrevealing, and we are forced to rely on supplementary evidence where it survives).

If papers concerning enclosure costs are plentiful, a number of questions may be asked. Thus the items which went to make up the total cost of enclosure can be discovered—the cost of the passing of the local Act, the sums paid to each commissioner (why did some receive more than others?) and to the surveyor(s). What did it cost to fence the allotments awarded in lieu of tithes; does this sum help us to estimate the total cost of hedging and fencing in the parish (not included in the costs of enclosure)? What did the newly-awarded roads cost to make? Were they to be metalled at enclosure; if so, what specifications were laid down by the commissioners for this—did they state where road-making (as distinct from road-repairing) materials were to be obtained; did they appoint a salaried surveyor of the roads to oversee road-making? What did it cost to dig new drains in the parish, and is there any indication of special drainage problems to be overcome? Were pre-enclosure rights to water safeguarded?

The greater the volume of the papers relating to enclosure, the greater the number and variety of the meaningful queries that can be raised. The precise way in which the group may apportion the work between its members or its sub-groups can be left to group decision, but as a detailed preliminary inspection of the papers proceeds (either in class sessions or as home-study between the sessions), the list of questions to be asked should be written down. Such lists of queries should be duplicated, made available for consideration by every member of the group and then discussed thoroughly by the group in class before more detailed work on the papers is undertaken. The purpose of such questions is to provide guidance for further work, and time spent in class discussion of such queries can save time later on: the queries should thus indicate precisely what needs to be known. A few examples of such questions may be helpful. If minutes of proprietors' meetings preceding enclosure exist, the group should ask such questions as these: who initiated discussion of this intended enclosure? How many owners attended these preliminary discussions? Who were these people, were they mainly the owners of larger acreages or did smaller proprietors also attend? (The names of people attending these meetings may be compared with the names of owners eventually awarded land.) Did discussions take place on the award of land to the tithe-awards in lieu of future tithes? If so, what were the terms reached for such compensation?[7]

To spend money on photocopying the commissioners' minutes, accounts and associated papers is good policy. Such papers can normally be used only in the place where they are deposited. Few members of most groups can get off work to make prolonged visits to the archive offices, so that these documents must be photocopied so that they can be fully used.

Presentation of the results

Any group which has enjoyed the privilege of working on the parish documents already mentioned has, in the writer's view, an obligation to make available to the parish the results of their work. The easiest method of doing this is by arranging public talks on the enclosure of the parish at which copies of the Award map, together with the re-constructed open field map of the parish can be on display. Brief duplicated notes about the local enclosure can be available for distribution or sale at these meetings. Such meetings should be arranged (and publicized perhaps in co-operation with the Parish Council and the Women's Institute or Townswomen's Guild) before any final writing up of the results of the group work for publication is undertaken. For by doing this the group is giving opportunities to a much wider group than themselves to ask questions and make comments on enclosure. Several of these questions and comments may raise points of real value which need to be considered and investigated before any writing up for eventual publication is undertaken. The location of missing documents may be revealed at, or because of, such meetings.

The possibility of publication of the group's work, in printed or duplicated booklet form, could also be discussed at such meetings. Such publication is desirable, not only (though this is important) for the satisfaction of the group, but also to make available the results of group work to a wider public locally and to other students and tutors nationally. A later chapter in this book deals with the possibilities of publication and so little need be said here, but the group itself should have sufficient faith in the value of its own work to explore the possibility of publication. First, approaches should be made to local libraries and local museums who either already issue occasional publications or who are willing to discuss the possibility of starting such. Publication is a natural extension of their existing educational functions and they should be urged to see it as such. In some areas W.E.A. Districts and University Departments of Adult Education have been glad to publish the results of group work arising from courses which they have sponsored: in other places it has been the local branch of the W.E.A. which has raised money for this purpose and recouped it from sales: occasionally a Parish Council or a Local History Society has financed such booklets. All such avenues should be explored; but in the last resort, the group itself may have to express confidence in the value of the results of its study by publishing the booklet itself.

Whatever method of publication is adopted, the group should give careful consideration to the form and content of the finished product. The body of the text can be duplicated (although the assembly of many separate pages of duplicated text is a time-consuming business), but the covers should be well-printed on thin card. Costs may well determine the length of the text and the number of maps to be included, but as a minimum the reader should be presented with the following information: two well-drawn maps of the parish before enclosure and immediately after enclosure, a summary list of all proprietors who were awarded land together with details of the acreage each was awarded, and chronology of the course of enclosure (which can be based on the commissioners' notices in the local county newspaper if such details are unobtainable from commissioners' minutes). Such content is clearly but a minimum and further material should be determined by a consideration of costs.

Notes and References

1 For examples of open field systems *see* Rex C. Russell, *The Logic of Open Field Systems* (1975).

2 *See* M. W. Beresford, 'The Commissioners of Enclosure', in *Essays in Agrarian History* ed W. E. Minchinton, vol. 2 (1968).

3 *See Hedges and Local History* (Standing Conference for Local History, 1971) and the paper by M. D. Hooper in *Landscapes and Documents,* ed A. Rogers and T. Rowley (1974).

4 *See Landscapes and Documents,* ed Rogers and Rowley, Fig. 4 p. 32; for field remains, *see* C. C. Taylor, *Fields in the English Landscape* (1975).

5 There are several sources for such dates. The first is the H.M.S.O. publication of 1914, *Returns in Chronological order of all Acts Passed for the Inclosure of Commons or Waste Lands* which is divided into lists by counties. For several counties there exist more detailed guides, two examples of which are R. E. Sandell, *Abstracts of Wiltshire Inclosure Awards and Agreements* (Devizes, 1971), and B. A. English, Handlist of West Riding Enclosure Awards (National Register of Archives, 1965).

6 *A Handlist of East Riding Enclosure Awards,* ed Vanessa Neave, Attic Press, Beverley, 1971.

7 *See* Rex C. Russell, 'The Enclosure of Wrawby cum Brigg' in *The Enclosures of Market Rasen 1779–1781 and of Wrawby cum Brigg 1800–1805* (1969).

8

Census Analysis and Village Studies

JOHN PHILLIPS

It is the purpose of this chapter to demonstrate how a local history group can centre its research on the published census reports and unpublished enumerators' books, with most of the attention being given to the latter source. A quick look at an example of one sheet from a census enumerator's book (8.1) will show clearly how rich a source it is if one wants to find out about people in the past; and a considerable amount of sophisticated analytical work has already taken place in this area. There is, for example, the work of M. Anderson, W. A. Armstrong, J. Foster, M. Drake, P. Tillott and R. Smith,[1] which not only provides essential information and understanding of nineteenth century society but which also provides a methodology. Hence it is essential for any group, either through its leader or as individuals within the group, to be aware of these more general studies in this field and to relate them to their own interests and work.

My own experience has been mainly with groups of people working on villages (especially Ruddington and Clifton, Nottinghamshire) and hence the methods described below relate to this type of community, although they may of course be adapted to work on towns. But work in urban areas involves special problems because of the scale of the study, and it may be necessary to employ sampling techniques in order to get an adequate picture of the whole.

From the beginning it is important for the group enquiring into the past of its community to realize that their village is a small unit and that such a small unit means that general statements about occupations or about household and family structure must be made with

27

Parish or Township of [illegible]	Ecclesiastical District of	City or Borough of	Town of	Village of —	B

No. of Householder's Schedule	Name of Street, Place, or Road, and Name or No. of House	Name and Surname of each Person who abode in the house, on the Night of the 30th March, 1851	Relation to Head of Family	Condition	Age of Males	Age of Females	Rank, Profession, or Occupation	Where Born	Whether Blind, or Deaf-and-Dumb
	Continued	George Cross	Son	—	5		[illegible]	Notts Ruddington	
		Emmily do	Daur			8		do do	
		Mary Foster	Servt	U		16	House servant	Leicester.	✓
105		Ann Smith	Head	Wido		35	Seamer	Notts Gotham	
		Emma do	Daur	—		9	do	.. Ruddington	
		Jarvas do	Son		11		Winder	do do	
		James Shaw	Lodger	U	57	-	F W K	Leicester	✓
		John Dring	do	U	56		Do Do Do	[illegible] Barroby	✓
		Mary do	Lodger	U		25	Seamer	Notts Ratby	
		John Dring	do	—	1		Infant	Notts Ruddington	
		Elizabeth Harrison	do	U		18	Seamer	Nottingham	
106		William Brooks	Head	Mar	26	-	F W Knitter	Nott Radcliffe	
		Ann do	Wife			28	Seamer	Darby	✓
107		Hannah Gunn	Head	Wido		40	do	Notts Plumtree	
		William do	Son		15		Winder	do Ruddington	
		[illegible] Gunn	Son		12		do	- do	
108		John Marshal	Head	Mar	41		Cordwainer	do do	
		Maryann	Wife			34	Seamer	Notts Bunny	
		Eliza Marshal	Daur			4	Scholar	d Ruddington	
		William do	Father	Wid	64		Milk man	do do	
Total of Houses	4 U B	Total of Persons			10	10	3 to other side		

8.1 A page from the unpublished enumerator's book for the 1851 census (Ruddington, Notts) (Crown copyright preserved)

caution. Indeed it will soon be realized that there is a need to correlate the findings from some other similar type of communities before useful general statements can be made.[2] Thus any conclusion reached about the behaviour pattern of any group of people such as the farm workers in one village, while it remains important for that village, must be seen in the light of the region or at least compared with other neighbouring villages. However this is not to underestimate the value of group work on census enumerators' books. Quite the reverse: it is an argument for more census anlysis so that the comparisons can be made.

Aims and objectives

Before a group begins to work on the census materials, it should be clear about its aim and have established a number of objectives which it feels can be achieved during the course of the programme. The general aim of the group may be concerned with the nature of continuity and change over time, a key concept employed by historians. Or the group may be looking for the 'dissimilarity' of the past in contrast to today especially if the members of the group live in what is today a commuter village and are examining the nature of their village in the nineteenth century. The evidence revealed by the census enumerators' books may show that the majority of the people in the village whose occupations are given in 1851 were craftsmen, farmworkers or those employed in some domestic industry, and so by inference, it could be claimed that those people were employed in the village where they lived. Yet having made this inference it would be necessary to realize that some of the farm workers, especially in an open village, may very well have been employed in a nearby village and would have travelled outside their village to work, most likely on foot.

From such a general aim, more specific objectives will follow. For example it will be necessary to find out about the background to the census of 1801 and perhaps about the nineteenth century statistical movement in general. It is important to understand the motives behind the establishing of the census in 1801 and how over the century which followed the techniques employed to count the population and to analyse the results changed.[3] It is also important to realize that the margin of error, which is hardly significant on a national scale, becomes very important in a study of the local community. In this context, the two main sources to the censuses, the published and printed reports on the one hand (8.2) and the unpublished and manuscript enumerators' books on the other (8.1) provide a significantly different range of information.

Another important objective of the group will be to find out about general population movements during the nineteenth century,

60 31 NOTTINGHAMSHIRE.—PARISHES. AREA; HOUSES, 1841, 1851; [DIV. VII

No. of District.	No. of Subdist.	DISTRICT or UNION. SUBDISTRICT.	No. of Parish.	Parish, Township, or Place.	Area in Statute Acres.	HOUSES. 1841 Inhabited	1841 Uninhabited	1841 Building	1851 Inhabited	1851 Uninhabited	1851 Building	POPULATION. PERSONS. 1801	1811	1821	1831	1841	1851
		438 BASFORD.															
438	1	GREASLEY - -	1	Kirkby-in-Ashfield - [a] Parish	5590	406	8	3	453	5	-	1002	1123	1420	2032	2143	2363
			2	Selston - - - - [a] Parish	2330	390	9	-	398	2	1	833	1102	1321	1580	1982	2101
			3	Annesley - - - - [b] Parish	3360	51	2	-	47	4	-	359	341	326	335	274	239
			4	Felley - - - - Extra Par.		6	2	-	8	-	-	33	70	71		41	44
			5	Greasley - - - - [c] Parish	8010	985	29	3	1047	13	1	2968	3673	4241	4583	5184	5284
			6	Eastwood - - - - [d] Parish	940	312	12	-	333	6	1	735	1129	1206	1395	1621	1720
			7	Codnor Park (*Derby*) [e] Extra Par.	-	131	2	-	131	1	-	309	708	693	637	815	735
				Heanor (*Derby*), part of Parish—[e]													
			8	Codnor - - - - [e] Hamlet	-	247	4	-	273	10	-	828	1103	1329	1439	1314	1439
			9	Loscoe - - - - [e] Hamlet	-	85	3	-	88	2	-					424	451
	2	ILKESTON - -		*Heanor* (*Derby*), part of Parish—[e] [f]													
			1	Heanor - - - Township	6870	568	34	5	676	2	6	1061	1912	2364	2672	3058	3427
			2	Shipley - - - Township		109	-	-	109	1	-	433	563	595	632	671	665
			3	Ilkeston (*Derby*) - [f] Parish	2290	1078	66	10	1224	11	6	2422	2970	3681	4446	5326	6122
			4	Cossall - - - - [g] Parish	720	63	3	-	59	-	1	353	328	317	341	334	303
			5	Trowell - - - - Parish	1570	70	-	-	69	-	-	235	482	464	402	380	392
	3	BASFORD - -	1	Beeston - - - - [h] Parish	1440	555	44	1	616	4	7	948	1342	1534	2530	2807	3016
			2	Wollaton - - - - Parish	2340	114	2	-	118	1	-	838	769	571	537	574	581
			3	Basford (w) - - - [i] Parish	2720	1679	82	20	1975	34	16	2124	2940	3599	6325	8688	10093
	4	BULWELL - -	1	Bilborough - - - [k] Parish	1090	51	8	-	43	3	-	307	269	291	330	267	255
			2	Strelley - - - [l] Parish	1050	47	2	-	51	1	-	250	298	350	426	284	279
			3	Nuthall - - - - [m] Parish	1644	136	3	-	135	4	2	378	326	465	509	669	685
			4	Bulwell - - - - [n] Parish	1210	604	9	1	739	10	7	1585	1944	2105	2611	3157	3766
			5	Hucknall-Torkard - - Parish	3270	537	17	1	581	9	5	1497	1793	1940	2200	2680	2970
	5	ARNOLD - -	1	Linby - - - - - [o] Parish	1190	50	10	-	58	4	-	515	434	439	352	271	310
			2	Newstead-Priory Extra Par. Lib.	5250	26	-	-	25	1	-	143	142	174	159	193	155
			3	Papplewick - - - [p] Parish		63	40	-	61	11	-	709	647	593	359	319	357
			4	Calverton - - - [q] Parish	3320	260	12	-	299	3	-	636	904	1064	1196	1339	1427
			5	Woodborough - - - Parish	1940	164	9	-	181	2	2	527	611	717	774	801	852
			6	Arnold - - - - [r] Parish	4670	885	69	1	959	36	1	2768	3042	3572	4054	4509	4704
			7	Lambley - - - - Parish	2170	183	6	3	186	2	-	467	583	690	824	983	951
	6	CARLTON - -	1	Burton-Joyce † - - - Parish [all except Bulcote; see 441; 1]	970	120	5	-	144	3	4	447	459	508	534	610	690
				Gedling Parish—‡													
			2	Gedling - - - Township	4490	82	3	1	90	2	-	554	525	499	458	411	402
			3	Carlton - - - Hamlet		408	24	1	474	5	9	819	1214	1345	1704	2015	2329
			4	Stoke-Bardolph - Township		35	1	-	38	1	-	157	164	173	181	216	191
			5	Colwick - - - - Parish	1255	20	3	-	21	-	-	116	102	120	145	109	129
				West Bridgford Parish—§													
			6	West Bridgford - Township	1720	41	1	-	48	1	1	235	210	208	231	229	258
			7	Gamston - - [s] Township		17	-	-	17	-	-	97	116	102	107	103	122
	7	WILFORD - -	1	Ruddington - - - Parish	2190	384	3	-	433	3	1	868	1017	[illegible]	1428	1835	2181
			2	Bradmore - - - - Parish	1560	82	1	-	74	-	-	325	407	410	369	416	401
			3	Bunny - - - - - Parish	2000	74	1	-	70	4	-	359	374	395	371	360	336
			4	Gotham - - - - Parish	2740	143	7	-	153	-	-	475	549	625	478	747	792

8.2 A page from the printed report on the 1851 census, showing Ruddington and Clifton (Notts)

especially within the region. This is a large and complex field, even within one region, but any local study must be set against the overall pattern of population growth during the century and the change from a rural to an urban society.[4] Again, an inquiry into the nature of employment during the period covered by the census enumerators' books available for examination (1841–71) will form part of the general research project. This will, for a village community, lead to a consideration of agriculture, crafts and services and village industry. One of the most difficult problems here is that of establishing useful categories of occupations so that the pattern that emerges in your village may be compared with that for other villages. One of the more common classifications is that devised by Tillott, but not all historians have followed his list.[5] But above all the group will want to enquire into the changing nature of the village under examination, to place the village within its historical and geographical context. Thus it will be important, from the first, to find out whether it was an open or close village and from there to consider briefly the nature of its social bonds—for example work, religion, welfare, education and government. An awareness of time and place is essential: the village under consideration must be seen in relation to others and, if possible, contrasted and compared with similar and different types of village, for example, a close village with another close village and also with an open village. Nor will the pattern necessarily remain static throughout the period. It will not be difficult to see changes in the community as the century progresses.

It will thus become clear that the censuses relating to any one village cannot be studied in isolation. They must be set against their general setting. Books on the general history of the nineteenth century, on population changes, on open and close villages and on rural life in that period, will form the background reading of all members of the group. Again the project needs to be seen within its regional setting. Other village studies from the locality should be searched for comparisons and differences. General discussions on the social, agricultural and industrial life within the region will throw a lot of light on the particular study. All of this reading can however be done as the research project progresses, but the books and articles may have to be acquired at the start of the work. It will also become clear that the source material to be pressed into service will not just be the censuses; it is necessary to relate these to other relevant source material. It will be hard to avoid the use of large scale maps (particularly the 25″ Ordnance Survey Maps) and other sources such as commercial directories and parish registers. This is, after all, part of the historian's craft of using more than one source in order to describe and explain the past.

Whichever approach is initially adopted, it is highly desirable to have some clear goal in mind right from the start. This could be the publication of the discoveries by booklet or exhibition, or it might be providing further information for a local museum or amenity group. Such a goal will help to ensure that the project is in fact completed. And it will dictate to a large extent the way in which the source material is handled and the information collected.

The Sources

With such considerations the way is clear to describe and explain the questions and methods which a group can use. The first and obvious need is to have photocopies of the census enumerators' books for the area under investigation. These are available for 1841, 1851, 1861 and 1871. The 1841 books are less satisfactory in that certain details returned are less precise, for example ages and birth places, while others are lacking altogether, for example relationship to the head of household. The hundred year rule prevents any group from seeing the full details of the census enumerators' books after 1871. This therefore means that groups customarily operate within the three censuses of 1851, 1861 and 1871. The photocopies have to be obtained from the Public Record Office, Chancery Lane, London, and they obviously cost money and take time to arrive. On the other hand, microfilm copies are often available locally (in the County Record Office or county or city library, for instance), and offprints of these can be made cheaply. The price depends upon the quantity needed. For a small village it will be possible to acquire complete copies of the books for 1851, 1861 and 1871. For larger villages or for towns, on the other hand, it may be practicable to consider only one of the series of books, or indeed particular areas of the town.

At the same time, the group should acquire copies of the relevant pages from the printed census reports which exist for each of the censuses from 1801. These published reports are normally held in the larger central reference libraries and are most useful in giving an overall picture. Thus the page from the 1851 census report reveals the growth pattern for Ruddington (Nottinghamshire), rising from 868 in 1801 to 1428 in 1831, 1835 in 1841 and to 2181 in 1851; at the same time, it gives some indication of the development of other villages in the same sub-district as Ruddington and throughout the wider region. Moreover since the printed reports are available after 1871, it is possible to collect useful information about the later period for every census year, for example total population and number of houses for your village and summaries of occupations throughout the registration district. This last point needs emphasizing, for occupations and ages are not listed in the printed reports for separate village communities. This information is only provided for the registration district. However it is necessary for the group to inform itself of the general regional pattern of occupations as a background to their more detailed local study.

Setting the Questions

Having acquired these two main sources, the group's work can now be planned in various stages. The first is clearly to discuss the sources and to establish the sorts of questions they can most conveniently answer about the village people of some 120 years ago—their numbers, their housing, the size and nature of their families, their occupations and their birth places. Further, the printed reports will enable some comparisons to be made with earlier and later years.

A task which seems to follow naturally from such a discussion, and which is indispensable, is to place the information contained in the enumerator's books on cards. The ways of doing this will vary according to the particular task in hand. There are, for instance, sophisticated systems such as those used by M. Anderson and W. A. Armstrong, but a simpler version may well serve the purpose of the group, leaving it to other people in later years to add to those cards extra information. The cards will always remain a useful index which will itself be a record of the group's activity. Such a card may be based on the head of household, whose full name and occupation is written on the top right hand corner. The date of the census (1851, 1861 or 1871) is written on the top left hand side. The number used by the enumerator must also be recorded, for there will be need on occasion to check back to the original sheet. All the information about the household is written on this card (using a continuation card

1851 Enumerator's No. 105						SMITH, Ann Seamer
Ann Smith	Head	Widow		35	Seamer	Notts. Gotham
Emma Smith	Daur.			9	"	Ruddington
Jarvas Smith	Son		11		Winder	Ruddington
James Shaw	Lodger	Unmar	57		F.W.K.*	Leicester
John Dring	Lodger	Unmar	56		F.W.K.	Lincs. Barrowby
Mary Dring	Lodger	Unmar		25	Seamer	Notts. Ratby
John Dring	Lodger		1		Infant	Notts. Ruddington
Elizabeth Harrison	Lodger	Unmar		18	Seamer	Nottingham

*Framework knitter

8.3 Sample card based on the census enumerator's book for Ruddington, 1851—*see* 8.1

clipped to the first card if necessary). A completed card would therefore look like the illustration (8.3).

As the major task of the group will tend to revolve around the name, occupation and date, these details appear for easy reference at the top of the card. The address, rarely given in villages, becomes less

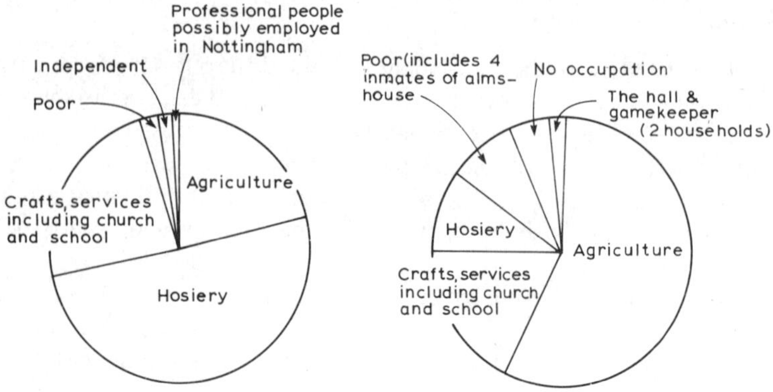

RUDDINGTON 1851 (total number of households 434)	
Agriculture	21·9%
Hosiery	50·2%
Crafts, services including church and school	23·4%
Poor	2·3%
Independent	1·4%
Professional people possibly employed in Nottingham	0·8%

CLIFTON 1851 (total number of households 90)	
Agriculture	56·6%
Crafts, services including church and school	17·7%
Hosiery	10·0%
Poor(includes 4 inmates of almshouse itemized as 4 separate households)	8·6%
No occupation	5·0%
The hall and gamekeeper (2 households)	2·1%

8.4 Occupation Structure—Heads of Household. Piegraphs showing occupational structures (heads of households) of different communities, Ruddington and Clifton (Notts.), 1851. (Ideally the righthand circle should be one quarter the size of the lefthand circle to indicate the size of the community)

important. If the location of people within the village is necessary, and sometimes this can be achieved where addresses are given, then the photocopies will have to be used rather than the cards. Such indexing has another useful function. It is a very quick way of enabling the members of the group to become familiar with the enumerator's book, for example, the writing and methods of registration, and above all with the people of the village and their work. Further, this work can usually be done in one or two group sessions—all three censuses for a small village, or 1851 alone for a larger village. From such work, some first impressions will be formed about the village 100 years or more ago—for example, the extent of a domestic industry, or the number of craftsmen such as shoemakers, or the nature of child employment. Certainly the continuity of family names over the last hundred years will be one source of interest.

After this initial task, a more systematic analysis of the occupations and age structure of the village population can be undertaken. We have of course to take the occupations given at their face value—we cannot for instance know how many people were at the time unemployed, nor whether the descriptions they gave to themselves were in fact accurate. There are for example few instances of dual occupations recorded, although other sources will show that this was a common feature of rural life in the mid-nineteenth century. A further difficulty may be experienced over the occupations of some of the wives and children (defined as those aged from five to fourteen

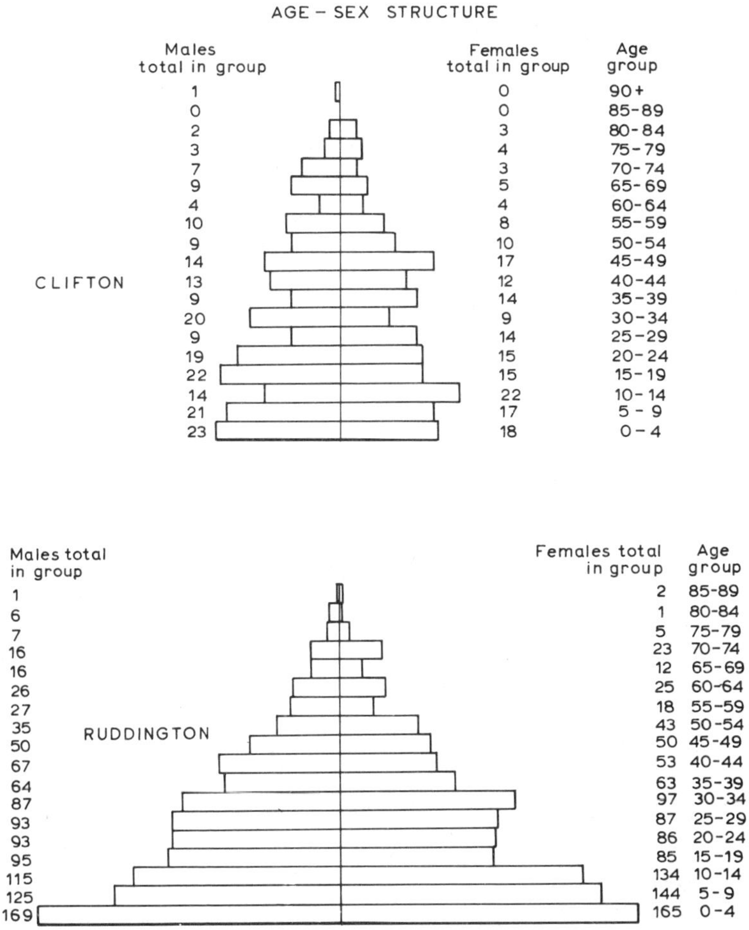

8.5 Age-Sex Structure for two contrasting communities, Ruddington and Clifton (Notts.), 1851

years inclusive[6]) as these are not recorded consistently. It is becoming clear, for example, as more work is done on the enumerators' books, that the role of women in agriculture may be underestimated in that the part-time nature of the work may not be recorded by the census enumerator. Moreover, the situation varies according to occupation. In domestic industry, for example hosiery in Ruddington, many wives of framework knitters were recorded as being occupied within the industry whereas the wives of agricultural labourers were not. There are reasons for this discrepancy which a consideration of the differing nature of the two forms of employment should provide. However a satisfactory overall survey can be obtained by noting the occupations of the heads of household as long as it is realized that this is not the total picture of employment. Such an analysis provides a fairly safe way of comparing and contrasting villages, a comparison which may be demonstrated by pie graphs (8.4).

The investigation into the age and sex structure of the village population may be carried out simultaneously. Here it is useful to use five-year categories starting from 0 (8.5). When portrayed in diagrammatic form, they can be very revealing for such visual representations of age structure compel the reader to ask further questions—for instance why two such diagrams differ, and what is the significance of the variations of shape in different age groups within each diagram.

The answers to such questions can only be sought from other information provided by sources other than the census, and they will reflect on the general characteristics of the villages being examined. Thus, in the present examples, the villages of Ruddington and Clifton (which included Glapton) were of very different sizes, Ruddington being 868 and Clifton being 381 in 1801. Further, Ruddington was an open village; Clifton was a close village. Other close villages in the vicinity, for example Bradmore (pop. 325 in 1801), Bunny (pop. 359 in 1801) and Wilford (pop. 478 in 1801), were of similar size to Clifton (8.6). These five villages are mentioned specifically by Francis Howell in his *Report to the Poor Law Board on the Law of Settlement and Removal of the Poor* (1848). He quotes Sir Charles Paget, who resided in Ruddington:

> In Ruddington we are affected by four close parishes, Clifton, Wilford, Bradmore and Bunny; we not only received the surplus population of those parishes to whom they do not choose to give accommodation, but we also have residing with us many agricultural workers who are employed in these parishes.

8.6 Part of Chapman's map of Nottinghamshire 1774 showing villages around Ruddington

Radford
NOTTINGHAM
Sneinton
Lenton
Wilford
West Bridgeford
Gamston
CANAL
Beeston
Ruddington Hill
Clifton
Clapton
Edwalton
Ruddington
Plumtree
Flawforth Church
Bradmore
Keyworth
Gotham
Bunny
Wysall
Cortlinstock
Willoughby
Rempston

In 1851, the populations of these five villages were: Ruddington 2,181; Clifton 401; Wilford 570; Bradmore 401; Bunny 336. Thus Ruddington had grown to more than $2\frac{1}{2}$ times the size it was in 1801, while the others had hardly grown at all and indeed Bunny had declined in numbers. A comparison with the general growth rate of south Nottinghamshire as a whole will soon reveal which were the particular growth points in the region.

The diagrams shown may then be related to the differing patterns of population growth for each of the villages. The broad base of the Ruddington diagram helps to suggest reasons for the increase in population in that village, while the narrow base at Clifton indicates that the proportion of child-bearing couples in the village was smaller than in its neighbour. But it will lead on to further questions such as mobility. Given that the broad base of the pyramid suggests a natural increase in population, does this fully explain the growth of Ruddington? Or were there also movements of people into the village as indicated by Sir Charles Paget above? Further examination of the evidence will be needed to answer these questions.

Further Questions: mobility

After these three basic tasks, card indexing the householders and analysing the occupations and age structure of the community, other enquiries can be made according to the nature of the village under consideration. The discoveries made so far by the group will raise a further range of questions. One of the most important of these is the problem of mobility. In villages such as Ruddington which show a considerable rate of growth, it is reasonable to assume that some of this increase was the result of movement of people into the village from other areas. But can their numbers and the date at which they came in be detected?

A look at the birthplaces of the inhabitants, as recorded in the censuses, will help to throw some light on this question, although it has to be realized that these do not give the total picture of migration. Nevertheless a comparison between any two villages can be achieved on the basis of the proportion of the people who were born outside its boundaries. A closer analysis of those people born outside, for example by looking at the birth places of their children, may provide more information concerning their movements before coming into the village. And if these immigrants turn out to have been young parents, then they will have been the very people who were most likely to have contributed further to the population increase of the village. These immigrants fell into several clear categories. There will have been those people who were born outside the village but whose date of arrival into it is unknown. These people could have been young children themselves who moved into the village with their parents. Others will have some children listed who were born in the village. In this case it may be possible to plot the timing of their movement into the village. The possible time span will vary, for it will depend on the ages of their children. If all the children were born in the village, then the span to be considered is from the birth of the oldest recorded child back to the birth of the parents, maybe twenty years or more. If on the other hand one of the children was born outside of the village and the next, say two years younger, was born in the village, then the time span to consider would be shorter, within two years. However one must be wary of such analysis. The children so recorded are those in the village at the time of the census. There may have been others, older or younger, who had left the village or died, and so the picture is essentially incomplete. But as long as the analysis is done with caution and is made in the light of knowledge of the developments within the area, some tendencies can be suggested. There certainly emerges a general impression that framework-knitters moved into Ruddington during the period 1831–51. The population of that village increased from 1428 to 2181 over those twenty years, and support for this tentative analysis is provided by the appearance in the censuses of lodgers, in most cases young male framework-knitters, usually bachelors but in a few instances with young families, and all born outside the village.

When it appears that people moved into the village, as in the case of Ruddington in the early part of the nineteenth century, the question arises of where they lived. Were there new areas of house building to which these people moved? It is unlikely that the census itself will throw much light on this problem unless addresses are given or unless we can be sure that the enumerators followed some topographical arrangement in making their returns (as indeed they usually did). The evidence for Ruddington suggests an area north of the village which seems to have been new in 1851. But here the use of other sources to help in this interpretation, for example maps and deeds, and street names and even the landscape itself, is essential.

Some of this work can be done by smaller sub-groups or by individuals within the larger group. The whole group can quite easily work on the card indexing and on the occupations and age structure of the village, but on the whole only smaller groups can effectively work on some of the other questions which arise. Thus one small group may wish to pursue the birthplace of parents and their children, using photocopies for this activity; indeed the photocopies are necessary if this group wants to try to find out where the newcomers lived.

Occupations

Another sub-group might start work finding out more about the various occupation groups in the village—the farmworkers, craftsmen, industrial workers and tradesmen, for instance. For this they can use the card index. Once again a number of questions can be addressed to these occupation groups: for example, their mobility. Do they have any specific pattern of movement from area to area as seen through the birthplaces of their children? What are the ages of the parents and numbers of children?—though here, of course, the picture will be incomplete in that the eldest children may have left the village and others may have died; older daughters may have married and hence changed their names. The parish registers should prove useful here. Parents, if born in the village, may feature in the marriage registers, as may the older sons and daughters who are absent from the household in the census books. Other members of the family may be detected in the burial registers. If the family is seen to be featuring in the registers, then the baptismal registers may be used to provide further clues to the number of children. And if there is a sufficiently large sample for each of the main occupation groups, then some general conclusions can be made.

Further questions may be asked concerning the nature of the households of the various occupation groups. Is there evidence of the extended family, households that is which include relations beyond the immediate parent–children relationship? For instance, were one or two grandparents members of the household; indeed was the grandparent the head of the household? Evidence of one or two grandparents living in the household of their married children gives us a different picture from that of married children with families living in their parents' household. Again, can the presence of other relatives of either of the parents be detected from the returns? All of these features of the extended family can provide useful clues about the way of life of the different occupational groups. The household may very well extend beyond family relationships. Were there servants resident in the household? Are there lodgers? And among which groups did these non-familial members of the household appear most frequently?

The employment of women and children will provide work for another group. It has already been suggested that the occupations of the wives of farm workers are not often mentioned although they may very well have been at work on the farms. Did the wives of industrial workers have stated occupations? The wives of framework-knitters in Ruddington frequently have their occupations stated, invariably within the trade. Again, some information is provided concerning the occupations of the children. Did they follow the same occupation as their parents? What were the ages of those children with stated occupations? Were there any different patterns for boys and girls? A background knowledge of the economy of the region at this time will provide a whole framework of questions, especially relating to the material standards and quality of life of the different occupation groups. However this is a major task and may very well form a follow-up project for the group drawing on a wide range of other sources such as parliamentary papers, reports of local health and poor law authorities and newspapers.

Comparisons

A group working on a small village may be able to study all of these questions on a comparative basis, using the enumerators' books for 1851, 1861 and 1871, for the total cost of the photocopies for a small village will often be no greater than the cost of a set for one of these censuses for a larger village. Thus the study over three decades of a village whether with a growing, stable or declining population, particularly in the second half of the nineteenth century, will provide a dynamic dimension which is missing if the group concentrates upon one census alone, and this dimension itself leads to a range of further questions. How do we account for the growth or stability or the declining number of people? Does the age structure diagram give any clues? Does its shape suggest that certain age groups were proportionately small? If a village was losing its population one may try to anticipate which age groups were likely to leave the village.

A first stage in this inquiry is to put all three censuses onto index cards in alphabetical order under heads of household. The whole group can then split up the packs of index cards, and working in pairs, sort out those households which feature in all three censuses. Other households may feature twice, either in 1851 and 1861 or in 1861 and 1871. The same sorting operation can be done with these, and the group will thus end up with six sets of cards: 1851, 1861 and 1871; 1851 and 1861; 1861 and 1871; and singles, 1851, 1861 or 1871.

Care must be taken over this, for surnames alone are not enough, but in most cases the clues are there: first names, ages, birth places. In the process of placing these cards into sets, the group has embarked on the first stage of family reconstitution, and in the case of households which feature in all three censuses, much information has been discovered.

Smaller groups may now analyze the sets and make their reports based on the question of 'the disappearing children'. If there are a number of older children disappearing, then this phenomenon should be investigated. Of course it must be emphasized that the group must be convinced that these people are not featured elsewhere in the enumerator's book. This is easier to do for boys than girls simply because they retain their surname. It may be possible to detect some of the girls who feature in the marriage registers. But when it is fairly certain that these people are not in the census, there are three alternative answers: either they were absent from the village at the time of the census; or they had died, a fact which can only be stated positively in the case of those who feature in the burial register; or they had left the village. Negative evidence would suggest either the first or the last alternative. A number of these examples may then suggest the trend, and it may be worthwhile to compare tendencies amongst the various occupation groups.

Such an analysis depends to a large extent upon the accuracy of the parish registers, in this case the burial registers. The chances of the 'disappearing' people being featured in these registers are greater if other members of the family have appeared there also. Indeed one useful small group project can arise over this correlation of the parish registers with the census enumerators' books. If the village was a close village at this time, owned and controlled by one or two landlords, then it becomes particularly useful to discover how many families itemised in the census enumerator's book appear in the parish registers, for such a correlation is valuable in testing the 'completeness' of the registers.

Households

This tracing of families makes a worthwhile study simply because it touches on the subject of family reconstitution. When households feature in all three censuses and when it can be seen by looking at the birth places of the children that there was a likelihood of their having been in the village for the whole of the twenty year span and indeed possibly longer and when these same families feature regularly in the parish registers, then a good deal may be discovered about the size and type of completed families, of age at marriage and fertility. Such work can be done also for those households which only appear in two of the censuses, although not so much information is forthcoming.

This more detailed analysis, drawing upon other contemporary sources, is particularly valuable in that it takes us beyond the analysis of the group to the people of the village themselves. For the ultimate aim of the study is to understand how people lived in the local community in the middle of the nineteenth century; and such an understanding involves the need to make that nice judgment between describing the people living in the village 120 to 100 years ago, and describing the behaviour patterns of groups of people with a view to comparison with the same groups in other villages.

Finally there are other more general points that groups might like to bear in mind when examining the census enumerators' books. It is fairly obvious that one piece of evidence easily extracted from these books would be the nature of the household; its size and composition. The whole question of family structure arises from a reading of this source; the evidence of the extended family and its role. What proportion of households contained relations other than parents and children? How frequently were the grandparents or parents heads of the household? How frequently were young married sons or daughters, with their children, living with their parents. Did the lodger appear regularly; and was he the young male bachelor who was born outside the village? Is there any evidence about those households which contained lodgers? Was the head of the household a widow, who may thus have been struggling financially and therefore took in lodgers to eke out her small income? Was there a similarity in occupations or birth places between the head of household and the lodger? Were there any whole families who were lodgers? What sorts of households had servants? And here there may have been the Hall with its army of servants which of course would provide some insight into how the large house was organized in mid-Victorian England. This is particularly an interesting exercise if the Hall is still standing, for then the servants can be seen in relation to the physical dimensions of the building, and there will almost certainly be oral traditions of service there surviving in the village.

There are many questions that may be asked about the household, and the answers so acquired can be tabulated with a view to making comparisons with other similar communities or different ones. Inferences can be made from some of these findings, for example, over the lodgers. The purpose behind the question about birthplaces is in order to ascertain whether strangers to the village would have tended to stay with people they may have known, or had been told about, in their home village. The questions about the position of grandparents in the household may provide answers which are helpful in assessing the economic position of that household. Were grandparents staying with their married children because there was a need to look after the old or because the grandparents may have been providing a useful function of looking after the grandchildren? Such a role for grandparents may be more obvious in a factory town where mothers may be absent from the home at work; but it is also likely to have been the case in a village where the womenfolk were either employed in a domestic industry or in agriculture part time.

Notes and References

1 *See* M. Anderson, 'Household Structure and the Industrial Revolution; Mid-Nineteenth Century Preston in Comparative Perspective,' in P. Laslett, *Household and Family in Past Time* (1972); 'The Study of Family Structure and Standard Tabulation Procedures for the Census Enumerators' books 1851–1891,' in E. A. Wrigley, *Nineteenth-century Society* (1972); and *Family Structure in Nineteenth Century Lancashire* (1972); W. A. Armstrong, 'Social Structure from the Early Census Returns,' in E. A. Wrigley, *An Introduction to English Historical Demography* (1966); 'A Note on the Household Structure of Mid-Nineteenth Century York in Comparative Perspective,' in P. Laslett, *Household and Family in Past Time*; 'The Use of Information about Occupation,' in Wrigley, *Nineteenth Century Society*; and *Stability and Change in an English County Town: a social study of York, 1801–51* (1974); J. Foster, *Class Struggle and the Industrial Revolution* (1974); M. Drake, 'The Census, 1801–1891,' in Wrigley, *Nineteenth Century Society*; P. Tillott, 'Sources of Inaccuracy in the 1851 and 1861 Censuses,' in Wrigley, *Nineteenth Century Society*; and R. Smith, 'The Early Victorian Household Structure,' *International Review of Social History,* Vol. 15 (1970).

2 A number of studies in the 1851 census have been published for many different counties; an enquiry at the county local history library will usually elicit whether there are such studies suitable for comparison with your own work.

3 A. J. Taylor, 'The Taking of the Census, 1801–1951,' *British Medical Journal,* 7 April 1951.

4 P. Mathias, *The First Industrial Nation* (1969) is perhaps as good as any other general introduction.

5 The problem is discussed in A. Rogers, *This Was Their World* (1972)

pp. 105–8; but *see* the essays by M. Anderson and W. A. Armstrong in Wrigley, *Nineteenth Century Society.*

6 R. Smith, in his article 'Education, Society and Literacy: Nottinghamshire in the mid-nineteenth century,' *University of Birmingham Historical Journal* XV (1969) p. 45, has defined 'child' for census purposes as those between the ages of 5 and 14 inclusive.

9

Urban Housing in the Nineteenth Century

MARTIN GASKELL

Housing and Society

When in 1966 the study of towns and cities was placed firmly on the academic map with the international conference of the Urban History Group, it is significant that Professor Dyos in his 'Agenda for Urban Historians' noted:

> Housing itself is oddly neglected. Two or three scholars have written briefly on housing conditions in Leeds, Nottingham, London and elsewhere, and the subsidised phase of housing has been investigated from the Whitehall end, but we have too few authentic tales of mean streets, or of the making and unmaking of slums. . . . How, one cannot help wondering, has this slow-moving complex machinery of urban renewal been set in motion, or brought to a halt?[1]

Since then, however, the history of the house has come to engage the attention of numerous scholars. This is particularly true of the nineteenth century where varied local studies are beginning to provide adequate foundation for the formulation of an overall concept of conditions. But the majority of such local studies have tended to be the product of research students' dissertations or of the peripheral interests of established academics.[2] As an area of consideration by amateurs, either singly or in groups, the subject has not yet gained the popularity enjoyed by other aspects of local history—demography, industrial archaeology or even vernacular housing in rural areas. The significance, as well as the teeming interest, of Victorian working class housing has still to be impressed on a wider audience. Its implications and the modes of investigation are only now beginning to be dealt with in any depth in general works on local history and in guides to sources and to methods.

Housing is one of the artefacts of a society which provides a clear, readily comprehensible and reasonably sensitive reflection of economic and social circumstances. The house does this, perhaps, more than any other building because it expresses the everyday needs, expectations and aspirations of all classes within society. But it is not only individual houses that one should examine, for the concentrations and expansion of housing in towns are fruitful areas of study. As the individual house is a visual expression of social status and ideals, so the pattern and method of housing development mirrors the economic conditions and serves to illuminate some of the complex workings of society.

Any study of housing, therefore, must clearly expand outwards from the specific building to the total urban context. At one level of society, the architecture of the house may be examined not only in its own right as an expression of the taste of the age but also as a reflection of social status and ideals. At the bottom of the social ladder, the evils of nineteenth-century insanitary dwellings serve as testimony to class oppression and degradation. Unlike the better quality houses, few of the former survive, but contemporary accounts, both national and local, provide a rich and eloquent source of condemnation.[3] In general terms, such criticism maintains a substantial consistency throughout the country and throughout the century; it is easy to find and is everywhere available. It is not surprising that such critical accounts proliferated, when one considers the speed of urbanization and the total novelty of the problems with which the Victorians were so ill-equipped to deal. To discover and to illustrate the evils of nineteenth-century housing is part of the historian's task and is an interesting and useful starting point for any group working on the subject. But it must not be the sum total. Far more important is the examination of the ways in which housing illuminates the problems of a particular town and of Victorian society in general.

Basically the housing question throws light on three particular aspects of nineteenth-century history. On the one hand, because the nature of its growth was so novel and because it was in itself a battleground between the forces of tradition and progress it provides us with a clear focus of insight into nineteenth-century attitudes and social *mores*. Secondly, the actual way in which the housing pattern of the nineteenth-century town grew—the physical addition of street to street, of house upon house—tells us much about the nature of Victorian business activity. While thirdly the reaction to the housing ills of the nineteenth century leads us into the question of Victorian social responsibility and aesthetic sensibility.[4]

To study how the Victorians dealt with a housing explosion of such magnitude is thus a most instructive introduction to their character and their approach to problems. Who, for instance, was responsible for the vast and rapid growth of housing in the Victorian town? Where did the finance come from, and how was it organized? The picture that emerges, of a multitude of little men individually responsible for this development, is in itself a revealing insight into the pattern of capital investment in the nineteenth century and the struggle for self improvement (9.1). The nineteenth-century housing

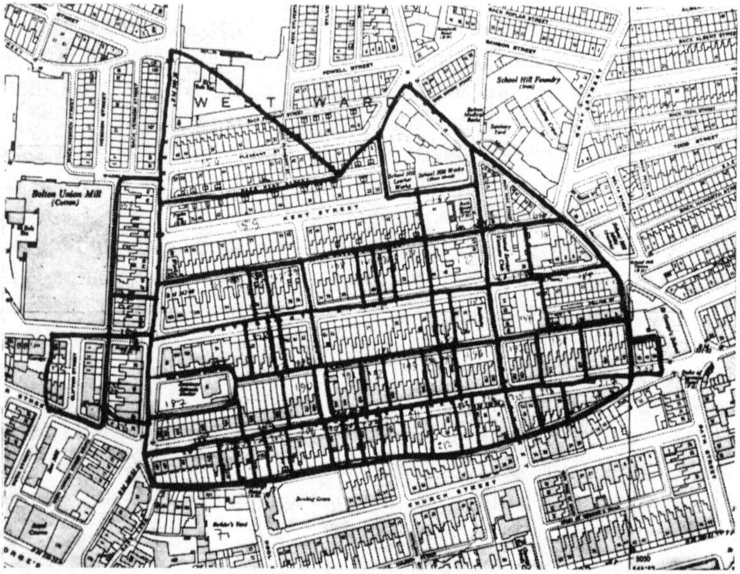

9.1 Bolton, the School Hill area developed with a mixture of factories and terraced housing during the second half of the nineteenth century. This map is the 1939 Ordnance Survey with the boundary lines imposed of the plots leased by the Tipping Estate to developers. This shows the small scale of development and the influence the original pattern of leasing had on the subsequent nature and layout of the buildings

estate was not customarily a single artefact produced by one controlling authority: it was rather created—often haphazardly and incoherently—from a multitude of separate interests. Most working-class housing, for example, was built in small groups of four or five houses at a time, which were financed and organized by individuals with limited capital such as foremen, clerks, professional people and widows. They invested in property since that provided, certainly until the Lloyd George Budget of 1910, one of the safest forms of investment. The nature of this financing meant that in appearance the nineteenth-century town did not have any uniformity; it was rather a collection of fragments, a confused muddle of roads and houses that reflected the myriad of interests in the land and in the control of property.[5]

Similarly from the lack of control over house building, combined with the lack of urban services such as drainage and sewerage, paving and lighting, there emerges evidence of the early nineteenth-century acceptance of *laissez-faire*. Later in the century the improvement in such conditions and the way in which improvement was secured reflect the emergence of governmental control and the acceptance of bureaucratic organization. The insight thus allowed into the local political situation and into the involvement of the Victorians in a multitude of local institutions should encourage modification of the traditional interpretation.[6] Similarly, the concern for the improvement of the environment involved a response at once theoretical and practical. And once again the housing debate provided the melting pot of ideas and ideals. The great development of housing, on the one hand, provided an example of progress and material advancement, while on the other it became a source of unease and disquiet leading to the intensification of the desire for a return to nature and a reaction to unhealthy mechanization. It encapsulated the romantic spirit of the century with its continuing search for 'nature' that was ultimately to culminate in that uniquely English combination of town and country—the Garden City.

Setting the Scene

In practical terms, therefore, housing development in the nineteenth-century provides us with numerous areas of enlightenment and investigation: the individual house—its size, design and architectural treatment; the quality of the housing, both in relation to contemporary building for different markets, and in relation to dwellings of a similar class in different towns; the lay-out of the houses both as it represents the financial fragmentation of the building industry and the social aspirations of the inhabitants; the expansion of the areas of housing in relation to the topography of the town, to the pre-urban pattern of land-ownership and to the nature of industrial growth; those responsible for organizing the provision of houses both in financial and practical terms; the social status of those who lived in the houses when built (9.2); the restrictions and social conventions that determined their character and their influence on the social pattern of the town as a whole. Considering that a large part of the early nineteenth-century industrial housing stock was initially both inadequate and insanitary, how did the local community begin to remedy the situation, and how did the activities of individuals and organizations complement national movements and reforming theories? How did the housing problem impinge on local politics, and ultimately how did the civic authority begin to tackle the problem, first through byelaws and public health legislation (9.3), and then through slum clearance and council housing? The house as a unit is clearly crucial to the family, as it is to the urban scene, and at both levels its study is invaluable not only in its own right but as an indicator of social change.

The approach to the subject must, as in all local history work, combine purely local material with the national picture. As yet there is no guide to regional variations in nineteenth-century housing types comparable to R. Brunskill's *Illustrated Handbook of Vernacular Architecture,* and indeed such a recording activity could valuably be undertaken by local history groups. However, studies of nineteenth-century housing on the national scale have begun to appear in recent years. Probably the most useful brief introduction, which places the subject in both an architectural and local setting, is the Historical Association pamphlet by Vanessa Parker, *The English House in the Nineteenth Century.* Professor Tarn blazed the trail in the study of the architectural implications of Victorian housing reform, and his *Working-Class Housing in Nineteenth-Century Britain* introduces the reader to the work of the large (and sometimes small) philanthropic housing associations, and begins to contrast provincial activity with the London pattern. He has recently extended this work, and in *Five Per Cent Philanthropy: An Account of Housing in Urban Areas between 1840 and 1914,* he has provided us with a clear record of legislative progress and housing reform as seen through the columns of the various nineteenth-century building journals. As yet there has been no thorough comparative study of slums, but a first attempt to see the housing problem and the attempts at reform in a national context is Enid Gauldie's *Cruel Habitations: A History of Working-class Housing 1780-1918.* This unfortunately ignores much recent research but is a more than adequate introduction for a class. The pioneer study in the field was *The History of Working-class Housing* edited by S. D. Chapman. This is a symposium with all the concomitant weaknesses, and students must treat the book with caution, though it provides a useful initial insight into local variations. The

9.2 Burngreave—a suburb of Sheffield with industry established in the valley and scattered housing appearing on the hillside in the second half of the nineteenth century. Here the topography clearly influenced development and the pattern of small landholdings is reflected in the terraces of houses climbing the steep valley slope in order to best utilize each plot

9.3 These mill houses at Hyde in Cheshire demonstrate the change in housing standards over the course of the nineteenth century. Those in the foreground are the 'model houses' built for his employees by Thomas Ashton in the 1820's, while those beyond date from the last decades of the century and reflect the higher standards of room height and size and of window area

bibliographies of all these books provide an indication of the various articles on particular facets of the question. As the study of the subject as a whole is still in its infancy, few of these have yet found their way into published symposia or monographs. A first attempt to do this for the question of flat building and habitation in the nineteenth-century is to be found in *Multi-Storey Living: the British Working-class Experience* edited by Anthony Sutcliffe.

In directing students' reading, as I would suggest in their own work, it is important to move away from the individual house to the house in the context of the estate and the town. As an introduction to town planning theory and legislation, Professor Ashworth's pioneer study *The Genesis of Modern British Town Planning* is still the classic. For urban housing of a grander kind, most instructive is D. J. Olsen's study of the aristocratic estates of London in *Town Planning in London: the Eighteenth and Nineteenth Centuries.* Housing reforms from a planning point of view, considering its development into the Garden City ideal, is dealt with in W. L. Creese's *The Search for Environment.* Planning, however, in the nineteenth-century was the exception and it is the incoherent spread of urban building with which most classes working in this field will be concerned. A most penetrating guide to the ramifications of this process is Professor Dyos' *Victorian Suburb,* which as a model of lucidity and scholarship in writing should be required reading for all students. Since then there have appeared numerous studies of particular towns which see the problems of urban growth in their total context, and many of the issues have been further investigated in that mammoth symposium, *The Victorian City: Images and Reality,* edited by H. J. Dyos and M. Wolff. Finally, however, in reviewing the secondary literature on this subject, one must remember that it is a new subject and much material is still in the thesis or article stage. The new *Urban History Yearbook* provides a regular survey of research on this and related areas.

General Survey

When it comes to the individual town, local historians by tradition have described the glories of civic pride and rarely given any balanced insight into housing problems. For the evils of the slums, at least in the growing manufacturing centres, the Blue Books provide eloquent material—in the 1840s, *The Select Committee on the Health of Towns* 1840, *The Report on the Sanitary Condition of the Labouring Population and on the Means of its Improvement* 1842, and *The*

Royal Commission Enquiring into the State of Large Towns and Populous Districts 1844, and later in the century *The Royal Commission on the Housing of the Working Classes* 1885, and *The Select Committee on Town Holdings* 1887–8. The indices of such Parliamentary Papers indicate the sections relevant to any particular area, which can then be photocopied for use by a class. The national building periodicals, pre-eminently *The Builder* but also *The Architect* and *The Building News,* provide criticism of conditions in different towns as well as a fairly thorough survey of reforming activity.[7] If a class has access to a large reference library with a continuous holding of such periodicals, a steady search through their indices can form a useful introduction which should provide not only a framework of local activity but at the same time an insight into the national scene.

Such national material can be supplemented at the local level. From the time a town appoints a Medical Officer of Health, his reports give an indication of basic housing standards; but prior to that one may be fortunate enough to have the comments of an interested observer—James Hole in Leeds, Dr. Holland in Sheffield.[8] With all such material the bias of the propagandist must be remembered. From later in the nineteenth-century and during the early years of this century local middle-class organizations or early Socialist bodies may comment on housing.[9]

One can never discover from written sources what it was like to live in these working-class homes. Victorian novels, which students should be encouraged to consult, can only portray the impression such houses made on contemporary observers; they cannot reveal the feelings of those who had to endure such surroundings every day.[10] Even the contents of the houses remain elusive in a period when the historian can no longer turn to inventories. For the style and fittings of individual houses one could be lucky enough to turn up a builder's copy book or ledger, but such finds are rare though still worth looking for. Some indication of general standards of furnishings in Victorian middle-class homes can be found in the developing collections of applied art and domestic artefacts in many museums, but the meagre trappings of working-class life cannot now be expected to have survived.

It is, however, possible to establish a housing typology for a town, which hopefully could ultimately contribute to a national survey of nineteenth-century urban house patterns of whose ramifications and classification there is as yet little knowledge. At the town level such an exercise can be not only a visual one, bringing awareness of different types of materials and treatment, but also an introduction as to how these changed over the century and how the design of the house developed and was adapted. This kind of recording can profitably be done by a group with the use of standard cards on which are noted the type of house (terraced or detached, through or back-to-back); the salient features of the ground-plan (parlour or non-parlour, tunnel-back, or separate privy); the number of rooms and their sizes; the building materials used and any ornamentation or noteworthy decoration (9.4).[11] Many elements of a house are readily apparent on external observation, while the interior features can be seen in houses that are being demolished or where access can be tactfully arranged. Such a record, combined with photographs, can rapidly develop into a picture of a town's housing stock.[12] In conjunction with a dating process this type of survey, on the one hand, brings to life the impact of legislative changes and bye-law developments and, on the other hand, illustrates the minutiae of class differentiations and social improvement. Meanwhile, it provides a group with a practical balance to the study of both primary and secondary material on nineteenth-century housing, and forces them to look with discriminating care at their own every-day built environment.

Detailed Surveys

So far, however, the work is only really concerned with the house as an individual unit. As such it is most suitable for introducing a group to the subject and would probably, with careful limitation of objectives, form a valid project for a year. If the group can stay together longer, the aims of such a survey could be widened, but it would be more valuable generally to broaden the perspective and begin to look at housing in a wider context. But in doing so one must ever be aware of the fact that the town is no single unit, it is a complex organ whose investigation involves the unravelling of confusion. The interested amateur tends to expect the nineteenth-century city to be well documented, and compared with earlier urban society it is, but the documents are rarely complete and if they were they would not present the historian with a ready-made picture.[13] The material is fragmentary and many things remain unrecorded, partly because of the wide range of casual involvement in urban growth, partly because of nineteenth-century dilatoriness in recording things that seem to us vital, and finally because of the very considerable (and continuing) destruction of documents since that time. So to understand the growth patterns of nineteenth-century urbanism requires, as does all historical research, detective work, but it is detective work of a kind that demands no

9.4 The Gothic gables and dormers and the heavy stone cornices distinguish these houses built in 1865 by Messrs Ripley and Sons in Bradford. It is features such as these that students should be encouraged to note because they often characterize a particular builder's work and reflect the precise social standing of the houses concerned

special technical skills, and no type of investigation that the interested amateur, with considered guidance, cannot readily undertake.

In terms of sources and of approach, therefore, it might be valuable now to consider the means by which a local history group can build up a picture and understanding of how a particular part of a town developed. It is probably wise to begin with the consideration of no more than a few streets and ask the questions: when were they built? Who was responsible for their layout and their building? For whom were they built and what was their character? Moreover, it is important that such a study should be combined with a thorough understanding of the advancing progress of the town, both economically and physically. The housing survey may be simply part of this wider investigation; but if the housing study is the prime interest, then the background information can be obtained from contemporary directories and guide books and the later standard civic histories. Also it is important for students to set the study of a particular area of housing in the context of the whole town's topography and of the pre-urban cadaster, for which the Tithe Redemption Commission Reports usually provide a readily accessible starting point.

As to when certain streets were built, a rough guide to their development is available in the form of the Ordnance Survey, though with this source the north of England tends to be better served than the south, and in any case large scale maps only begin to appear from the 1840's. Even then there are often large gaps—maybe from 1850 to 1890—between revisions of the Ordnance Survey. Few towns can be as well served as Sheffield where there were revisions at two or three yearly intervals throughout the 1850s to the 1870s. Obviously in such a case one can get a very clear picture of the date of development, but in general the Ordnance Survey will provide merely the broad parameters (9.5). It is however a picture that can be narrowed down from the use of a variety of sources. Directories and rate books, for example, indicate when street names and house numbers first appear. Once the group has worked backwards to establish an initial date of building, it can begin to advance and formulate a picture of development. It is however a laborious process, and therefore one to which a dedicated group can make a valuable contribution.

The picture of development that emerges must inevitably involve both time and personnel. Who built the houses and who financed them? These are often very difficult questions to answer and require more painstaking research. To trace the origins of property ownership is no easy matter. Deeds, for instance, are not always readily available and rarely in bulk, except where a council has purchased extensive

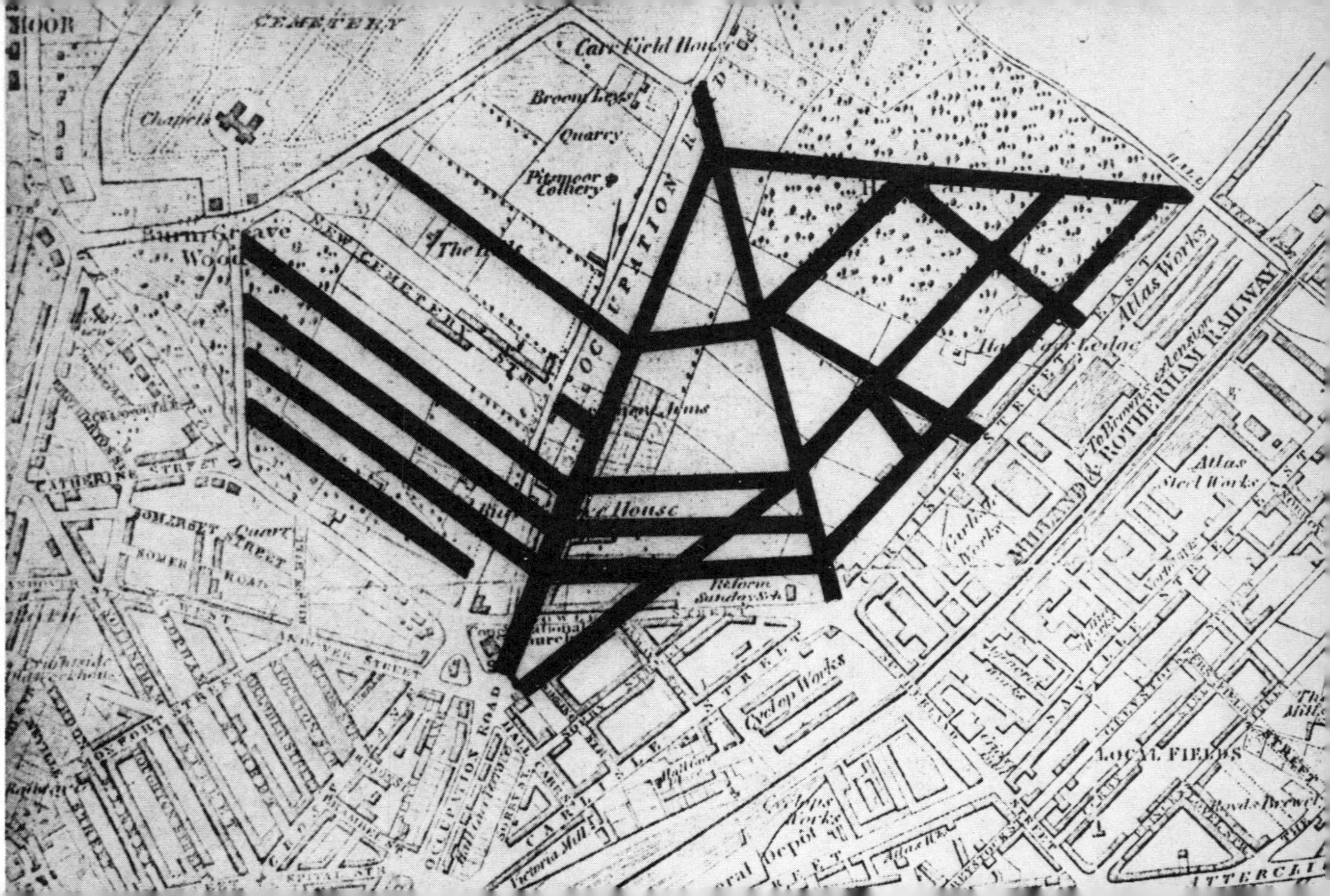

9.5 This diagram illustrates the use that can be made of Ordnance Survey maps in establishing the date of urban expansion. Here maps for 1868 and 1873 relating to Sheffield have been compared and those streets laid out between the two dates marked in. Thus the student has an approximate guide to the initiation of development in a particular street or area

properties for clearance. Lacking deeds, one might again work backwards through rate books, but these would only establish the ownership of the property. The crucial missing link in this story is the relationship and interaction between financier, builder and ultimate owner of the property. If one is investigating a period after the imposition of local bye-laws which required the deposition of plans with the local council for their approval, then the name of the 'builder' (presumably meaning the person financing the building) will be recorded in council records. But in some cases these have not survived or have done so intermittently. With regard to the other characters in the story, patient searching through local newspapers may reveal snippets of information, particularly at times of not infrequent bankruptcy, while a local group with its local contacts may be able to secure access to the ledgers of old-established building firms, to the records of building societies and to the files of solicitors. The various pieces of information from such sources may seem of little relevance to the individual class member, but with careful structuring of the whole and with detailed building together of such minute and multifarious sources, there can emerge a picture of housing development —a pattern of houses growing up not in sequence but haphazardly, of streets slowly and hesitantly expanding to meet the market requirements. It is a pattern that seems to demonstrate that the Victorians in their urban development, as in so many other fields, largely responded to the needs and problems of expansion in an *ad hoc* manner.

Once the development of an area of houses has been examined, then the character of the houses, the kind of people who inhabited them and the social complexion of particular streets must be assessed (9.6).[14] For this purpose, at ten-yearly intervals prior to 1871 we have of course the census enumerators' returns. But these give only broad guide-lines, and if we wish to know the detailed picture of occupation and the changing social character of an area (which could often go up, and more frequently down, very rapidly in the nineteenth century) then we need to fill the ten-year gap. If the houses were owner-occupied, a more detailed picture may be obtainable from the rate books—but both the survival rate and the nature of the information provided in these vary from town to town. For the mass of working-class property we have very little information as to the pattern of occupation—the directories, however frequently published, rarely provide any information as to occupation below the professional class. In their houses, as in their lives in general, the Victorian poor have left few records, their passage goes unmarked and their thoughts and reactions remain an enigma.

9.6 This characteristic group of working class houses photographed in Brightside in Sheffield shows the range of houses within a short terrace. The observation and recording of such variations provides students with a guide to the social complexity of an area and the way in which the housing stock reflects this

We are, however, on surer ground when we try to evaluate the character of these buildings. Admittedly we do not know what the people who had to live in them thought of them, but we can often get some appreciation of the design and quality of the buildings themselves at least for the second half of the century. Most of the housing stock of the earlier part of the century has since been demolished and gone largely unrecorded. But for property built later in the century, the more scrupulous municipal building departments should have kept plans and specifications. It is important to try to look at these and to recreate the original image—the new red brick and machine cut ornamentation—not as we see it now after a century's grime and increasing neglect. As a further guide to the original spirit of an area, the increasing availability of Victorian photographs can be useful. Occasionally local guides and later nineteenth-century newspaper articles on 'our suburbs' give some indication of the character and quality of building in the relevant area. But in the end one must walk the streets, where they survive, and obtain some impression of what happened for oneself. As J. D. Marshall noted in *The Study of Urban History,* 'personal observation is an indispensable part of the study of urban history' (9.7).[15]

And so we come back to personal observation, and perhaps this is where we should begin and end. From looking at and assessing one's own environment one can begin to build up a picture of how an area developed, its character and significance, and from that go on to relate it to the town picture as a whole, and ultimately to see its relevance in terms of a wider context of social and economic history.[16]

For the latter purpose there are certain aspects of the housing question in the nineteenth century which provide useful case studies. The housing work of enlightened industrialists, the philanthropic reforming societies or the lower-middle class self-help groups, all present valuable insights into the social relationships of Victorian England.[17] For project investigation the work of the self-help societies is probably the most fruitful. Within the confines of a small estate developed by either a building society or a freehold land society, one is able to build up a pattern of investment, of housing types and of changing environmental standards. More importantly, the microcosmic study of an estate provides illustration of the general problems of Victorian self-help, of housing reform and of social adjustment. As a working class movement, for example, the freehold land societies, misled by unscrupulous trustees and often crippled by unexpected road charges, quickly exhausted the enthusiasm of their founders. Yet it was just such hesitant and inconclusive movements that went to make up the

9.7 Nineteenth century working class housing cannot be studied in isolation, and this picture of the East End of Sheffield shows the way in which houses must be judged within their total environment of the overshadowing mill, the surrounding chimneys, the adjoining railway and the vista of the works' wall

process of housing reform in Victorian England. They may not have been too successful in living up to an ideal, but they did provide the first practical lessons in co-operation in estate development. In Sheffield, for instance, the Walkley societies gave a distinct character to the layout of one part of the town, while the later middle-class societies secured a picturesque environment that was to be the model for the later working-class suburban estate (9.8). The practice of co-operation involved in the freehold land society was applied to housing problems by the Co-operative Societies and later, and much more successfully, by the Co-partnership Tenants. The combination of this approach with the environmental ideals of a suburban arcadia came to fruition in the Garden City and Town Planning Movement at the end of the century.

It was such hesitant steps that went to make up the housing reform movement of the nineteenth century. It was equally such hesitant steps that contributed to the growth of the town as a built environment. To this end a local history group's detailed study of a particular area of housing may be considered within a broader social context than the mere limited local character of the pattern of urban expansion. The group could investigate an area of housing in terms of previous ownership, rates of development and quality of building. This in turn can provide the basis of a comparative study with other peripheral areas of the town. Thus one set of housing may be viewed within the total context of the growth of a township or suburb. Such a study, based on maps, planning records or title deeds, would be able to chart the development of the area and show how and why various portions of it catered for different classes and were built in different styles. It would also show how the historical development of an area determined, to some extent, the subsequent changes; how the provision of services, of schools and clubs, of shops and pubs, or the development of industry, or the intrusion of workhouses or prisons, both determined and reflected the rise and fall of the social barometer of an area. Moreover, with the use of broad cartographical evidence, census material, directories and town guides, it would be possible to set the development of particular area against the growth, irregular and ill coordinated as it may be, of the town as a whole. In this way the social characteristics and chronological development of housing would be placed in the total urban context.[18]

Working the group

There are then a variety of possibilities in using nineteenth century urban housing as the basis of a group study; there are various depths

9.8 The small estates of nineteenth century building and land societies provide useful case studies of housing development. Such self-help societies were numerous in most industrial cities. On this map of Sheffield in 1868 the freehold land society estates have been delineated in order to illustrate the impact that such schemes could have on the pattern and character of Victorian urban development

of investigation and levels of approach. That chosen will depend, of course, on the interests and capabilities of the members of the group, on the length of time they can stay together and on the particular circumstances of the area in which they are operating. These factors will equally influence the work resulting from such studies. Fieldwork, documentary and library work by individuals must be all combined, along with the reporting of such activity to the group as a whole, and subsequent analysis and assessment.

As suggested, the recording of visual evidence makes a valuable starting point for a class and, with a little experience, students begin to operate speedily the recording on uniform cards of the character of particular houses and terraces (9.9). As yet there is no standardized recording code which can allow the ready computerizing of results—but the drawing up of such a recording card for a particular area

Note book refs. in red by entry. Colony/Village/Town
COUNTY NGR

Name prev. hamlet/village
Type - scattered, nucleated etc.) INDUSTRY (GENL)
IF CLEAN-SLATE DEVT. Single firm dates
First industrial houses built c. Double " s
by Multiple " s

Names of leading partners/industrialists. (Connections with instins. to be shown with arrow)
Cotton famine etc.

	1801						1851	61	71					1901	
Population at dates (appr).															
Movements of migrants; note skill source, nationality.															
Institutions															
Co-ops															
Friendly socs.															
Mech. intns.															
Schools national															
factory															
charity															
Political clubs															
socs.															

URBAN FORM Extended
Nucleated
Gridiron etc.

9.9 A specimen card for recording the housing character and social development of a community (J. D. Marshall, University of Lancaster)

would not be difficult and would be especially worthwhile if the group has easy access to computer facilities and if the exercise is being undertaken on a large scale. Normally, however, the sample of properties will be small enough to allow their correlation and analysis by the group itself, and indeed this process can provide a useful class activity and an interesting starting point for discussion. The results should be collected and assessed in terms of date, pattern of the houses, style and quality. It would be the responsibility of individuals within the group to present this material in either cartographical or written form, and this would be an exercise at which to aim. In giving greater interest and depth of meaning to this process, groups of students should be encouraged to investigate and report on the wider issues of nineteenth-century housing—legislative changes and in particular local bye-laws and their effect; contemporary information on the housing of the area, whether it be critical reports and investigations or guides and commentaries on the character of particular districts; secondary material on national housing trends and architectural developments. The discussion of such general questions should serve, over the year, to put the practical surveying and recording into perspective.

This concern for a balance of work should be as equally obvious in the case of the study of housing development. It is best if each member of the group undertakes, either individually or in pairs, detective work on one street or maybe a few streets. Organizing the research this way allows everyone to handle a wide range of material, and it is useful if each student is able to follow the whole process through, because often its disentanglement depends on seeing the inter-relationship of events and people. It is, however, important to maintain a uniform pattern of transcribing material so that it can be readily referred to by the rest of the group. The pattern of development that emerges will gradually become clear in the course of group discussion, but it will probably fall to the lot of the group leader to pull it together into a coherent whole. In this process it is important again to keep the wider impact of housing development ever in view. Though a general survey of cartographical evidence will have been essential for all students, one or more should plot, with the aid of deeds and tithe records, the pattern of landownership prior to development on to a later map. This early investigation would give the whole of the group a structural basis for their work and provide a constant reference of explanation for later anomalies in the building pattern. Other members, in addition to their particular survey, should also be involved in the investigation of, and reporting to the group on, wider influences in the housing pattern: land availability; the lubrication of urban growth through developments of transport and social movement; the impact of local government and municipal control on the regulation and expansion of urban growth; the economic and demographic process; and the mechanics of urban development as evidenced by the local building industry. The depth that such studies would give to the detailed research into housing expansion is vital if the significance of housing study is to be made apparent and if the interest of the subject is to be maintained. It would give body and meaning to the examination of a particular area of housing development or its housing typology, especially if this is written up by the group.

The value of the subject for an adult group, in the last resort, is that it combines so well with the examination of other facets of local history, or with the explanation of contemporary urban social problems and environmental issues. Moreover, it is to be urged because of the increasing need to record the housing stock of the nineteenth century as it is constantly diminishing, and the opportunities for field work become continually scarcer. Alongside the need to record the details of property before demolition is the problem of securing, and indeed rescuing, local authority records and documents in the hands of private firms, which are all too frequently destroyed. Not only does examination of urban housing enable the student, at his own basic local level, to gain greater awareness of his environment and its often neglected qualities, but even more its study should make him ever more conscious of the complex historical forces behind the development of towns and cities. Its consideration also imparts a greater degree of understanding of that complexity of interaction of man and events, of people and place, of human and material interests, which all go to make up the general picture of society and therefore of social change in history.

Notes and References

1 H. J. Dyos (ed) *The Study of Urban History* (1968) pp. 37–38.

2 An indication of the range of such work is to be found in the *Urban History Newsletter,* 1963–74, and in the *Urban History Yearbook,* 1974–.

3 Documentary evidence of this nature is readily available for students in the various collections of documents edited by E. R. Pike, *Human Documents of the Industrial Revolution in Britain* (1966); *Human Documents of the Victorian Golden Age* (1967); *Human Documents of the Age of the Forsytes* (1969).

4 In encouraging students to look at the question of housing in a wider

aesthetic concept, a valuable introduction is E. Johns, *British Townscapes* (1965).

5 Here students could usefully be introduced to the wider problems of the building cycle through such works as W. H. Beveridge, *Unemployment 1860–1914* (1930); C. E. V. Leser, 'Building Activity and Housing Demand', *Yorkshire Bulletin of Economic and Social Research* (1951); J. P. Lewis, *Building Cycles and Britain's Growth* (1965); M. A. Shannon, 'Bricks—A Trade Index, 1785–1849', *Economica,* vol. 1 (1934).

6 A valuable general survey for students of the growth of the social services in nineteenth-century England, which places housing reform within the general pattern of development, is D. Fraser, *The Evolution of the British Welfare State* (1973).

7 *The Architect,* 1869–. *The Builder,* 1842–. *The Building News,* 1854–69.

8 J. Hole *The Homes of the Working Classes, with Suggestions for their Improvement* (1866); G. C. Holland, *An Enquiry into the Moral, Social and Intellectual Condition of the Industrial Classes of Sheffield* (Sheffield, 1839); *The Vital Statistics of Sheffield* (Sheffield, 1843).

9 Indicative of such sources in two northern towns are Rochdale Housing Reform Council, 'Housing Reform Suggestions for Rochdale' (1913, typescript in the Mattley Collection of Rochdale Public Library) and W. J. Bridge, *A Municipal Programme for Barnsley* (Barnsley, 1910).

10 Contrasting descriptions of housing at different periods can be found for example, in C. Dickens, *Dombey and Son* (1848) and *Hard Times* (1854); E. C. Gaskell, *North and South* (1850); G. Gissing, *The Nether World* (1889); and *In the Year of Jubilee* (1894); G. and W. Grossmith *The Diary of a Nobody* (1892); and in H. G. Wells, *Anne Veronica* (1913).

11 Good visual awareness is encouraged by F. M. Jones, in 'The Aesthetic of the Nineteenth Century Industrial Town', in *The Study of Urban History*.

12 An example of work of this nature for housing in South Wales is recorded in *The Iron Industry Housing Papers*.

13 There is a useful commentary of this problem in H. J. Dyos, 'Agenda for Urban Historians', in *The Study of Urban History*.

14 Any group working on housing in London will, of course, have the benefit of the cartographical surveys in C. Booth, *Life and Labour of the People in London* (17 vols., 1889–1903). Elsewhere, groups could usefully draw up social distribution maps for their own areas at particular times.

15 J. D. Marshall, 'Colonisation as a Factor in the Planting of Towns in North-West England', in *The Study of Urban History* p. 230.

16 An example of this kind of study for Victorian Leeds is M. W. Beresford, *Time and Place* (Leeds, 1961).

17 *See* for example, the author's article, 'Self-Help and House Building in the Nineteenth Century', in *Local Historian,* vol. 10 no. 2 (May 1972).

18 The outstanding example of this comprehensive approach remains H. J. Dyos, *Victorian Suburb* (Leicester, 1961).

10

Industrial Archaeology

M. J. T. LEWIS

Industrial archaeology is the study of the material remains of our industrial past. One can interpret industry in as wide a sense as one likes, to cover workers' housing, crafts, or even agricultural buildings. Archaeology should mean investigation of physical remains (although the study of written records is an inseparable part of the process) and is far from synonymous with excavation—one does not dig if one's evidence is still above the ground. The time scale involved ranges in theory from the year dot to yesterday, although it seems sensible to leave the Iron Age pottery kiln or the early medieval bloomery to the expert in excavation techniques, and plant that is only recently obsolete may be comprehensible only to the specialist engineer. In practice the subject tends to concentrate on the period from the seventeenth to the early twentieth centuries, and particularly on the industrial revolution (however one defines it). Industrial archaeology serves not merely to clothe the bare bones of the written word with the flesh of confirmation and illustration; it often contributes completely new information not obtainable from the documents, although it is not yet long-established enough to have reached its full potential of general as opposed to particular contributions.

As a study, industrial archaeology is a reflection of the present-day trend away from the time-honoured emphasis upon the military, the ecclesiastical and the grandiose domestic. It is a part of the rising interest in the life and work of ordinary men and women, part of the acknowledgment that social and economic and technological history matter. Its scope is enormous and even bewildering; it is one thing to set out to study the corn mills or the limekilns of a limited rural area, but quite another to undertake a comprehensive project on the huge and densely packed factories of an industrial conurbation. But provided that impossibly large mouthfuls are not bitten off, it is admirably suited for local group work. Unlike excavations, where unskilled labour is liable, without careful supervision, to destroy evidence unrecognized and unrecorded, industrial archaeology can be fruitfully practised by the amateur who possesses few skills and without the need of constant surveillance. Indeed its future, like its past, lies in the hands of the amateur. Its relevance moreover to local studies is total, since industry in some form or other played its role in practically every community; and such is the rate of destruction these days—especially in towns—that countless buildings and machines are disappearing totally unrecorded. Any information we can rescue before it is too late will surely bring down the blessings of future historians upon our heads.

It is of course important to set all such studies in a framework both of regional history and of the general development of English industrial history. There are now many books dealing with particular areas or particular industries; the David & Charles series of regional studies and the Longmans series of studies by industries may be mentioned. In addition, there are many accounts of the national scene: P. Mathias' book *The First Industrial Nation* is perhaps the most useful.

On industrial archaeology itself, R. A. Buchanan, *Industrial Archaeology in Britain* (1972) and Neil Cossons. *The BP Book of Industrial Archaeology* (1975) are the best general works. Arthur Raistrick, *Industrial Archaeology* (1972) is useful, though, in its exclusive approach, not to everyone's taste. For fieldwork, students should turn to Neil Cossons and Kenneth Hudson, *Industrial Archaeologists' Guide 1971–3* (1971) which is a most valuable compendium of practical detail, while both J. P. M. Pannell (ed Kenneth Major), *The Techniques of Industrial Archaeology* (1974) and J. Kenneth Major, *Fieldwork in Industrial Archaeology* (1974) contain much useful guidance. Above all there is the journal *Industrial Archaeology* to which all who work in this field will need to refer regularly.

Starting the Group

The choice of a specific topic for an extra-mural class or local history group to pursue is regulated by such considerations as the

Bridge over HULL AND HORNSEA RAILWAY

Name of Bridge SUTTON STATION BRIDGE | Grid Ref. TA. 117. 331.

Material LOCAL BRICK | CAST IRON

Design: arch (+ shape) | girder (+ type) CAST IRON VAULTS | other

Number of spans 1 | Approx. span of each 33' 0" | Overall length 102' 0"

Width over parapets 34' | Max. headroom above ~~water~~ TRACK 20' 0" | Skew /

Function of bridge ROAD OVER RAIL TRACK | Disused ✓

Inscription, plaque, date stone CLOSE AYRE & NICHOLSON PHOENIX FOUNDRY YORK | Approx. date 1863

S.T. CRAWSHAW CONTRACTORS

Special features (e.g. stone approach, cutwaters, refuges)

NONE

Is setting specially picturesque? YES

History and references

BRIDGE STILL FUNCTIONS IN CARRYING THE MAIN WAWNE-SUTTON RD OVER DISUSED RAILWAY CUTTING. THERE ARE 7 CAST IRON VAULTS AND INDIGENOUS BRICK ABUTMENTS. ALL IN GOOD CONDITION. THERE IS A STATUTORY WEIGHT LIMIT.

Recorder P. GRAVES | Date 21/1/73

Photographed: Yes/~~No~~ If no, does it deserve photo: Yes/~~No~~

If yes, is a.m. or p.m. the best time? A.M. | Neg. Ref. No. 109 - 14/15/16/17

Add sketch and further details over if necessary

attach contact print

10.1 Specimen completed proforma for recording bridges in Lincolnshire and Yorkshire

threat of destruction, the previous neglect of an important site or series of sites, the completeness or paucity of the remains, the ease of access, the size of the task and so forth. The tutor or leader must be prepared to arbitrate on the suggestions put forward by the group members—as well as to have suggestions of his own. In most areas, there will be a wealth of possible projections to engage the interest of the students.

In organizing the work, the group can choose one of two rather differing approaches to fieldwork. One is to undertake a fairly wide-ranging comparative study. As an example of this, two surveys are now under way of all the bridges in the East Riding of Yorkshire and in Lincolnshire. The participants are divided into small teams of two or three and assigned particular rivers or particular areas to work on. Either these teams or different teams can be deputed to carry out library research as well. Everyone is provided with supplies of standard proformas for filling in on the site (10.1); these will ultimately be drawn together, conclusions drawn from them, and outstanding sites will be examined in greater detail. But unless the organiser gives a fair amount of preparatory advice, novices often hesitate to jump in at the deep end and fail to do their stint. All members should be given a briefing on the history, geography and technology of—in this case—bridges, including a statement of the purpose of the exercise, the kind of information required on the proforma and how that information can be obtained. It can prove helpful as a starter for all members to visit a typical site together where the organiser can explain these points on the spot. Some unevenness in reports is inevitable, but such an introduction should keep it to a minimum. Similar wide-ranging surveys, covering in outline all the industries of an area, can also be done on the standard record cards of the National Record of Industrial Monuments.

Alternatively the group can launch an all-out assault on a single site that is of enough interest and importance in itself (or is about to be demolished) to justify detailed recording. Again, the group should be split up to prevent too many cooks spoiling the broth: in the case of a watermill, say, one group can be assigned to the mill building, one to its machinery, one to the water supply, one to the miller's house, and so forth. The organizer should be there too, to encourage those who lack confidence, iron out problems that crop up, and prevent overlapping and omissions. This blitz approach can also be used as a follow-up to the first alternative: a wide survey will reveal the best examples, which can then be singled out for detailed treatment.

Setting to work

Work of this kind falls into four main categories: locating, examining, interpreting and recording. So wide is the range of industries which may be involved that only general guidance can be offered here: a commonsense approach is worth far more than erudite knowledge. Location of the sites to be examined will entail not only fieldwork but the other usual tools of the local historian, such as old maps, directories, street names and folk memory. For example, in our instance of river bridges—a simple one—a detailed perusal of the 6 inch Ordnance Survey maps will give all the required sites. Examination is inserted in the list merely to emphasize that there is no point in swarming on to a site, tapes and notebooks at the ready, expecting to get it all down in black and white without any deliberation. This approach will only lead to subtler points—changes of use, rebuildings, long-abandoned sections—being missed. A more thorough examination of every site is required.

Interpretation is perhaps the most exacting of the four activities. A knowledge of the history of the site and of the industrial processes involved is necessary, or access to somebody who does have that knowledge, such as an old employee. But even if such knowledge is available, it is rarely complete—especially if the site has a long history—and back-up work is essential to fill in the picture. This involves library and archive research of the usual kind—maps, newspapers, tithe apportionments, census returns, company papers and the rest. Group members can often do this themselves, and should be encouraged to do so. Consulting other published works to see what sources were most useful in those cases can often give pointers for current work. But the necessary information may well not be available in local libraries and record offices, in which case it will no doubt fall to the lot of the tutor or whoever has access to such specialised sources as Parliamentary Papers, or to manuscript sources in repositories such as the British Museum, Public Record Office or British Transport Historical Records, to take on this part of the task. In my experience, with an individual site of any complexity of age or layout, the best order of visits is either library-site-library, or site-library-site. A library visit followed by fieldwork almost invariably results in points arising on the site which can only be resolved by a return visit to the library. It is a combined application of all this information acquired from general knowledge, from documents, from informants and from the site itself, which results in the final picture of the purpose of the site, its plant, history, builders, workers, economics and so on. Almost inevitably queries and gaps will remain; but in essence it is an exercise in detection, using all the clues available.

Recording, though ostensibly the main object of industrial archaeology, is thus only a part of it. It is not, generally speaking, difficult, though it may be prolonged. This is no place to describe the techniques, for there is no right and no wrong way to do it: some prefer this method, some that. So long as the end result is accurate and satisfactory for the purpose, the means are immaterial. With experience, short cuts and aids are discovered for particular purposes, such as estimating the height of an inaccessible gable end by counting brick courses and measuring an accessible sample, or gauging the width of an uncrossable gap by tying a weight to the end of a tape and throwing it across. Recording techniques boil down to a conjunction of simple geometry and a goodly dose of mother wit. This is not to say that in some instances more sophisticated equipment is unnecessary. Surveying, other than the simplest kind, does demand instruments. Ordinary group members cannot be expected, unless they are very dedicated, to provide more than the basic tape, notebook and, when needed, spade, trowel or other clearing equipment. The organizer will have to find such things as level and staff, prismatic compass, clinometer, ranging poles and often (very necessary in some circumstances) safety helmets. If the group includes members with relevant skills, it is foolish not to use them. Such people as surveyors, architects or engineers of various brands are normally happy to indulge in a busman's holiday simply because the job is so different from their normal work; but it pays to add amateurs to their particular teams to pick up the rudiments.

Just how much detail needs to be recorded is a question that only the circumstances can answer. Much depends on how important (nationally as well as locally) the site is considered to be, though the typical must not be ignored in favour of the unusual or the outstanding. Much too depends on the degree of urgency: if a textile mill is being flattened tomorrow, it is useless to start on a full-scale architectural drawing—only an outline record will be possible. But should some rare monument—a glass cone or a seventeenth century blast furnace or an old lead ore crusher—be due for demolition, then, if time allows, a detailed record is desirable with plan, elevations and sections on a reasonably generous scale. In general, this close attention is probably not necessary. In our example of the survey of the river bridges of a county, which might involve a thousand examples or more, it would be excessive to make detailed drawings of them all. The salient features of each should be noted—building material, arch shape, size of spans, width, ornamentation etc. When these results are compared, it may prove sensible to record a few specific bridges of different date, design or material, in some detail. But not all.

Two hints to avoid frustration. First, make sure in advance that drawings do not already exist. They probably will not, but makers of machinery or owners or county authorities or record offices may have drawings. Likewise the need for making a small-scale plan of a complex is often obviated by the adequacy of 25 inch and 50 inch Ordnance Survey maps. Nothing is more aggravating than the discovery, after the event, that fieldwork has been a mere duplication of existing sources. Secondly, organizer and members alike should check and double check that all necessary measurements have been taken on site. All too often the draughtsman finds in mid-work that a vital dimension is missing from the field notes and that a return visit is necessary. It often needs to be impressed on the novice that to draw a scale elevation of a wall involves more than measuring the wall, the door and the window; he tends to forget that the location of window and door in the wall is important too. But even the expert is fallible. There is no solution to this problem except care and visualizing the final drawing as the field notes are made. It is sometimes possible to draw to scale on site, especially if a van can reach it; but otherwise the problems of carting drawing board and equipment to the site and dealing with it in rain and high wind are excessive. Field sketches will normally be rough and even messy; their virtue should lie not in neatness but in being complete for their purpose and in being legible, at least to their maker. But memory is short, and notes should be translated into scale drawings before it fades. Something that is clear as crystal on the spot is easily forgotten a month later.

Photography is an essential part of the work. It not only on occasion makes measured drawings unnecessary, but it supplements them by adding another dimension. A small series of good photographs, the work of only a few minutes, can give as much information as a whole day's work at measuring and drawing, and if time is of the essence has an obvious advantage. A scale should always be included. Likewise photographs can be a great help when putting detail on drawings. This is no place for a dissertation on photographic techniques:[1] but it is fair to point out that cheap cameras can produce excellent results just as expensive ones can produce failures. For really fine prints, the 35 mm camera is too small, but it is now accepted as the standard and few will have larger ones. For many purposes interchangeable lenses are desirable and sometimes essential; the chances are that some member of the group will possess them. More people these days use colour film than black and white; but though the former can bring out features which the latter cannot, it seems that black and white prints are still the best medium for general record photographs—easier to consult, easier to reproduce and possibly longer-lasting. It must be emphasized, too, that record photographs are not expected to be works of art: they are purely functional, to show what is there in the most straightforward manner possible. Again, if a skilled photographer is in the group or otherwise available, his services should be snapped up.

A further and under-used method of recording is sketching. Many people are over-modest about their abilities in this direction, but these drawings are not intended for the Tate Gallery. A quick sketch or even diagram can often show as much as a photograph by concentrating on the essentials, and may show more if the light is bad or the subject tucked away in an awkward corner.

On anything more than the smallest project, then, each team will with luck produce results in three forms:

a written reports incorporating observations that cannot be indicated on drawings or photographs, information derived from documents and from the oldest inhabitants, and interpretation of the site or part of the site;
b scale drawings (or at least notes and sketches for them, since far from everyone has facilities for making accurate drawings);
c photographs, duly labelled with subject, date, and other useful details.

To tie all this together there must be a master mind—normally the organizer himself who alone will be in a position to see the overall picture. Collation by committee suffers from the usual disadvantages of the committee and may well yield no fruit at all. It is better for one person to take on the job of assembling, editing, comparing, drawing overall conclusions and producing the final report. But he may—and should—consult the members who did the donkey work, whether by communal discussion or by inviting their individual criticisms of a draft. If he has an expert draughtsman at his command, he should of course use him, otherwise the labour of final drawing will fall on his own shoulders. For publication, the drawings should ideally be of the same style and to common scales—one scale for all machinery, for example, another for buildings and a third for more general plans. It normally happens, in my experience, that three stages are necessary for each drawing: field notes, working scale drawing, and final standardized drawing for publication.

The final aim will most often be publication, whether in the journal of the local archaeological or history society, in a national periodical like the new *Journal of Industrial Archaeology* or in a separate monograph such as the series produced by the East Yorkshire Local History Society. It is said that archaeological work which is not published may as well not have been done; but this seems an unduly harsh judgment. Where publication is not practicable for financial or other reasons, provided the results are deposited in the local library or museum where future researchers can consult them, they are far from wasted. It is only when the results are hoarded inaccessibly in the home and probably thrown out at the owner's death that the exercise becomes futile. But any publication is bound to be selective, and it is good practice to deposit the original drawings, reports and photographs with a library or museum in any case, so that those who want more detail than the publication contains can find it.

Case Studies

Let us look in more detail at a few actual projects, beginning with the smaller and simpler and progressing to the more complex.

Eight members of a Lincoln adult education class in industrial archaeology (and myself) spent a summer Saturday working on a suspension bridge across the River Ancholme at Horkstow. Since this very fine structure, built by Sir John Rennie in 1835–6, was practically unknown to the world at large, it was felt that it deserved full recording as an outstanding and unaltered monument of engineering. It proved to be just the right size for a day's work, and more people would have been superfluous. The eight were divided into pairs working on the anchors, the towers, the chains and the deck, and two of us took time off for photography. It was a straightforward job in most respects, except that the higher portions were inaccessible from the ground. We would have benefited from an aluminium ladder, but limited access to the upper parts was obtained by shinning up the chain like a monkey. The archway in each tower is semi-elliptical, an awkward shape to plot even if within reach; here we simply took a photograph of the arch square-on, which was ultimately projected on to the drawing board and the curve traced off (10.2 and 10.3). The other difficulty lay in the absence of any continuous horizontal datum line to measure heights from, since the chains naturally sagged downwards and the deck climbed markedly towards the centre of the span. So, sighting with a level, we put chalk marks on the towers and suspension rods in an arbitrary horizontal line, from which measurements could be taken up to the chains and down to the deck. Each team's field sketches were handed over to me (as the only one with a suitable drawing board), and the drawing up proved reasonably simple, though the multiplicity of chain links and suspension rods made it tedious. One essential measurement, however, was elusive (it was not made plain from which points the main span had been measured) so that a quick visit to check was necessary. The documentary side was no problem at all: the Lincolnshire Archives Office has the minute books of the Navigation Commissioners and other papers such as the specification for the ironwork of the bridge, from which the relevant information was easily extracted. The task fell to me of writing the report on the structure and its history (and the questions which remained unsolved), illustrated by three pages of drawings and by photographs, and rounded off by a brief comparison with other early surviving suspension bridges for which my own knowledge, aided by a little research, was adequate. This was published in the obvious place, the local group's periodical.[2]

Another project by members of the same group was carried out over several weekends one winter on the pithead buildings of Appleby ironstone mine near Scunthorpe, which worked during the 1870s. At a later date a building had been installed over the shaft to house pumps for lifting water to the mains. The site was unusual in that practically all ironstone extraction in the district is by opencast working, not underground mining; and the buildings and spoil tips were to be levelled in a programme of reclaiming derelict land. Since the machinery had all long since been removed, it was largely a case of clearing away the undergrowth and even trees from inside the engine house, to expose the massive walls that once supported the engine (10.4). A study of these walls and the marks on their surface revealed the type and approximate size of the engine. The foundations of the boiler house were traced beside the still-standing chimney. These buildings not being of great interest in themselves, we were satisfied with an outline survey—enough to draw a small-scale plan and elevations, without much detail. One member who lived nearby was responsible for the drawings and documentary work: the sources proved to be scattered and incomplete since the records of the Appleby-Frodingham Steel Company (successors of the lessees) are minimal. But enough was discovered from the official history of the company, the lease of the site, the Memoirs of the Geological Survey, a few minor sources and from interviews with old inhabitants, to yield

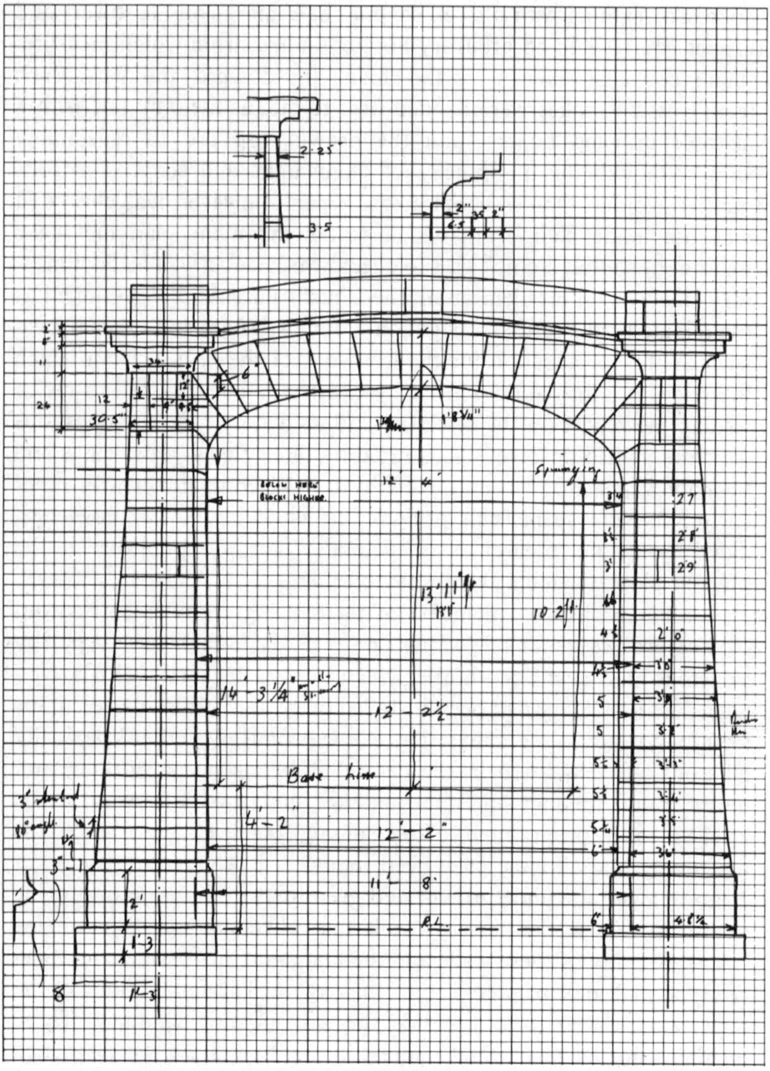

10.2 Rough drawing made on site: Horkstow Bridge Lincs

an outline history. Comparison of successive large-scale Ordnance Survey maps shows the changes which took place in the buildings. Again, the report was published in the local journal;[3] it was written up by a student, as authorship is very much a part of the learning process and wherever feasible students should be asked to undertake it, with due checking from other group members and the tutor. Soon after our work was completed, the bulldozers moved in and the site is now completely levelled and absorbed into the adjoining field.

A very much larger project was the survey of Rhosydd slate quarry in North Wales carried out basically by members of two week-long summer schools held in 1971 and 1972. The slate industry, for all its importance in the local society and economy and as a supplier of

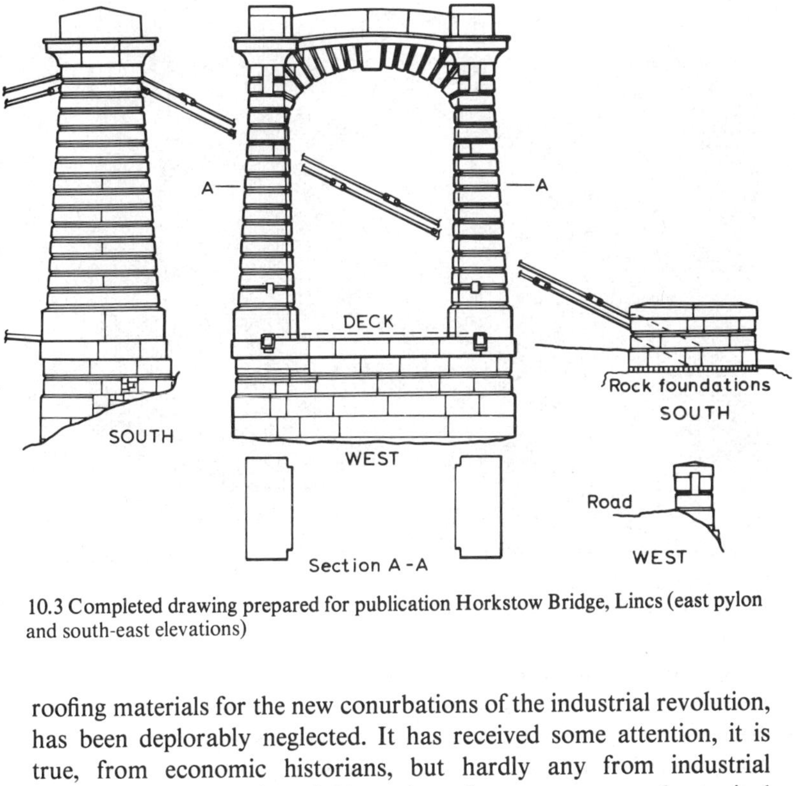

10.3 Completed drawing prepared for publication Horkstow Bridge, Lincs (east pylon and south-east elevations)

roofing materials for the new conurbations of the industrial revolution, has been deplorably neglected. It has received some attention, it is true, from economic historians, but hardly any from industrial archaeologists. The aim of this project, then, was to record a typical slate quarry in considerable depth as a case study in the industry, in the hope that other quarries would be similarly treated in the future for comparative purposes. Rhosydd, was chosen as being average in size and in date (its effective life was from 1853 to 1930); because it possessed a wide variety of buildings and power sources; because it was at the time under threat of partial destruction from a hydroelectric scheme; and because (a not insignificant attraction) it is set in magnificent surroundings.

The summer schools each consisted of about twenty-seven members and two tutors. The students came in from all over the country in response to national advertisements, and most were novices to the subject; the schools were intended not merely as working parties but to give practical instruction in techniques as well.

10.4 Interior of Engine house of the Appleby Ironstone mine, north Lincolnshire, after clearance of undergrowth (1970)

After a communal inspection of the site, members were divided into teams of two or three which were assigned specific projects—a barracks complex, a dressing mill, the water supply system for the water-wheels, roads and tracks, and so forth. The size of these projects varied, and some teams worked faster than others according to the complexity of their sites and the degree of their skill; so that the pattern of work was constantly changing as teams finished one job and were redirected to a new one. The tutors were constantly on the move from one team to another, advising, consoling and encouraging when problems arose. Their work was made the more energetic by the sheer size of the quarry—its various works cover an area $1\frac{1}{2}$ miles by $1\frac{1}{4}$, with a difference in height of 1200 ft—and the tutors could rarely visit any one team more than twice a day. Wandering teams—those concerned with reservoirs or transport—might be anywhere within the area and were hard to locate. Some teams had suitable equipment and were able to take their own photographs of their sites; for those who were not, one of the tutors photographed for them and was also responsible for general photographs. But altogether the photographic side raised problems of getting contrasty shots of ruined slate buildings whose colour merged in with the background and of recognising suitable atmospheric conditions for long shots, not helped by the fact that many camera owners preferred colour to black and white. For final publication, costs prevented large numbers of photographs being used, and sketching—either on the site or from photographs—seemed the best answer; but we had no artists and the need was not fully met.

Specialist equipment such as surveying instruments, ranging poles and a mine detector for tracking buried ironmongery was provided for common use. Members who had special skills—notably a surveyor and a hydraulic engineer—were gladly put to work in that capacity. For the rest, it was a case of commonsense on the part of the workers and (when they were able) informed explanations on the part of the tutors. But plenty of queries arose where everyone was equally at sea, such as whether the gradient and surface of a track implied the use of packhorse or cart. Generally speaking, the actual recording raised few difficulties: these came in the interpretation. Each evening was set aside for writing up reports, making a start on drawings and discussing the day's problems. After the course was over, each team finalized its report by circulating carbon or xerox copies to each other by post. Longer-term progress and queries were discussed at winter reunions which practically every student attended.

In our innocence we thought that one week would see the work completed. Far from it. By the end of the second year's week the surface remains were more or less covered; but the very extensive underground workings (10.5)—for it was a mine rather than a quarry—were not touched on during the summer schools. This was mainly because they are potentially dangerous and adequate supervision of large numbers was impossible. Instead, I returned to survey the mine at many weekends over the two winters with small parties drawn largely from an evening class but sometimes including members of the summer schools. None of us had any previous experience in underground surveying and we had to evolve our own techniques for surveying and photography which, even if time-consuming, nevertheless proved satisfactory (10.6 and 10.7). The expert services of a caving club were borrowed for exploring places

10.5 Rhosydd Slate Quarry, North Wales; underground workings
a (above) One of the adits
b (below) Piccadilly Circus (Junction of main adits)

beyond our amateur reach. An understanding of the workings threw considerable light on the surface arrangements, and vice versa.

One of the reasons for choosing Rhosydd was that the documentary sources are comparatively slight and scattered, so that archaeology would have to play a much larger part in deciphering the palimpsest than would be the case with a well-documented concern. This certainly proved to be the case. The difficulty of the sources and the impossibility of mass access to them meant that the students could not be introduced to them as they were to the site, and I had to take on this side of the task myself. Though unavoidable, this was a pity;

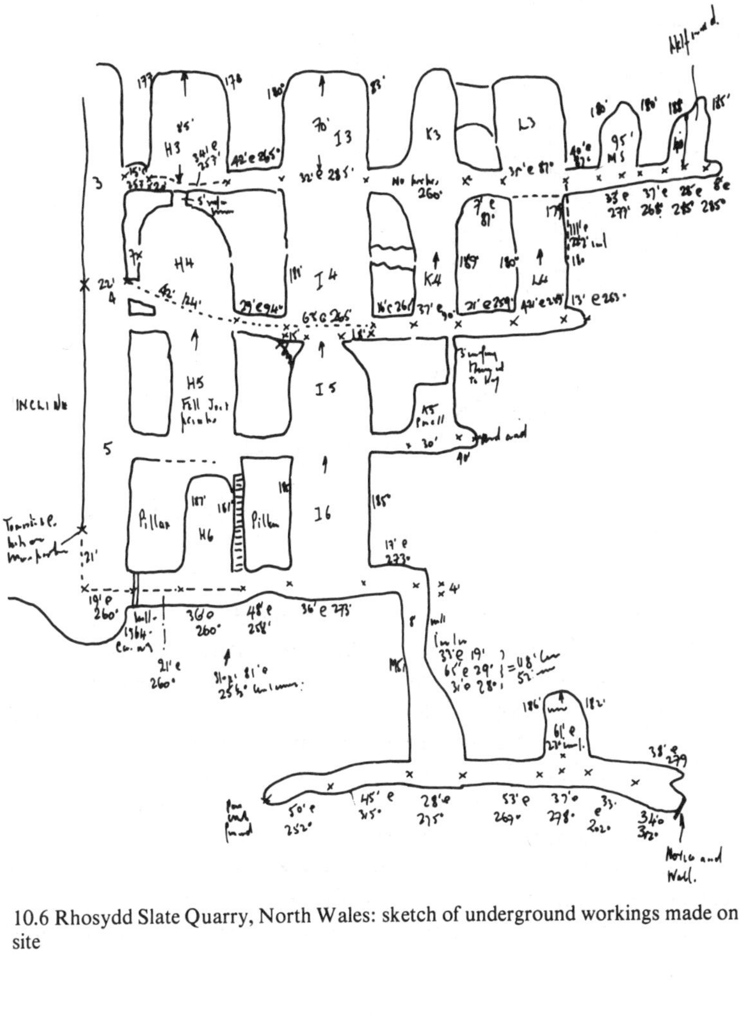

10.6 Rhosydd Slate Quarry, North Wales: sketch of underground workings made on site

10.7 Rhosydd Slate Quarry, underground workings drawn to scale

but at least as information came in from the documents it could be passed on to individual teams, if of restricted interest, or (xeroxed) to all members if of general significance, to shed light on their own projects. Scattered pieces of information emerged from the National Library of Wales, the University College of North Wales Library, the Carnarvonshire and Merioneth Record Offices, the Festiniog Railway Archives, reports of Inspectors of Mines, census returns, files of dissolved companies, local newspapers and so on. In the absence (with one minor exception) of the quarry company's working papers, it became very much a case of detective work, piecing fragmentary clues together both from documents and from the site. A great deal of help on the last days of the mine was obtained from a few elderly local men who had worked at Rhosydd, but beyond living memory we were on our own.

Because I alone had an overall view of both the physical and written evidence, I took on the job of compiling the final report, based on the reports—many of them excellent—produced by the various teams and on my own documentary findings. The draft was sent round to others for criticism. The team's drawings—many of high standard and some of them capable of reproduction as they stood—were nonetheless all re-drawn for compactness (one cannot afford to waste space in publishing) and for uniformity of scale and style. The report[4] has been published privately and runs to about 34,000 words and 27 drawings large and small, plus a limited number of photographs. This may seem excessive treatment for a single quarry—though it could have been made even longer—and is indeed something of an experiment. Its reception will be a guide for future parallel projects. But the quantity of work that has gone into it is also large: about 240 man- (and woman-) days in fieldwork alone, plus an uncounted amount of drawing, library work, editing and writing. A project on this scale cannot be lightly undertaken; but everyone involved worked with enthusiasm and intelligence. The job (and the place) got into their blood in spite of the physical effort involved, or possibly because of it: Rhosydd is an hour's hard climb from the nearest road. The majority of the students in the first year's school returned for further punishment in the second, which suggests that the work was felt to be both enjoyable and worth while.

In 1973 a similar summer school was held at the great Dinorwig slate quarry at Llanberis, once the largest slate quarry in the world. The aim here was to record as much as possible of the mills, barracks, mess rooms, inclines, aerial ropeways and the like before the CEGB built a pumped storage power station in the quarry and flooded the lower levels. As it was a rescue operation and as the quarry is so much bigger, the work could be nothing like so detailed as at Rhosydd. This matters the less since the quarry records are voluminous and can provide the outline history by themselves. But a great deal of very useful work was done, with the aid of three tutors (rather than two, in view of the size of the place) and of a Landrover for internal transport. We also had the benefit, as we did not at Rhosydd, of an artist to sketch buildings and scenes. It is not intended to publish the results as such (to put them into the context of the documentary evidence would be the work of years), but simply to deposit the reports, drawings and photographs with the National

Museum of Wales which already runs the quarry workshop as a branch museum. The material will thus be available for the Museum to draw on for its own future publications and eventually, one hopes, for the author of a full-scale history of the quarry to consult. By then our work will be the only source of information since many of the structures themselves will be no more.

This, in short, is one of the chief justifications of industrial archaeology—to record for posterity (if not for the present) the physical side of earlier industries which before long will be destroyed; though it should not of course ignore those remains whose future is safe. For local history bodies it is ideally suited, since it lends itself better to group work than purely library-based research and can usefully employ, interest and educate the novice who starts with only the minimum of background knowledge.

Notes and References

1 *See* Brian Bracegirdle, 'Photography for Industrial Archaeology', *Industrial Archaeologists' Guide* 1971–3 pp. 157–71.

2 M. J. T. Lewis, 'Horkstow Bridge', in *Lincolnshire Industrial Archaeology*, vol. 8 no. 1 (1973) pp. 2–12.

3 M. J. G. Upton, 'The Appleby Ironstone Mine', in *Lincolnshire Industrial Archaeology*, vol. 6 no. 4 (1971) pp. 66–72.

4 J. H. Denton and M. J. T. Lewis, *Rhosydd Slate Quarry* (1974).

11

Change Within Living Memory: the Rural Community in the Twentieth Century

REX C. RUSSELL

Some of the really valuable and vivid books which deal with local history are those in which change within living memory is recalled. Five examples of these immediately come to mind: Flora Thompson's *Lark Rise to Candleford* (1939), Richard Hillyer's *Country Boy* (1966), Raphael Samuel's 'Quarry Roughs' in *Village Life and Labour* (1975), and of the books of George Ewart Evans, especially *The Days That We Have Seen* (1975) and *Where Beards Wag All* (1970). Books such as these help adult students and others to appreciate the importance and relevance of the changes within their own lifetimes and give them greater respect for the importance of the memories of their own parents and the recollections of an older generation. Such books bring home to their readers the fact that history does not stop at some date before they were born. They remind them that their own earlier participation in Sunday School outings, in Chapel anniversaries, in work on the farms with horses and with now obsolete agricultural instruments are all aspects of past (or passing) history. Their memories of days at school in the nineteen-twenties and thirties, when temperance lecturers could bring along models of juicy red hearts to contrast with the models of yellow-fatted hearts to demonstrate the health and vigour of the teetotaller and the degeneracy of the drinker, are memories of past history. Their mother's recollections of the procession of costumed men riding white horses behind other men in regalia who carried banners can help them recall perhaps the former importance of friendly societies—Oddfellows, Foresters, Druids and Sons of Temperance. The memories of Miss Clara Gant (in *St. Paul's Church, Ashby: 1925–1975*) include this passage:— 'The highlight of the year besides the Feast was the procession of the Oddfellows Club, which marched from the bottom of the High Street to the Crown Inn for a dinner in the covered yard at the back. The men wore coloured sashes (mostly blue and gold) across their shoulders. They processed with a large banner, the local band, and were led by two men on horseback (J. Steeper and Mr. Goy) . . .' One of my students recalled that she walked to her school which was several miles from her home: she and her friends brought their dinners with them but were strictly forbidden to eat these within the schoolroom; their use of the school porch was tolerated but not encouraged. This recollection came back to me when I read the following entry in the Log Book of Tealby (Lincs) School:

30th May, 1879: The Revd. S. Levin forwarded to me a note, at the request of the Committee, containing the terms on which the use of the school is granted and are as follows:—

The School to be kept in repairs and a regulation enforced that the children are not admitted during meal and play hours.

I have given notice of the above to the children today, and have commenced to lock the school up and carry the key with me. Eight children including the p[upil] t[eacher] were obliged to eat their dinners in the street, and were afterwards exposed to a drenching rain.

The memories and recollections of people like these are important parts of the source material for group work on 'Change within living memory'.

One of the main difficulties which faces tutors and leaders of local history groups is that of ensuring that every member is able to participate in the work of the group. One period of history, that from 1900 (or from 1918) onwards which is perhaps not studied enough, is precisely that time for which we can expect our students both to draw upon their own experiences and knowledge and to get co-operation from local people who are not members of the group. It is also essential that our groups should make some impact on the community in which they meet, and a study of change within living memory may well provide one profitable method through which we can reach two desirable ends: the active participation of all students in the work of the group and the involvement of other local people in the activity of our group. We need the latter involvement because the memories and knowledge of local people will be part of our source material.

How can group work on this theme be planned and carried out? The writer has worked almost exclusively in rural areas and the suggestions which follow are made with village and market-town classes in mind. Nevertheless the theme of 'change within living memory' can be pursued profitably in urban areas, provided that the range of change to be studied be carefully delimited. Urban groups would need, of course, a list of topics to guide their research different from that suggested below: it would probably be essential to restrict the scope of enquiry considerably to achieve any worthwhile results, or to keep a group of students together over four or five years.

The first list of questions which tutor and students together should compile to guide their studies should be based upon easily accessible sources. Some such valuable sources are the relevant county directories for the period. The names of the local incumbents, the farmers, tradesmen, shopkeepers and school-teachers can help to recall relevant recollections, and the very fact that relatively recent directories do reveal just how much change has occurred within living memory helps the group to appreciate the worthwhile nature of their task. It is helpful if photocopies of all directory entries for the parish to be studied are obtained, copies for each member of the group. Repeated reference to these entries will be essential; the more they are read the more questions will come to mind, and the entries themselves may well suggest sources (both personal and institutional) to be approached for answers to such queries. It will be helpful if the questions compiled from these sources be grouped under several main headings: these may offer adequate *initial* guidance:—

1 Changes in parish population and housing.
2 Changes in farming and employment in agriculture.
3 Changes in local trades, industries and transport.
4 Changes within Church and Chapel and their relationships with the village community.
5 Changes in local education and schools.
6 Changes in the voluntary local movements.

Under each of these general headings the group members together can list more detailed questions to which they will hope to find answers. It can be helpful here to include facts given in directories, or already known to members of the group—the date of the rebuilding of a chapel or of the closure of a chapel, the date of the enlargement of the school or of the closure of the school, the date of the foundation of the local Women's Institute, the date at which local children of secondary school age left the village for secondary education. The inclusion of some dates of national decisions or of national events may also well be helpful—how many of us can recall accurately the date of the coming of old age pensions or the date of the decision to work for national (and local) Methodist unity? The figures for local population increase or decrease should certainly be included; very few people know these and many assume, often quite wrongly, that a modern spread of new housing denotes population increase.

Examples of the kind of questions which can be grouped under our suggested main headings might include the following as a minimum useful outline:

Changes in parish population and housing

Population has changed as follows:—

		Increase or decrease
1901	595	
1911	505	−90
1921	472	−33
1931	461	−11
1951	498	+37
1961	602	+104
1971	756	+154

Why has there been first decline and then increasing growth?
How many houses did these people occupy, and how has the density of people per house changed over the seventy years?
When did the building of Council houses start?
How much new building has been provided by Council and how much by private enterprise?
Has there been demolition of older housing? If so, where and when? What can the 25 in Ordnance Survey maps reveal about building change?

Changes in farming and employment in agriculture

How many farms were there in 1901 and how many are there today?
What changes in farm-tenancy or owner-occupation have there been?
Have there been major changes in land-use in our period? What new crops (for example, sugar beet) have come in, and when? What changes in farm-stock have taken place?
How many horses were used on each farm? When did the use of horses cease?
How many regular farm-workers were employed on each farm and

how many are now? Where was extra seasonal labour recruited?
How have farm wages changed during our period?
When was the local branch of the National Union of Agricultural Workers started? When did local farmers first join the National Farmers' Union?
What farming changes were brought about by the Second World War?

Changes in local trades, industries and transport

Which trades listed in the Directories no longer exist in the parish, and when did they cease?
When did the carriers cease? When they existed, where did they go and how often?
When did the local railway close? What effects did this have?
When did motor-buses start and where did they go?
What new trades/industries have been started in our period? From where did they recruit their labour?

Church and Chapel changes

A list of the incumbents with dates of incumbency can be drawn up. When was a change in the status of the incumbent noticeable?
What changes are noticeable in the Church parish magazine between *c.*1910 and today?
Have some Sunday Schools been discontinued and if so, of which denominations and when? Have annual Sunday School outings ceased? If so, when?
National Methodist Unity came in 1932: when did local Methodist Unity come? Was there a long delay between 1932 and the achievement of local unity? If so, why? How was it decided to close one chapel rather than the other, and with what results?
What changes have there been in Church/Chapel relationships?

Changes in local Education and Schools

Have there been any private schools in the parish since 1900?
What have been the local results of secondary education for all since 1944? When did local children over the age of 11 leave the village for secondary education?
Where were children of the middle classes sent to secondary school before this date? How many went?
In some cases where the local school has been closed, an assessment of whether the closure affected parish life and in what ways is

useful. Again, when did adult education come to the village? who sponsored it?

Changes in Local Voluntary Movements

The village W.I. was founded in 1921. Why was it started and by whom? Why did women become members? What contributions has the W.I. made to village life? Do records of the local W.I. exist from foundation onwards? Who has them?

Which Church and Chapel societies have ceased to exist: for example the Girls' Friendly Society, Mothers' Union, Women's Bright Hour?

What new voluntary societies have been started?

Have women rather than men been served by local voluntary societies?

Once such a list of questions has been drawn up, it should be duplicated in numbers sufficient not only for each member of the group, but for selected distribution beyond the group to local people (and former local people no longer living in the parish) whose help and co-operation can be sought. The local history group will itself wish to add many other questions to its lists as one line of enquiry opens up others. It will be sensible to note down the location of relevant source material which can be used to answer some of these queries, such as the school log-books; often the school-managers will allow the group to consult their past minutes. It will be necessary to find out who has the custody of the local chapel records and who has kept runs of the parish magazine; and whether the local newspaper or the local library holds a file of local newspapers covering our period. Again the local library or the County Records office may well possess sale catalogues and maps of local farms or estates which have changed hands, while the Rural District Council or its successor will often be able to provide information on the dates of building of local council houses. Students will, of course, be encouraged to ask their own questions, and to seek out information for themselves which can be brought back for group information and group discussion and use.

It can prove valuable if the leader or members of the group will accept invitations (and even seek invitations) to speak to local societies on the work in hand. The more members of the community who know of the group work being undertaken the better, for this may well result in hitherto unknown sources coming to light. Picture post-cards of villages and market towns were formerly much more common than they are today: several local people may have these and they can be invaluable as records of buildings which have gone. The appearance of a village can change rapidly and drastically over forty years. Unmetalled roads with wide grass verges become metalled roads with tarmac and curbed pavements. Trees which were an important feature in the street scene can be felled and their places taken by street-lights, telephone kiosks, bus shelters. Such changes are by no means too trivial to record. Old photographs of classes of schoolchildren can be revealing documents of social change: how many boys in that photograph of 1923 are clearly wearing cut-down versions of adult garments? Are they all still wearing heavy boots? Is poverty really apparent in such photographs? It is these kinds of source material, together perhaps with photographs of carriers' carts, of Sunday School outings, of the annual Foresters' parade, that can become available as a result of a talk to the local Women's Institute or the Senior Citizens' Club. Valid and vivid facts about farm service, seasonal work on the farms and in some industries such as brick and tile-making, information about the realities of life in domestic service together with figures of wage-rates can all be gleaned from discussions at such meetings. The whereabouts of lost parish documents —accounts of the surveyors of the highways or of the overseers of the poor—have sometimes been discovered at such meetings. Such documents may not be relevant to change within living memory, but the family who held on to the records of *their* chapel, when *their* chapel was closed, may be delighted to talk to members of the history group about why they valued their chapel so much and why they were unhappy about the local results of apparent unity.

A great deal of the gathering of factual information from interviews and informal talks with local people must of course be done outside the regular meetings of the group. This is, in part, why it is so essential for the tutor and group together to work out the series of questions to be asked. A minority of informants may be happy to come to a group meeting and pass on information to the whole group; people who have held office in local organizations and have gained confidence and experience in speaking should certainly be invited to meet the research group, for the results of questioning by several people can be markedly more productive than questioning by one. Retired teachers, local Methodist preachers, a past president of the Women's Institute, the chairman of the parish council, the secretary of the local branch of the National Union of Agricultural Workers or the secretary of the parochial church council may all be willing to meet the group.

There are still very few good guides to the techniques of recording oral history. Probably the best is J. Vansina, *The Oral Tradition,* published by Pelican in 1973, and membership of the Oral History Society will give access to its journal and other publications.

It is essential that oral history should be supplemented and checked by written sources wherever possible. Minutes, local newspapers, parish magazines for the recent past are rarely used and as a result of this are too often not valued sufficiently to be kept and stored as carefully as older records. The least cared-for documents in many church safes are those which deal with the recent past. Courses on change within living memory may well rescue some of these records from destruction.

It is of course important to put all this information into the context of the general history of England since 1900. There are now several good histories of this period which group members can obtain from their local libraries. Such works of reference will of course vary, depending on whether the study is being conducted within an urban or a rural environment. For a village, students might well consult W. P. Baker, *The English Village* (1953) which contains a useful bibliography, C. S. Orwin, *Problems of the Countryside* (1945) and R. Samuel (ed.) *Village Life and Labour* (1975). In addition, there are two new journals, the *Journal of Social History* and *History Workshop,* both of which contain much local material of relevance to this subject.

It seems unnecessary to discuss the putting together of the material collected. The techniques of assembling and writing up the material which tells of change within living memory are very similar to those for earlier periods of history. What is needed is the stress on the importance of this theme. Too many local histories end with no consideration of recent changes. The scholarly author of the volume on *Lincolnshire* in the Cambridge County Geographies (the Lincolnshire volume was published in 1913), ended his chapter on the history of the county with this sentence:

> 'Since the Civil War there has been little in the way of history to record in connection with our county' (p. 111).

We have different ideas now, but all too rarely do we and our students tackle change within living memory.

12

Writing and Editing

BERNARD JENNINGS

It will be assumed for the purposes of this chapter that the local history groups under consideration are open to all interested people, and are not confined to people with qualifications or previous research experience; and that in the case of adult education classes, the group research grows out of normal class work. It is noteworthy that a considerable proportion of the classes which have produced substantial published work began with no such objective, but were gradually drawn towards it through attempting to satisfy their own intellectual interests. 'Normal class work' needs further definition. Some local history classes are essentially lecture courses in which the tutor provides most of the information, sets occasional written exercises, and encourages any keen students to work on records which interest them. Other classes may work busily on documents, but never progress beyond the stages of transcription and compilation. It is assumed here, however, that the students have agreed to work on local records and other historical evidence in order to give them some insight into historical methods and to develop their powers of critical analysis and constructive thought. Regular written work is an essential tool for these purposes, and the students who eventually make contributions to a published work will find that their training for this began in the earliest stages of the class. This also holds true for non-formal local history groups.

Initial steps

A study of this kind need not necessarily begin at the chronological beginning. Ideally the first term's work should centre upon a topic and/or period for which suitable material is easily accessible or can be made available, to which the students can relate without serious difficulty and in the study of which they can employ a variety of talents. The launching pad could be a topic, such as transport or aspects of agrarian history, which lends itself to an integrated approach using documents, maps of various kinds and dates, and the present landscape. Or it could be a period which is suitably documented and has left a tangible focus of interest in the form of buildings, town layouts or industrial remains. A consideration of these issues has led groups interested in both medieval and modern history to begin their work in periods as far apart as the Dark Ages and the nineteenth century.

The principles being advocated here, and the essential link between the way a group starts to operate and the approach to the subsequent problems of writing a local history, can be demonstrated by citing the example of one particular class held at Hebden Bridge in Yorkshire. It began as an ordinary three-year tutorial class studying the history of the upper Calder Valley, and the decision to write a history of the area was not finally made until the class had been extended into a fourth year. The industrial revolution in the upper Calder Valley caused a relocation of industry, communications and settlement along the valley bottom, leaving the older villages, farms and routeways virtually untouched on the terraces above. Probate inventories, which offered virtually a valuable and easily understood source for the study of the economic and social life of this older community, survived from the 1680s. It was therefore decided to begin the course with a study of the late seventeenth and early eighteenth centuries. A selection of probate inventories was duplicated for class use, and the students were asked both to undertake a simple analysis of their contents and to try to identify some of the houses described in the inventories. Several of the latter were quickly recognized and were drawn or photographed by some students for the benefit of the others. At the next stage a set of about fifty Xeroxed original inventories was used, both to teach the elements of palaeography and to increase the volume of material available for study. When these had been transcribed and analysed, the study of farming, industry and housing was broadened by the use of other relevant sources.

An initial project of this kind gives the students the stimulus of using primary sources, the boost to confidence which comes from learning a new skill, and the satisfaction of making a small contribution to acknowledge even in the first term. It also provides a good base from which to move out into a more flexible situation, with some projects being undertaken by the whole class and others by small groups or individual students, who feed back their results to general group meetings. It is never too early to inculcate sound academic habits. Students should be encouraged from the beginning to include accurate references in all their written papers and notes, whether derived from documents, from specialist articles or from background reading. This will not only help the students to keep their own work in order, but will also avoid time-consuming searches at the editorial stage. (I would urge this with all the fervour of a reformed sinner.) Wherever possible standardized systems should be devised for the collection and analysis of data, using forms or record cards. It will probably be necessary to modify some of these systems in the light of experience, but they can help the students by giving a definite shape to their research projects and by ensuring that team work proceeds along similar lines.

Large-scale Projects: Organization

If the group undertakes a major research commitment, the tutor or leader's task of providing general guidance becomes more complex. Increasingly the research will be done by individuals and small groups away from his eye. A good deal of it will involve work in the areas where his own knowledge is thin. Some of the members will in any case be better equipped, by virtue of special knowledge and skills acquired through their professional roles or amateur interests, to tackle particular topics. The tutor or leader must however keep in touch with the work of each individual or group, and ensure that the members as a whole are made aware from time to time of the main features emerging from the research. In the early stages periodic discussions between the tutor and members working upon a particular project will probably suffice. Once the research has passed a critical point of volume and complexity, however, it is important to have regular written reports, drawing together the main features of the analysis and indicating which problems remain unsolved, which are the priority areas for further investigation, and so on. This method, as well as allowing the leader to offer guidance where appropriate, will prevent the members contracting the disease which might be called 'antiquarian's palsy'. This is a condition in which the accumulation of a mountain of unsystematized data paralyses the will of the student to analyse and write, and leads him to take refuge like a drug addict in the collection of further information.

Once the project has begun to take shape, provisional decisions can be made about publication. Is the group aiming at a comprehensive history of the locality or a coverage of certain topics and/or periods? Does it intend to publish its work as a single book or as a series of booklets? Are there plans for other forms of presentation, such as an exhibition or a slide-and-tape unit? There are obvious advantages in producing a single substantial volume, if satisfactory arrangements can be made for publication. On the other hand, publishing in parts can encourage the members, by the sight of their work in print and by the reception which it is accorded by readers. If a comprehensive book is in prospect, there may still be a case for producing a 'trailer' in the form of a booklet dealing with some theme of general interest, or for mounting an exhibition, both to encourage the students and to prepare the market, and indeed on occasion to elicit new information or source material.

Schemes of work

It will be assumed here that a single comprehensive publication is planned, which will be arranged partly by subject and partly by period (and not, V.C.H. style, village by village). The main topics will suggest themselves—agriculture, industry, trade and transport, social organization, religious life, politics—but there are many ways of grouping them together and dividing them into periods, depending upon the nature of the locality and of its historical experience. Some of these themes will already have been studied in detail by the whole class or group, while others may as yet have been considered only in general terms. An important question is whether, for the final stages of the work, each member should concentrate on one chapter or whether each chapter is to be the collaborative work of two or more members. If the latter course is followed, each member will probably make a contribution to two or three chapters. The choice will depend partly on the size of the group, partly on the tastes and temperaments of the individual members. There are, however, two arguments in favour of a collaborative approach: it gives the members a broader view of the project as a whole, and it provides a framework for mutual support.

It may be that for certain parts of the scheme there are no takers, through lack of interest or lack of confidence in tackling particularly complex subject matter. Perhaps the first question to ask of an unwanted topic is, can we do without it? Would its omission unbalance the book, or can it be left for later treatment by another person or group? When *A History of Nidderdale* was being written, neither I nor any of the students had the necessary specialist knowledge and skills to make a serious study of vernacular architecture. We therefore decided to deal with the development of housing functionally and not structurally. Currently a research group made up of former tutorial class students is working on vernacular architecture in Nidderdale under the guidance of one of my colleagues who is an expert in the subject.

If the topic is an essential one, it may be possible to make a virtue out of necessity by treating it as a collective project for the whole group in which the leader guides the members through all the stages of research, analysis and writing. The experience will help them to deal with the parallel problems which appear in their chosen topics. The members can take it in turns to act as rapporteurs of discussions. The written reports of the latter can provide the basis for the first draft of the chapter, which everyone can have a hand in shaping.

A third way out of the difficulty is for the leader to write the 'unpopular' sections himself. There may be no other way if the sources for the latter are effectively outside the members' reach. To illustrate the latter point from the experience of *Nidderdale,* in the Middle Ages the upper dale was developed as a series of monastic estates, and the Forest of Knaresborough stretched across most of the lower dale. Some of the monastic charters were already in print in English, and the bulk of the other monastic records was not too great for the whole of them to be transcribed and translated by the tutor and duplicated for class use. This procedure was quite impracticable for dealing with the principal source for the Forest of Knaresborough, the court rolls housed in the Public Record Office. They were much too extensive for more than selective microfilming, and in any case many of them contained membranes too badly rubbed and faded to reproduce satisfactorily. Extracts were transcribed for use in class, but otherwise the bulk of the research and the preparation of the first draft of the appropriate sections were left to the tutor. (It also happened that none of the students had more than a smattering of Latin, but having a few good Latin scholars would not have solved the problem.)

The provisional scheme will indicate the broad treatment agreed upon by the leader and members. It will probably be found useful at this point for the members responsible for each chapter to work out a more detailed plan, indicating priorities for further investigation and listing the relevant secondary sources with which they are acquainted. The latter will help the leader to search out specialist articles for the members. The former is necessary to concentrate effort where it is most needed. Students should not try to 'leave no stone unturned' if there are too many stones.

The production of written drafts by the members can be planned in a variety of ways, depending upon the structure of the topic, the amount of information and the inclinations and capabilities of the members. It is often helpful, however, to break a complex topic down into sections for the first stage of drafting and then attempt a synthesis. Let us take the example of a group working on the industrial revolution in a textile district who have collected, on forms or record cards, a mass of information arranged or indexed under the heading of mills or enterprises. They can draw the material out first in the form of a series of specialized papers dealing with parallel as well as consecutive aspects of the subject, for example early fulling/scribbling mills; the development of the mechanical spinning of different fibres; details of water power—sizes and types of wheels, volume of water flow, construction of reservoirs, etc.; the advent of steam power, sizes and types of engines; the effect of steam power on the location of mills; the mechanization of weaving and other processes; the emergence of local engineering firms serving the textile trade; sources of capital; the fortunes of local firms in booms and slumps; the building of mills, extensions and closures; the detailed history of a few key firms. From such papers the shape of the chapter can be worked out.

Any topic can be treated in different ways according to the inclinations of the students. In one class, for example, two people were working side by side on local Methodist history. One of them dealt primarily with organization—the development of circuits, the building of chapels, the routine of ministers, the class system—the other with the work of the local preachers. The former worked on her own through the chapel, circuit and district records of both of the Connections (Wesleyan and Primitive) which were active locally. The tutor never saw any of this material, although he had seen similar records elsewhere; the student handed in a comprehensive account of her topic which needed only a little polishing and rather more compressing to be ready for the printer. The other student however preferred to work in stages, asking at each for the tutor's comments. As a first step, he read the minute books of the local preachers' quarterly meetings and made what was intended to be a balanced selection of entries from which to construct his account. The tutor went over the same ground and found that the selection was unbalanced; the student, himself a greatly respected local preacher, had noted as 'newsworthy' all the references to the failings of local preachers—neglect of duties, drunkenness, even moral depravity—and had passed over as commonplace every tribute to a lifetime of devoted service! A revised selection was then made, a skeleton account prepared in note form and finally an excellent literary draft written. After each of these stages, the tutor made critical comments. It would be impossible for a tutor to shadow the work of all his students in this way—to the extent of going over all the records used the latter—but the step-by-step approach is often a great help to some of the students. The heterogeneity of such adult groups usually means that those who want guidance at every stage are balanced by those who work, both happily and effectively, without much supervision.

The Editorial Process

There comes a point at which the tutor or leader becomes the editor. Although one role shades into the other, the tutor's main concern is with the intellectual development of the students, and the editor's with the production of the book. The tutor would like to make another effort at improving the written expression of the less fluent students, the editor cannot afford the time; he has problems enough. In addition to securing the competent academic analysis and exposition of each subject, he has to achieve some degree of literary unity—or at least tone down the stylistic contrasts between one section and another—and reduce the book to the required length. The most difficult task of all is to make the book both conceptually and verbally suitable for the target readership.

To take the latter point first, an adult class or research group is unlikely to want to write a local history which only professional historians or other trained amateurs can read. The members will probably have a picture of the non-specialist readers at whom they are aiming—reasonably intelligent, interested both in history and in the locality but with little or no background knowledge of many of the topics dealt with, prepared to make some effort with difficult subject matter but unable or unwilling to plough through long stretches which appear to them to be either particularly complex or excessively dull. At the same time the group will want to produce a work of lasting value, judged by the highest professional standards.

Specialist terms provide the lowest hurdle to be cleared. A sound rule is to avoid them whenever possible, but to explain them adequately when they must be used. To illustrate this point from agrarian history, 'selion' is a precise term for a unit of common-field arable land. Neither 'land', 'ridge' nor 'strip' are adequate substitutes, partly because each of these words has other meanings. In any discussion of common-field agriculture it is therefore useful to define the term 'selion' and use it freely. On the other hand, the expression 'reversed-S curve' will do just as well to describe one of the physical legacies of common-field ploughing as 'aratral curve' and can be explained more easily. A glossary is useful, but it is still desirable to define unfamiliar terms and concepts on first acquaintance, and leave the glossary as a reminder when the words recur later in the book.

More serious, but not insoluble, problems may arise from the inherent difficulties of the subject matter. The solution can often be found within the group, as it will have a wide range of what one might call negative skills, for example in people who find technical descriptions baffling or suffer mental cramp when they try to think in statistical terms. The latter can be used as catalysts to separate the essential exposition from other material (such as details of a mechanical or chemical process or the statistical reasoning behind a table of figures) which could be put into appendices. A topic remote from the understanding of the non-specialist reader, like bondage in medieval society, may be easier to comprehend when re-interpreted through the experience of mature people who have been conscripted, subjected to Essential Works Orders, sent down coal mines as 'Bevin Boys', or have lived in tied cottages or been compelled to suffer an overweening master through economic necessity.

The most intractable problems are those which arise out of the intrinsic difficulty not of the subject matter itself but of the evidence. Any sound piece of historical writing must show, either implicitly or explicitly, how the main conclusions have been reached. To provide only the latter and the references is to miss out the meatiest part of the intellectual sandwich. But, to pursue the metaphor, the meat may be tough and full of gristle. The evidence may be substantial in total but made up of many separate fragments, each of which has to be carefully analysed. The resultant chapter could represent an intellectual *tour de force,* and yet demand for its proper understanding very close attention even from the specialist reader. There is no easy solution. One can hardly put three-quarters of a chapter into an appendix. It goes without saying that a thin stream of text flowing through great sandbanks of footnotes will repel the general reader. It may be possible to turn the chapter round, presenting the general argument first and then embarking upon a detailed analysis of the evidence which could be skipped by readers who found it too difficult to follow. One could argue that as a comprehensive local history is not suitable for reading straight through from cover to cover, it does not matter very much if some readers abandon the effort to understand one particularly difficult chapter. On the other hand the latter may provide an essential link in a chain of economic or social development which runs through the whole work.

The literary aspects of the editorial process should present fewer difficulties. Drafts may have to be reduced in length, in some cases drastically. This should, of course, be done in collaboration with the author or authors of each chapter, but the editor will need to have a fairly free hand as only he can effectively balance the claims of one chapter against those of another. Even if general clarity of expression has been achieved, either spontaneously or as a result of the critical processing of earlier drafts, there may be jarring contrasts of style between one chapter and another. Sometimes a greater uniformity can be achieved by breaking up long and complex sentences in one chapter and welding together short, jerky expressions in another. The deletion of over-used adverbs can sometimes work wonders. In other cases a paragraph can be rebuilt around a key sentence or felicitous phrase in such a way that the student-author is not robbed of the pride of literary parentage. Of course, drastic surgery may be needed, and often the students, particularly those less fluent in literary expression, are only too happy to see their ideas emerge in a more elegant literary garb.

The tutor or leader need not, however, discharge his editorial responsibilities unaided. He may share the load with an editorial sub-committee drawn from the group, perhaps asking them to go over his edited version with a particular eye to its readability. The group as a whole should also have its say. Many of the drafts, or the notes on which they were based, will have been circulated for comment at an earlier stage. Before the text is finally settled, the members as a whole should have every opportunity to comment on both the substance and the presentation. After that, all that the tutor/editor needs to do is to give some instruction in proof-reading and index-making while waiting for the galleys to arrive.

The acknowledgement of such assistance is, of course, essential. It may be expressed in formal co-authorship or less formally in a preface. At the same time, a longer list of acknowledgements may not be out of place, particularly to those who have provided access to their premises or who have lent photographs, documents or other material. It is advisable always to inform such people that you plan to mention them in the published work, for they may—for a variety of reasons—object! Few original documents are now copyright but photocopies may still be (as from the Public Record Office and the British Museum), and it is necessary to seek and to acknowledge their permission before quoting the material in print. Ordnance Survey maps too are subject to all sorts of restrictions. Above all, the rule is to be courteous—you never know when you may need to ask another favour.

One last point: if the group does decide to publish privately, do remember to deposit copies with the five copyright libraries and with your local library and records office, so that others will learn of the existence of your study. And do mark the book clearly with information of where it may be obtained and (if possible) with some indication of the price. Elementary mistakes like this can be costly and result in large numbers of unsold copies remaining on your hands, unread and useless—a waste after all the effort which has gone into its production. And that would be a pity.

Bibliography

The following lists comprise a number of the most important books and articles of relevance to each project discussed above. Articles and books referred to in the text of each chapter are not repeated here.

Chapter 1 Starting the Group

(a) Local History

Bloch Marc, *The Historian's Craft* (1954).

Carr, E. H. *What is History?* (1961).

Elton, G. R. *The Practice of History* (1967).

Dymond, D. P. *Archaeology and History* (1974).

Finberg, H. P. & Skipp, V. H. T. *Local History . . . Objective and Pursuit* (1967).

Hoskins, W. G. *Local History in England* (1972) 2nd ed.

Rogers, Alan *This was their World* (1972), new ed. 1977, *Approaches to Local History*.

(b) Sources

Cheney, C. R. (ed.), *Handbook of Dates for Students of English History* (1970) 2nd ed. Royal Historical Society.

Munby, Lionel M. (ed.), *Short Guides to Records* (1972) Historical Association.

Richardson, John *The Local Historian's Encyclopaedia* (1974).

Stephens, W. B. *Sources for English Local History* (1973).

West, John *Village Records* (1962).

(c) General History

Relevant works are listed in the text.

(d) Examples of Local Histories

Ashby, M. K. *The Changing English Village 1066–1914* (1974).

Harvey, P. D. A. *A Medieval Oxfordshire Village* (1965).

Hey, D. G. *An English Rural Community* (1974).

Hill, Sir Francis *Medieval Lincoln* (1948).

Hill, Sir Francis *Tudor and Stuart Lincoln* (1956).

Hill, Sir Francis *Georgian Lincoln* (1966).
Hill, Sir Francis *Victorian Lincoln* (1974).
Hoskins, W. G. *The Midland Peasant* (1957).
Jennings, Bernard (ed.), *A History of Nidderdale* (1967).
Jennings, Bernard *A History of Harrogate and Knaresborough* (1970).
Spufford, Margaret *Contrasting Communities* (1974).

Chapter 2 Reconstituting the Medieval Landscape

(a) General

Kerridge, E. *The Agrarian Revolution* (1967).
Tate, W. E. *The English Village Community and the Enclosure Movement* (1967).
Thirsk, J. (ed.), *The Agrarian History of England and Wales 1500–1640* (1967).
Titow, J. Z. *English Rural Society 1200–1350* (1969).

(b) Evolution of the Landscape

Baker, A. R. H. & Butlin, R. A. (eds.), *Studies of Field Systems in the British Isles* (1973).
Hoskins, W. G. *The Making of the English Landscape* (1952).
Thirsk, J. 'The Common Fields', *Past and Present* 29 (1964) pp. 3–25.
Thirsk, J. 'The Origins of the Common Fields', *Past and Present* 33 (1966) pp. 142–147.
Titow, J. Z. 'Medieval England and the Open-Field System', *Past and Present* 32 (1965) pp. 86–102.
Orwin, C. S. & C. S. *The Open Fields* (1967) 3rd ed.

(c) Local Studies

Baker & Butlin (above) provides a comprehensive bibliography for most parts of the British Isles, but the following are particularly recommended for their methodology:

Sheppard, J. A. 'Pre-Enclosure Field and Settlement Patterns in an English Township: Wheldrake, near York; *Geogafiska Annaler* xlvii (1966) pp. 63–70 (in English).
Skipp, V. H. T. & Hastings, R. P. *Discovering Bickenhill* (1964).

(d) Field Names

Field, J. *English Field Names, a Dictionary* (1972).
Smith, A. H. *English Place-Name Elements* (1956) EPNS xxv and xvi.

(e) Sources

Baker, A. R. H. 'Local History in Early Estate Maps', *Amateur Historian* 5 no. 3 (1962) pp. 66–71.

Beresford, M. W. 'Maps and the Medieval Landscape', *Antiquity* xxiv, no. 95 (1950) pp. 114–118.

Harley, J. B. *Historian's Guide to Ordnance Survey Maps* (1964) National Council of Social Service.

Harley, J. B. *Maps for the Local Historian* (1972) National Council of Social Service.

Legg, E. 'Title Deeds', *Amateur Historian* 6, no. 3 (1964) pp. 86–90.

(f) Field-Work

Beresford, M. W. *History on the Ground* (1957).

Beresford, M. W. & St. Joseph, J. K. S. *Medieval England: An Aerial Survey* (1958).

Bowen, H. C. *Ancient Fields* (1962) British Association for the Advancement of Science.

Crawford, O. G. S. *Archaeology in the Field* (1953).

Hoskins, W. G. *Field Work in Local History* (1967).

National Council of Social Service, *Hedges and Local History* (1971).

Taylor, C. C. *Fields in the English Landscape* (1975).

Chapter 3 The Study of Traditional Buildings

All relevant works are cited in the text.

Chapter 4 Hearth Taxes and Other Records

Ashmore, O. and Bagley, J. 'Inventories as a Source of Local History', *Amateur Historian* vol. 4, nos. 4, 5, 6 and 8 (1959–60).

Barley, M. W. *English Farmhouse and Cottage* (1961).

Camp, A. J. *Wills and Their Whereabouts* (1974) 2nd ed.

Gibson, J. S. W. *Wills and Where to Find Them* (1974).

Havinden, M. A. *Household and Farm Inventories in Oxfordshire 1550–90* (1965).

Hoskins, W. G. *The Midland Peasant* (1957).

Jones, B. C. 'Inventories of Goods and Chattels', *Amateur Historian,* vol. 2, no. 3 (1954) pp. 76–79.

Merion-Jones, G. I. 'The Use of Hearth Tax Returns and Vernacular Architecture in Settlement Studies', *Transactions of the Institute of British Geographers,* vol. 53 (1971) pp. 133–58.

Meeking, C. A. F. *Dorset Hearth Tax Assessments 1662–1664* (1951).
Patten, J. 'The Hearth Taxes 1662–89', *Local Population Studies,* no. 7 (1971) pp. 14–27.
Schofield, R. S. 'Estimates of Population Size: Hearth Tax', *Local Population Studies,* no. 1 (1968) pp. 32–34.
Spufford, M. 'The significance of the Cambridge Hearth Tax', *Proceedings of the Cambridge Antiquarian Society,* vol. 55 (1962).
Steer, F. W. *Farm and Cottage Inventories of Mid-Essex 1635–1749* (1969) 2nd ed.
Vaisey, D. G. *Probate Inventories of Lichfield & District 1568–1680,* Staffs. Record Society 4th series, vol. 5 (1969).

Chapter 5 Historical Demography

All relevant works are cited in the text.

Chapter 6 Local Nonconformist History

The necessary works to be consulted are listed in the text.

Chapter 7 Parliamentary Enclosure

The following books provide an essential minimum background.

Beresford, M. W. & St. Joseph, J. K. *Medieval England: An Aerial Survey* (1959).
Chambers, J. D. & Mingay, G. E. *The Agricultural Revolution: 1750–1880* (1966) especially Chapter 4, 'Enclosure'.
Curtler, W. H. R. *The Enclosure and Redistribution of our Land* (1936). Especially Chapters XIV, XV, XVI, XVII, XVIII, together with appendices I to IV.
Fussell, G. E. *Village Life in the Eighteenth Century* [undated].
Hoskins, W. G. *English Landscapes* (1973). Especially Chapter 7 'The Landscape of Planning'.
Hoskins, W. G. *The Making of the English Landscape* (1955) especially Chapter 6, 'Parliamentary Enclosure and the Landscape'.
Jones, E. L. (ed.), *Agriculture and Economic Growth in England, 1650–1815* (1967). Especially Chapters 2, 4 and 5, 'Agricultural Progress in Open-Field Oxfordshire', 'Enclosure and Labour Supply in the Industrial Revolution', and 'The Cost of Parliamentary Enclosure in Warwickshire'.

National Council of Social Service, *Hedges and History* especially papers by D. M. Hooper and W. G. Hoskins.
Russell, Rex C. *The Logic of Open Field Systems* (1975). Standing Conference for Local History.

Chapter 8 Census Analysis

In addition to the works cited in the text, the following are of particular relevance.

Best, G. *Mid-Victorian Britain* (1971).
Burnett, J. *Plenty and Want; a Social History of Diet in England from 1815* (1966).
Burnett, J. *Useful Toil: Autobiographies of Working People. From the 1820s to the 1920s* (1974).
Chambers, J. & Mingay, G. *The Agricultural Revolution 1750–1880* (1966).
Cullen, M. *The Statistical Movement in Early Victorian Britain* (1975).
Harrison, J. F. C. *The Early Victorians, 1832–1851* (1971).
Horn, P. *The Victorian Country Child* (1974).
Mills, D. (ed.), *Rural Communities* (1973).
Samuel, R. (ed.), *Village Life and Labour* (1975).
Thompson, Flora *From Larkrise to Candleford* (1963).
Thompson, F. M. L. *English Landed Gentry in the Nineteenth Century* (1963).
Tranter, N. *Population Since the Industrial Revolution* (1973).

Chapter 9 Urban Housing in the Nineteenth Century

Ashworth, W. *The Genesis of Modern British Town Planning* (1954).
Benevolo, L. *The Origins of Modern British Town Planning*, translated by J. Landry (1967).
Booth, C. *Life and Labour of the People in London*, edited by A. Fried and R. M. Elman (1969).
Briggs, A. *Victorian Cities* (1963).
Brunskill, R. W. *Illustrated Handbook of Vernacular Architecture* (1971).
Chapman, S. D. (ed.), *The History of Working Class Housing* (1971).
Cherry, G. E. *Urban Change and Planning: History of Urban Development in Britain Since 1750* (1972).
Choay, F. *The Modern City: Planning in the Nineteenth Century* (1969).

Cleary, E. J. *The Building Society Movement* (1965).
Creese, W. L. *The Search for Environment* (1966).
Dyos, H. J. (ed.), *The Study of Urban History* (1968).
Dyos, H. J. *Victorian Suburb* (1966).
Dyos, H. J. & Wolff, M. (eds.), *The Victorian City: Images and Realities*, 2 vols. (1973).
Fraser, D. *The Evolution of the British Welfare State* (1973).
Gauldie, E. *Cruel Habitations* (1973).
Gloag, J. *Victorian Comfort* (1961).
Hitchcock, H. R. *Architecture: Nineteenth and Twentieth Centuries* (1968). 3rd ed.
Jackson, A. A. *Semi-Detached London* (1973).
Jordan, R. F. *Victorian Architecture* (1966).
Mumford, L. *The City in History* (1961).
Olsen, D. J. *Town Planning in London: The Eighteenth and Nineteenth Centuries* (1964).
Parker, V. *The English House in the Nineteenth Century* (1970).
Pike, E. R. *Human Documents of the Industrial Revolution in Britain* (1966).
Pike, E. R. *Human Documents of the Age of the Forsytes* (1969).
Pike, E. R. *Human Documents of the Victorian Golden Age* (1967).
Pollard, S. *A History of Labour in Sheffield* (1959).
Redford, A. *The History of Local Government in Manchester*, 3 vols. (1939).
Sutcliffe, A. (ed.), *Multi-Storey Living: The British Working-Class Experience* (1974).
Tarn, J. N. *Five per cent Philanthropy: An Account of Housing in Urban Areas Between 1840 and 1914* (1973).
Tarn, J. N. *Working Class Housing in Nineteenth Century Britain* (1971).
Thompson, F. M. L. *Hampstead—Building a Borough, 1650–1964* (1974).
Thorns, D. C. *Suburbia* (1972).

Chapter 10 Industrial Archaeology

All the relevant items to be consulted are referred to in the text.

Chapter 11 Change Within Living Memory

In addition to the books mentioned in the text, other items which students will find helpful are listed below.

Bennett, E. N. *Problems of Village Life* (*c.* 1914).
Bourne, George *Change in the Village* (1912).
Goldman, Joan M. *The School in our Village* (1957).
Home, Michael *Autumn Fields* (1944).
Home, Michael *Spring Sowing* (1946).
Jenkins, Inez *The History of the Women's Institute Movement* (1953).
Kitchen, Fred *Brother to the Ox* (1940).
Moreau, R. E. *The Departed Village* (1968).
Robertson Scott, W. *England's Green and Pleasant Land* (1947 ed.).
Rose, Walter *Good Neighbours* (1942).
Rose, Walter *The Village Carpenter* (1937).
Sturt, George *The Wheelwright's Shop* (1923).

Acknowledgements

The editor and contributors acknowledge their debt to the following for permission to reproduce copyright material: Cambridge University Press and Dr M. Spufford (4.1, 4.5, 4.6); SSRC Cambridge Group for the Study of Population (5.1, 5.2); Nottinghamshire Record Office (6.2); Cambridge University and Dr J. K. St. Joseph, Curator of Aerial Photography (7.2: Crown Copyright reserved); Public Record Office and HMSO (8.1, Crown Copyright reserved); Nottingham University Library (8.2, 8.6); Sheffield City Libraries (9.2, 9.6, 9.7, 9.8); Dr J. D. Marshall, University of Lancaster (9.9); Bradford City Library, Local History Collection (9.4).